Seven Times Brighter

a story of identity, purpose, hope
&
the battle for our treasure

by
Cath Sheridan
A Creative Retelling

**Kingdom
Publishers**

A catalogue record for this book is available from the
British Library.

All Scripture Quotations have been taken from The
Passion Translation, New International Version,

Good News Translation, New Living Translation, New
King James Version, King James Version, The Message,
Berean, International Standard Version, Amplified Bible

ISBN: 978-1-911697-52-7

1st Edition by Kingdom Publishers

Kingdom Publishers, London, UK.

You can purchase copies of this book from any leading bookstore
or email **contact@kingdompublishers.co.uk**

Dedications & Acknowledgments

Firstly, and most importantly I humbly dedicate this retelling - *in so much as I am able to accurately recall the details and discern that which my earthly eyes can merely imagine* - to my Heavenly Father. The one who designed the unique and crazy-wonderful parts of me on purpose, for purpose. The one who wove priceless treasure deep within my feeble earthly flesh and bone. The one whose glory, I pray, violently explodes off every page of this account. The one who agonisingly allowed His only boy to hang on a tree for me - That one day, at the appointed time, this story (His story) might be read.

And to His boy, Jesus. The Carpenter from Nazareth. The one who caught me when I fell. The one who is love, whose love never once let me go. The one whose secret desire was to take upon himself the unimaginable suffering and weight of *that* tree, yet again, for me - To set me up for victory, for freedom, for eternity - To set me up for greatness!

And ohhh, to His Holy Spirit. My comforter, my teacher my wonder-bringer. The one whose light I pray continually burst forth from the deepest parts of me, so that as I *'go'*, others might unexpectedly encounter Him - That Spirit of grace and truth, who bears witness to the truth of all that is recorded here.

So too, I lovingly dedicate this account to all those who hurt, who feel broken and lost, who have lost their hope, who have forgotten who they are, who are desperately searching for their treasure; their own kind of crazy-wonderful. How I pray - within the pages of my messy, beautiful, outrageous story - you meet the one who is even more 'desperately waiting' to help you find it again.

More *personally,* I dedicate each and every page of this book and remarkable, yet unconventional, journey to

The Carpenter from Lancashire - My wonderful earthly dad, whose [patience, wisdom, character, love, practical skills, workshop lessons and affirming words], nurtured, encouraged and amplified all that my heavenly Dad originally established; placing in me a hard-wired sense of identity and a belief that anything is possible!

K&T – My beautiful, beloved girls #original3 My heart, my life, my reason, my seed. Without you (without us) there would be no story worth telling. What Jesus ignited in this stunning love of ours during the wilderness years is something that will forever blow my mind. There is something of the divine in the '*oneness*' of three!

My big Sis – For always refusing to stop petitioning heaven on my behalf.

My irreplaceable Brother-in-law - Who made me make two promises and then held me accountable. Who fought with holy anger for me and my girls in the courts of Heaven (*and still does*).

Mrs Dunlop – For seeing '*me*' first.

Orly – For uncovering my '*shine*' and inviting me to dance on the table.

H – My wingman, prayer warrior, sounding board, travel buddy and bestie. I will be forever thankful for your fierce friendship, love and wisdom. For your *holding space* for me to just spill out, or simply '*be*'. For your constant cheerleading and encouragement. And for our many late-night chats and giggles - That balmy August night in the garden was surely appointed!

Cath's Literary Tribe [Han, Mum, Rita, Marina, Su, my Baby Sis, & my Big Sis, Nikki, Nicey] — All for taking the time to lovingly read, feedback and encourage me as I attempted to faithfully write what at times felt impossible to write. Again, to this special group (particularly my **Mum**) *and* to a few other heroes (you know who you are) for loving me hard through the snot, the tears, the sad germs, the questions and the confusion; when quite honestly, I didn't feel easy to love. Then, for cheering me on through every glorious victory, miracle and breakthrough (and crazy Cath adventure!) It has meant more than you could ever possibly grasp.

Dr Brian Simmons – Lead Translator The Passion Translation. Founder, Passion & Fire Ministries. Author, Bible Teacher and Speaker.
Madison Prewett – Author, Speaker, TV Personality.
Brian and Madi, words cannot do justice to how crazy-blessed I feel that you would take time from your busy schedules and precious ministries to read, encourage and endorse this book. I thank God for you both!

Finally, I commit this book as a written record of all the amazing things God has showered on this family. The unmerited favour He has shown to me and my girls, their boys and their own delicious bubbas. I believe with all my heart that this is only the beginning. I pray each of you, and those that are to come after, abide in that same favour and grace, knowing fully the extent of a Fathers love, discovering the precious treasure He has created within you. Then, running *the race set before you* in PROMISE, PURPOSE, TRUTH, HUMILITY and *crazy-bonkers* FAITH.

This is my testimony...

This is my story...

Cath
[Momma|Nannie]

PREFACE

Satanic monitoring – now there's a statement and a half. But before you rapidly throw the book back on the shelf and run, let me encourage you that this is a story about love and light and victory and purpose. It's written to inspire you and to bring truth and hope. As I walk you through my story, let your eyes be opened as never before to the astonishing patience, determination, and skill of the one whose strategy is set on crushing your spirit and derailing the calling on your life.

My professional background is that of a strategic marketer. I've always thought of myself as pretty good at what I do and fairly switched on to the games people play; well-seasoned in discerning what's really going on in the gap between what a person says and what they actually mean (or indeed, what they're actually thinking.) Having been a Christian for over twenty-five years I thought I knew a good bit about spiritual warfare and the schemes of the master marketer himself. Turns out I didn't know the half of it.

As I navigated what I can only describe as the most painful journey of my entire life, God gave me a peek behind the veil to what was really going on, and it blew my mind.

What I discovered about the *fantastical* diligence and application of satan not only brought a brand new reality and illumination to my whole backstory, it also created in me a greater desire to get to know myself as well; if not better; than he did – to dig deep into my unique kind of wonderful, to pinpoint the source of my power and my treasure, to brave the murky water where my blind spots hid just below the surface, and to drive a few red flags into the furrows of my tender places. I had to get to the bottom of who I was *really* created to be and not who the world thought I should be. Victory was promised, but the guarantee required participation and I was about to discover just why satan was so interested in me; and in all those woven into my story.

We are being watched from the moment our tiny precious feet first rest in our momma's cupped hands and by the time we hit our teens, satan probably knows more about what makes us tick and where our treasure lies than we do ourselves. We're so busy trying to create a *world-friendly* version of '*me*' that we take virtually no notice of the exceptionally wonderful human being whose heart we drag around every day in fancy dress. But *he's* taking notice. *BOY IS HE* taking notice. Wide angled zoom lens at the ready, earpiece turned to just the right frequency, well-thumbed grubby note pad with our name on the front, clasped in his sullied hands; arrogantly and confidently keeping watch, as he painstakingly schemes and plots our downfall.

He is tireless and his monitoring relentless; so we must fine tune our *voice recognition* skills, making certain we are armed and ready for him.

For a while back there, I wasn't.

This is my story. The story of a good girl, a girl full of light and love, a girl full of dreams and imaginings. A girl with a price on her head, who's calling made him tremble. A girl who first caught his eye many years ago, barefooted, carefree, on a swing, at the bottom of a garden.

A girl that Heaven never once let go.

Contents

It is the Lord who directs your life, for each step you take is ordained by God
to bring you closer to your destiny.

So much of your life, then, remains a mystery!

Proverbs 20:24 TPT

Prologue

Journal

Thursday 18ᵗʰ August 2016: A good place to start

10.55am GMT

Well, my precious grown-up girl, like a dutiful momma under instruction, here I am starting my lovely new journal today, just as I promised you I would. There was such sweet, yet desperately rehearsed, optimism and encouragement folded into the crinkled tissue paper and pretty ribbon wrapped around it; as if, in some small way, your gift might bring a sense of adventure and expectancy. As if, writing down and capturing every step of the unimaginable journey ahead might somehow upcycle the dark cloud that has been hanging over us all these past months. You have both tried to be so brave for me, continually cheering me on, reminding me of who I am; even sitting silently in the dark with me when words simply failed. Yet each time I look at your gorgeous faces, the physical pain that has penetrated your own sweet souls is etched across them and it's almost more than I can bear.

It seems as if every weary conversation, every attempt at light-hearted banter, every 'see you later' hug is stained with tears for a life lost. And for the very first time I feel like I've failed you, because there is simply nothing I can do to fix it. The Mom badge of honour which I've always displayed so proudly, now feels awkward. An unfamiliar embarrassment accompanies frequent disorderly tears and swollen eyes and my renown as a wonderful wife, a supermom and the beating heart of this extraordinary family (the things I've built my entire world around and invested my heart and soul in), now lie in tatters; leaving me spinning off my axis, with neither anchor nor identity.

I have no idea how all this is going to work out, sweetheart, but as I sit here, pen in hand with my seat belt fastened, waiting for the thundering roar of the jet engines to signal that it's time to leave this drizzly Manchester morning behind, I can't help but feel a little unnerved by the uncanny similarities with another day just like this; 7th March 1996 – exactly twenty years ago (but for a few months). Then, sitting on a runway in Atlanta waiting to fly back home to England; a newly single mum and a new Christian, with two wonderful little girls and no idea what lay ahead. I was filled with determination to build a happy and special life for the three of us back in the UK.

Having always been pretty strong and independent and an eternal optimist, I knew I could make a good life for us; one where there was no shouting or bad language, where we didn't have to permanently tip toe, as if walking on glass. One where our home was bursting with love and giggles and dancing and just space to be silly and to be us.

And we did it didn't we, us girls, #original3 It was such a wonderful carefree time, full of God's provision and blessings. But in the evenings, prayers said and you girls snuggled up asleep in bed with Geggy & Sam, I'd sit downstairs with the lights off, candles lit and music playing and wonder whether God might choose to be even more gracious to me than He'd already been. Though I still didn't know Him well enough yet to be totally sure how He felt about me being divorced, I often wondered if He'd ever allow me a second shot at real happiness? Not that you girls didn't make me amazingly happy, it's just, well, you know how it is, now that you've found #theone; it's a different kind of joy...

Wow, how time flies when you're busy reminiscing; can't believe we've been up in the air three hours already· The pilot just prompted us all to set our watches to Eastern Standard Time and with the sound of his voice, I was rapidly jolted forward twenty years and back to reality· Back to 2016, airborne over the Atlantic Ocean again but this time heading west instead of east and staggeringly, as a newly single Mom, yet again; still with two absolutely wonderful, but now *grown-up* girls (and you just married) and three amazing step-children·

None of this seems real· In the last twenty years God has given me my complete hearts-desire – My Boy; that *once in a lifetime* love I'd so earnestly prayed for and, Oh, what a crazy wonderful rollercoaster journey it's been· If I die today, I can honestly say I have loved unconditionally with all my heart, which few can claim (not that I am going to die today, God has given me *His Word* and so much more besides)·

Yet, here I sit; crushed and overwhelmed because My Boy has decided that he doesn't want *us* anymore· Like all marriages, there have been mistakes for sure, yet for so long we both gave extraordinarily of ourselves; too much sometimes, I think, and in the most part, to others· Then came one reckless choice, a *moment of impact* and through the hurt, the disappointment and the self-preservation, blended with the usual practical family stuff and the demands of busy careers, somehow, we seem to have lost each other *and* ourselves along the way·

For quite a while I've felt as if I haven't been fully living· I can't remember the last time I felt free to be the *daft* me I used to be – He once said I was the person who taught him how to love· He described me as *a breath of fresh air,* but now he's insistent that, as people, we're just too different· I guess he forgot· The uniqueness and enthusiasm for life he so loved about me in the beginning became an obstacle; my love of making our home beautiful, somehow a burden· And in the end,

I have come to feel un-loved, un-cherished and a mistake·

My Boy always said he had never met anyone more comfortable in their own skin than me and he was right, I can't remember a time when I've ever wished I was someone else – even now· But rejection, particularly from the man who once loved me most in all the world, the man who was my go-to guy, whose name spelt home to me, who held and continues to hold my heart's free lifetime membership card; is probably the most painful thing I have ever experienced· There is an instinctive urge to transform yourself into something different to accommodate the discontentment, but truthfully, that's an impossible path to tread·

So here I am, sitting on a plane, six months from goodbye, with no home, no job, no boy, two hurting girls, a splintered family and a heart more broken than I ever dreamed possible· I'm wondering if the next twenty years will hold yet another adventure worthy of the optimism woven into my little journal here; a brand new blockbuster – or whether God will super-naturally piece together the perfectly imperfect pieces of the old love, the old life· And the truth is I have absolutely no idea· My insides tighten just contemplating a new start because I can't imagine loving again this completely· Quite frankly, navigating someone new through this deep, complex, emotional, imaginative, chaotic, impulsive, dream-filled inner sanctum where my soul hides, is not currently on my bucket list: Yet...

I'm so very tired·

11.00am EST

I watched a movie on the plane today· I'll be honest, it was a little kooky, but the main character kind of reminded me of me, and I found myself smiling as an inner fire started to flicker inside of me, thinking, Yes, this IS who I am: I'm fun and I'm kind and a little unique and actually, I quite like being this way·

Don't get me wrong, I have plenty of faults, rambling on too much being a major one, but this girl I saw (I remembered), she's been gone for quite some time - and I miss her. I found myself thinking what a fool My Boy is to close off and quash all of that *spirit*, but at the end of the day it's his choice, his life. God gives us all the freedom to choose the path we want to take and the sort of life we want for ourselves, none of us have the right to control someone else, nor can we force another to love us - love is a choice and given freely. I guess at some point I need to stop calling him My Boy.

Things have been moving so crazily fast at home. I've really needed this time away to get my head around it all, plus it will be great to see everyone and soak up some of the lovely Bama sunshine. And feel useful again. I've set myself a mini challenge whilst I'm here; to get to the bottom of this whole *total abandonment* thing - fully surrendered, trusting God with everything - no helpful suggestions from me, no creative strategies, no sleepless nights wondering and guessing, no tossing and turning in fear, just a calm simple hand-off to Him; whatever the outcome, whatever the cost.

Seems like a no-brainer hey? Why the heck wouldn't you? Well for a *problem solver extraordinaire* like your momma it feels like a total pipe dream. That old poem keeps going round in my head - yes, you know the one:

How amazing would it feel to say,

> Here you are, have it all, Lord, it's yours - I'm off the hook for this one,
>
> I'm going to be over here just getting on with regular stuff whilst you do your thing; let me know when we're good to go, when the palace is in sight.

Now that sounds like a plan doesn't it.

In twenty more years, I'll be seventy-two (that sounds so old) and I pray with all my heart that I'm able to remember this exact moment; the fear, the bruises, the doubt, the uncertainty, the unanswered prayers, the stripping back of everything familiar, this sense of defeat; and gaze back in total awe at what God has done. What a testimony to tell that would be... *will be*, for there is one thing of which I am certain, sweet girl, though we can't, He most certainly can and this *Epic* is going to make one heck of a script for Mr Gibson.

11.25am EST

Three hours and zero minutes exactly to Orlando, then on to Atlanta and then Sweet Home Alabama with your bright shining sun and Hardees Cinnamon Biscuits here we come.
Love you girls so much and missing you already
Momma x

As children bring their broken toys with tears for us to mend,

I took my broken dreams to God because He was my friend,

But then instead of leaving Him in peace to work alone,

I hung around and tried to help with ways that were my own,

At last I snatched them back and cried how you could be so slow,

My child He said what could I do, you never did let go.

Author Unknown

Glossary

Y'shua - Deliverer

Abba - Father

Ruach – Breath/Spirit

Ora - Her Light

Rasha' - Guilty One

Hephzibah – She is my delight

ESTABLISHING THE CITY

Rasha'

She intrigues me, Yeshua. I watch her as she wanders off alone in child-ish chatter and make-believe. Her eyes seem to see things one so young has not yet had time to know; her thoughts drifting, drifting, drifting... as if they're going to fall off the very edge of my kingdom?

And that *Ora*, what is that?

.... yes, she definitely is a curious one.

Y'shua

Always meddling, Rasha'(amused). She'll never be yours. (smile)

Before I formed you in the womb I knew you,
before you were born I set you apart.

I appointed you as a prophet to the nations.

Jeremiah 1:5 NIV

1

The Carpenter's Daughter

*She had a gypsy soul and a warrior spirit. She made no apologies for her wild heart
She left normal and regular to explore the outskirts of magical and extraordinary...
....and she was glorious.*

MICHELLE ROSE GILMAN

Monday 6th March 2017

I stand before you a regular girl... well not *regular* exactly, but regular*ish*. Apart from maybe one small area of my character. Ideas... thoughts... I get lots of them, and I mean lots. I'm not quite sure where they come from, they just come; erupting uncontrollably out of my chest at the most inappropriate times. Now I know what you're thinking; ideas come from the brain, right? From a thought which, having been bounced around inside your head for a period, is subconsciously analysed, formed into an intelligent concept, then rationally articulated to an appropriate target.

This *is* indeed true for most. Frustratingly, however, not for me – mine start somewhere else completely, somewhere deep inside my very soul, where initial chatter feeds a habitual fountain of ideas and thoughts, stirring all of my senses and awakening my impressionable heart, sending out simultaneous messages to my brain and mouth, akin to lighting the blue touch paper on a firework. These bright multi-coloured pockets of energy, fuelled by an insatiable level of enthusiasm and an ideology that is hard-wired in my brain, inform me that, *You can do this Kid, you can make this happen.* Now you must understand, none of this is my fault, seriously, its 100% my dad's. He taught me from a very young age that nothing is impossible and boy did he open the floodgates. I'm sure he taught my two sisters the same thing and we're all extremely industrious, but sometimes I think I received a double dose and, quite frankly, it's exhausting. Now sadly my dad isn't here to defend himself, but on this occasion, I'm afraid he's going to have to *(posthumously)* take one for the team.

Increasingly, over the years, I have tried to teach myself to better recognise the warning signs and honestly, this really did seem like a great idea at the time. Give up work, forfeit all sources of income, rent an apartment, live off the savings intended to help me buy a new home and, Yay, write a book. Not any old book, oh no...in true *Cath* style, this was going to be an epic story that recorded the monumental (unplanned and undesired) journey that has totally transformed my life over the last year, changing my perspective on everything. A story of courage, boldness and defiance, a story of grace, a story of warfare and illogical faith. A story I felt certain would reach out to the battered places of the human soul, digging into a harvest of brokenness and rejection to bring healing and hope. A story that would present the possibility of replacing disappointment, anger and bitterness with grace and unconditional love; something almost unthinkable for most of us who have experienced the terrible pain and burden of rejection and loss.

What a dummy - I really ought to master the art of procrastination, at least once in a while. As I sit here, with my chin resting in my hand, staring sideways out of the window beside me, across the courtyard; not yet sure whether spring has finally arrived or whether winter is still keeping us guessing, I'm beginning to feel like a complete fraud. Some kind of deluded and arrogant con-artist, detached from reality, from her own diminished capabilities; someone with ideas well above her station. Who am I that I should think I have anything of value to offer; anything to say of significance that could possibly make a difference in anyone's life? One look at my personal *shop window* would clarify, *You don't*. It's not exactly inviting these days. OK, so I know it doesn't reflect truth, but to a watching world, to the people who might wander by and gaze in, on the face of it the goods are looking decidedly second hand and shoddy; quite different to the unique inspirational *one-off* finds it once offered? And there are so many others who have suffered and survived much more than I. With such despair and devastation out there, how could I have been so audacious as to think my little story could possibly make a difference to any of it, to any of them?

Anyway, where would I begin? How far back do I go? How do I tell the *real* story whilst wrapping my arms around those I cherish so dearly, buffering them from the unwanted tittle-tattle that inevitably accompanies a public unlocking of the soul? And for the most part, I have been truly blessed: it's hardly the story of lifelong heartache and neglect.

All rhetorical questions. I don't have any of the answers. I'm not even sure I have the courage or the energy to do this, but in my impulsive state, I have declared it – to friends, to family, to myself; and besides, for several months...no, from the beginning if the truth be told, I have felt the gentle nudge of God on my shoulder urging me *to use what I gave you*. Over and over again this past year I have heard His voice boldly say, "write down all that I have told you, write down what you have been shown, so that there is a record." For those who have never heard the direct voice of God, please don't leave me here - I'm not crazy, well maybe a little crazy, but not about *Him*. Stick with me a while and hopefully as we walk together through the tatty pages of my story, you'll come to realise that we're not so different, you and I. As we hang out more, I'm pretty sure that this *madness* of mine will eventually start to make a whole lot more sense.

Anyway, separating madness from plain old common-sense, most smart girls on hearing the voice of God urging them to stick it all down on paper would at least wait until there was at a complete story to tell,

25

right? Not me - I'm straight in there as always; full steam ahead. *Let's do this* an excited voice inside my head declares, *He will give me an ending, by the time I reach the final chapter.*

You've got to be kidding me, that same voice whispers this chilly spring morning, in blind panic.

December 1963

I'm not sure what was going on in God's head when he designed me, but he sure did create a powerhouse of passion, raw emotion, romance and big picture dreams (in other words *mush*). From as far back as I can remember, this has typically manifested itself through written or verbal prose or the demonstrative waving of arms and hands, wilfully attempting to gift this raw emotion and enthusiasm to whoever might be willing (or not) to listen. The label hanging from my *gift* announces that I just discovered something amazing and now I want to bless you with it too - *right now.*

It's not uncommon for reality to fight back, plunging a sharp knife deep into my eager heart as I see the eyes of my audience glaze over, just as the familiar discerning voice in my head whispers *they're not that interested kid; not everyone sees the world through your rose-tinted glasses.* I know it, I do. I understand not everyone wants to live in this chaotic world of possibilities and adventure, most are quite rightly content with their own version of *normal;* happy, established, settled. I've learned over the years that sometimes I exhaust people and to be honest, I exhaust myself most of the time too. Though I've tried for most of my life, I just don't know how to turn off the voices in my head that continually throw around these new ideas, new thoughts, unexpected feelings, the what ifs: What do they really think? How are they really feeling inside? What if we tried that differently?

The surface has never been a barrier to me, in fact, it's a bold invitation that says *come right on in.* With a head full of restless curiosity, I want to know more, I want to know what lies beneath, what lies inside. I want to know what their eyes are saying that their words aren't. I often hear what people *don't* say. It's not just a mind thing either, because in addition to digging deeply, I also *feel* very *deeply*. I don't just mean a casual deeply, I mean a physical feeling in my chest that's as real to me as my fingers or my nose. It's like I have some innate ability to intuitively feel and perceive others and situations around me.

A few months ago, as I was unpacking boxes that had been in storage, I came across a pile of old junior school English books. Flicking through them I was horrified to read some of the poems and stories I'd written at such a tender age. The maturity and emotion I saw on each page did not reconcile with one so young – my teachers must surely have thought me quite unique. With age now on my side, I chuckled as I was transported back to one of my earliest (and probably most enlightening) memories from those school days.

The year is 1973, I'm ten years old and having studied a poem in class called *The Highwayman,* we were tasked with going home and writing a story based around the themes we'd learned. If you haven't read *The Highwayman* by Alfred Noyes, go look it up; it's a story of treachery and heartache and loss, but fundamentally; for those of us willing to look closer, it's a story about the power of love and the willingness to sacrifice ones own life for another. I have to say, re-reading it now, it seems wholly inappropriate for a bunch of ten-year-olds, however, our form teacher that year, Mrs Dunlop, was a tiny but fierce Scottish lady, who was different to most of the other teachers. I think, looking back, she was probably ahead of her time; but what my heart remembers most, is how expressive she was – I sensed a *kindred spirit.* Whatever it was, I loved her and just lapped it up. She clearly must have felt some kind of empathy or affinity with me too, because my class report for that year (which I still have) reads: *Catherine's reading is both fluent and expressive, her stories and poems are exceptionally good. She writes with flair and imagination.*

She probably wanted to write: *This girl has issues.*

Moment of Impact

Having embraced the writing assignment with my usual gusto, I eagerly handed back my book for marking. Now let me just say, whilst on the inside I might have had a headful of imagination, dreams and big adventures, on the outside I kept a low profile, preferring either my own company or that of my small circle of elite friends. I certainly wasn't one of the *in-crowd,* mostly because I didn't particularly want to be. I've never felt the need to fit in or be a certain way. My friends are usually great friends, always have been, in fact some of my closest friends today were in that class with me. So here I am, waiting to get my marks back for this story into which I'd invested blood sweat and passion, when the headmaster, Mr Dunne, called me into his office to say that Mrs Dunlop had showed him my story and he was blown away by it; so much so, that he wanted me to stand at the front of the weekly school assembly and read it out loud for everyone to hear.

Every budding writer's dream, right? ...*Wrong.*

It's all fine and dandy sitting in your bedroom crafting a romantic saga of love and beauty, passion and rescue, but for this ten-year-old girl, speaking those words out loud to an audience of 150+ peers came a decade and a half too soon. They just weren't ready for the kind of romantically graphic thoughts that frequented this weird brain of mine. The only thing in which the boys had the slightest bit of interest was football or teasing us girls, and the only thing on the minds of most girls was how many tricks they could master on elastics (or the previous night's episode of Shangalang - our version of MTV)...they certainly weren't equipped for a dose of *me* anytime soon. How could this be happening, I'd cleverly kept this alter ego hidden from every-one for so long; this beautiful, joyous, perfect world I occupied in my head was my secret place. How could I have been so dumb as to let it spill out onto the pages of my English exercise book?

Friday arrived; the day of the school assembly. Mr Dunne made this big fancy announcement to the whole tribe, then signalled me to come up to the front. I took a deep breath, stood up, straightened my skirt and my jumper, cleared my throat and fumbled to find the first page of my story. Then, slowly but surely, I began to read aloud. Silence... all eyes on me. My heart started to beat so loudly that it felt like a huge drumroll, announcing my imminent downfall. My mind drifted – *This must have been how Bess the landlord's daughter in the poem felt as she waited, wondering what she could do to save her love?* My forehead started to perspire as big red blotches appeared around my neck and chest. The words rising up into my throat were screaming at me to stop; willing me to leave them on the pages for which they had been intended; not throw them out into the lion's den, into that large and by now, very attentive school hall full of unappreciative spotty juveniles.

The reality hit, I wasn't playing make-believe in my bedroom anymore, dreaming up all the things little girls dream of in the safety of their castles, this was real and it was pure torture. I read another line and looked up, out into the sea of faces staring back at me, waiting with baited breath to hear this amazing masterpiece unfold. Boys, lots of *boys;* my mind diverted again - I was going to be such a laughing stock. Suddenly the discerning voice inside my head kicked in and instructed me assertively: *cut and run kiddo.* By now my mouth was dry and my teeth were sticking to the inside of my top lip. I fell silent, looked up at Mr Dunne, pleading with eyes that cried out, *you've got to help me out here.* And then came the miracle...

He smiled, reached down and sweetly took the book from my sweaty hands and at once, with the comforting sound of his gentle Irish tones filling the air, I realised I was off the hook.

After that everything else was a blur, I was way too busy analysing the situation in my head to take the slightest notice of the reaction on the ground. My reputation seemed to survive unscathed and with a renewed sense of confidence, back in the safety of my bedroom that evening, I congratulated myself for the huge contribution I'd made to mankind that afternoon; imagining that maybe, just maybe, my story had given a bunch of clueless ten year old boys a heads-up on what their future Princesses might be hoping for from their Prince (aka them in ten more years) when he finally comes to woo and rescue her.

And that, if he plays his part well, there was every chance she'd be willing to lay down her life for his.

They say that your core character is evident from a very early age and I've certainly always been an open book; often too open I think. If you ask me a question there's every chance your answer might involve some bonus information you never expected (or wanted), because as I've already said, I like to equip people with everything they need. Professionally and privately I'm a problem solver and as all good problem solvers know, to solve a real problem you need to understand the root cause, the effects and the options available - *simples*. My girls often say to me, "Mum, why did you tell them all that, they only wanted to know..." I'm not going to lie - it's an issue. I've spent years trying to address it and have finally come to terms with the fact that this is just who I am. Plus anyway, those around me generally benefit *big-time*. If I discover some new interesting piece of helpful information or listen to an amazing podcast or *TED talk,* boy am I going to go out of my way to make sure that everyone who's important to me gets to hear this *essential,* life changing set of facts. You see, somewhere deep inside of me there's a fundamental need to build, shape, encourage and enable others.

Growing up most of my dreaming and scheming was done at the bottom of my garden, close to an orchard full of apple trees, on a two-man swing my dad had built from scratch. That swing had to be the sturdiest, most impressive apparatus on the block (well on our little lane anyway). It was far enough away from the house so that the only things I could hear were the birds singing, the hum of a distant tractor in the fields behind and the sweet internal murmurs of an imagined future in far-off shores, along with the well-rehearsed declaration of undying love from a handsome hero on horseback; but not so far off that I couldn't hear my Mum calling me in for tea (unless of course it was salad). In those days salad was a punishment, sadly, now it's become more of a necessity.

I was a low maintenance child, one that rarely needed to be stimulated or kept occupied. With my chores out of the way, I had a busy schedule, which frequently took me around the world, meeting interesting people and doing *happy* things, but often meant that getting home in time for tea could be a real challenge. It regularly took Mum four or five hollers of *Catherine!* before her voice dragged me back to reality and to the tea table. My chosen form of transport was *always* the swing and once on-board, I'd dream away hours lying on my tummy, my toes controlling the forward and backward thrust, my face staring down at the grass and the creatures that occasionally appeared from its willowy depths.

Sometimes, my partner in crime, my best friend Nicey (she was actually called Denice but to me she was Nicey) would join me and we'd make great plans together. They were such glorious and carefree days, though I don't think she ever fully understood how worryingly real those plans and dreams were to me – how completely interwoven they were with the very core of who I was (am). Back then, I'm not sure I did either, I just knew there was something different about me, something that caused me to feel things so much more deeply than others, something that often drove me to seek solitude.

My amazing dad raised me on the belief that anything is possible. If I went to him with some wacky, crazy idea about something I wanted to do (and there were many, believe me), once he'd established that it wasn't dangerous or undesirable, he'd sit me down and say, "OK, so tell me about it Kiddo – why do you want to do it?– how do you think it's going to work?" He was a carpenter too, my dad, just like Jesus (I mean his trade was just like Jesus' earthly trade, not that my dad was just like Jesus, though to me he came awfully close). It wasn't his day job, in his day job he was a *Boss*, but his skill as a carpenter defined him to me. He could make anything from wood, he even built the house we all grew up in and if something was broken there was nothing my dad couldn't fix.

When I moved in to my first flat at twenty-one and desperately wanted to equip it with designer furniture at zero cost, I'd find pictures in magazines, tear them out and take them to Dad in his big workshop and say, "Can you make one of these for me Dad?" He always did. He was my true hero, my first true love. I adored standing and watching him at work in his garage, listening to the squeals of his big industrial circular saw; breathing in the smell of sawdust and always, the thud, thud, thud of his well-worn hammer with its home-made handle that had been replaced many times over the years.

He took great care with everything that passed through his hands, but it was in the detail that his true craftsmanship shone. That's when his real skill (and the tools he'd had for years and lovingly looked after and sharpened and oiled) came into their own. It was in the small stuff you didn't see; the hidden elements, the critical joints that would eventually be invisible, yet hold everything together. He would meticulously sketch out a diagram, calculate all the precise measurements, work out what material he needed (most of which he usually had lying around somewhere). Then he'd create a space on his workbench, switch on a bright light directly over the object he was going to work on and, doing what he did best, the magic would begin.

He used to let me stand on a small stool beside him, watching everything he was doing. If I reached up uninvited, interfering with his work of art, he'd say "Don't touch, it's not ready yet – you don't want to break it again do you Catkins?" Most of the time I listened to him, but sometimes I'd want to get more involved, especially if he was fixing something precious that belonged to me, because then I had a vested interest. To make sure he was really clear what needed to be done I'd point out the exact root-cause of the problem and how best to repair it; like I hadn't told him twenty times already on submission of the work request (my problem-solving prowess has always been somewhat dominant). Yet he remained patient and diplomatic, always offering me a choice (as if there was ever really any choice to be made) – he would raise his eyebrows comically, tilt his head to one side, lean down to my level and with a hint of sarcasm lovingly enquire "So are you going to keep hold of it then and have a go at fixing it yourself or are you going to let go and let me have it so I can sort it properly for you?" And of course, I'd leave it with him; childlike impatience...*guilty as charged* – stupidity...*absolutely not!*

In the job of miracles my dad and his workshop had form. He shaped joints so accurately that they always fitted flawlessly, he glued broken pieces together again with such gentleness and precision that you could barely see the cracks, and once he'd done the intricate work with his hands, he'd place the repaired item carefully into the press on his workbench, holding the pieces firmly in place until he was satisfied they wouldn't come apart again. When he was sure of that, he'd lift the restored item out of the press, sand it down to remove any blemishes or irregularities, polish it up and then give it back to us, usually in a better condition than it started out.

I can remember pestering him night after night, when I knew full well my precious item had been completely repaired, yet remained idle in the garage instead of in my hands (waiting for what I had no idea?), but my dad seemed to think it was a necessary part of the process, seriously... "Will it be ready yet Dad?" I'd ask with eyes that flirted with his heart, much the same way I had done a few days earlier. His reply was always the same: "Be patient," he'd say, "I'll give it back to you when I'm finished with it - If I give it back to you now it will only break again and next time we might not be able to fix it."

Occasionally, when time wasn't an issue, he'd say "Come on then, jump up, I'm going to need your help with this one," and working together, father and daughter, we'd create something special he and I. As my small hands tired, I'd hold my breath, desperately trying to concentrate on keeping steady my *piece de resistance,* hoping my dad would think me a gifted apprentice and, as if he intuitively sensed my need for reassurance, he'd smile encouragingly, cup his big strong hands over the top of mine to provide a little extra support and say, "Come on, you've got this Kid, you can do it." Those affirming words, in that workshop planted a strong, deep-rooted self-belief within me; a resilient inner voice that says defiantly over and over again, *You can do this Kid, you have what it takes; you are enough.*

33

Though the path I have walked since those perfect days may not have been all that I had imagined they would, they prepared me well and there have been few proverbial brick walls that I have not managed to scale. And, when all else fails, I learned early in life from a great teacher how to pick up a sledge hammer with finesse - *and simply swing*.

It's pretty clear to me now, looking back, that there was method in this protracted approach, because each night when we'd go into the garage to check on progress, whilst I had the opportunity to critique (observe) Dad's craftsman-ship, he actually had one-on-one time with me and my full attention. Oh, how I loved to spend time with my dad. There was never anything I couldn't tell him or ask him - he never seemed to be shocked with my numerous hair-brain ideas, nor did he lose his temper with me. Don't get me wrong, I knew when I was in trouble, but it was never a scary trouble, it was a calm, wise, "Come on kiddo, get your act together and let's not do that again," kind of trouble.

> You can do this Kid; you have what it takes; you are enough!

I remember an old-fashioned three-wheeler bicycle that I and my two sisters had as children – it had three very large wheels and a white leather saddle. That bike started out as a brand-new blue and white shiny Christmas present for my older sister, Angie. It must have felt like a huge amount of money for Mum and Dad to pay when they first purchased it, they hadn't been married many years and wouldn't have had much money, however, over time it was to prove an extremely shrewd investment. Seven years after it first showed up, Santa kindly brought me one just like it, it was a high gloss bottle green colour with a little silver thumb bell and I was in love. Finally, I had my own *big-girl* wheels and I was poised to explore my world, which I did enthu-siastically for a good few years, wind in my hair, scars on my knees.....
What I found quite remarkable was that a full six years later, when it was time for my baby sis, Elizabeth, to get her first bike, the shops were still selling the same model and somehow, as if by magic, Father Christmas showed up again with a beautiful brown and cream one especially made for her.

Of course, you've probably guessed by now that this was the same bike. Over what was probably a fifteen-year period, that bicycle served each of us loyally, giving us all years of joy and fun, but, in turn, as we each out grew it or got bored with it and cast it aside to play with something new and more interesting, my dad would discretely take it away and hide it somewhere until it was time for the next big reveal. None of us ever saw the bike in exactly the same way, we didn't ever realise our particular bike had previously been in our midst; each time it was passed on it looked completely different, lovingly and skilfully transformed into an even more beautiful version of itself by the careful hands of my dad – a gift, as if seen for the very first time, perfect for that very moment. Below the layers of paint and polish the original structure always remained fundamentally the same, but the outside told a very different story.

As the years went by, the bike became more and more precious to our family - it came to represent so much more than the physical; it was a significant link to each of our pasts, to idyllic childhoods, to memories of carefree days full of laughter and love, to family and close community. Despite the many fences into which it had been crashed over the years, despite the number of paths it had ridden off the edge of, or the amount of stone chipping that had bounced up off the pavement and chipped its paint, it always seemed to survive. Yes, it encountered a few dents and scratches along the way, but through the painstaking work that Dad put in, night after night in secret, which none of us ever really understood until we were much older, its beautiful transformations were always a source of wonder.

> Lovingly and skilfully transformed into an even more beautiful version of itself by the careful hands of my dad – a gift, as if seen for the very first time, perfect for that very moment. Below the layers of paint and polish the original structure always remained fundamentally the same, but the outside told a very different story.

As I capture these memories; words that are merely my past's truth - words meant only to provide a backdrop and some understanding to where I've come from; even I can't help but be stirred by the revelations of current truth within them. Remnants of ordinary moments, whispering down the years, "See, do you see now, do you see what's taking place here?"

Dad died much too young. I was only twenty-eight, he had just turned fifty-nine. Sometimes things happen in life that will never make sense, things that you simply cannot put into words. Things unexpected, which change your world so completely that they leave an indelible scar on your heart. Thankfully there haven't been too many of these moments in my life but that one on the 16th of March 1992 was my first. Love is such a strange thing to fathom. It's invisible, there is no tangible matter, no atoms that scientists can dissect to explain what causes it or how it's made up, you can't take it and get a part replaced when it's not working as well as it once was, you can't nip out to the local store when you find it's been stolen and buy a replacement and yet..... it is one of the most powerful forces on earth. A force which drives our behaviour, our thoughts, our feelings and often our physical wellbeing. It inextricably binds one to another via an invisible cord and when that cord is severed, it delivers a pain so intense and so deep that nothing can console.

That was my first experience of true love lost. I understand much clearer now that there is really only one way that love is ever lost, but back then I was a novice. I figured, you dump, you get dumped or someone dies. Up to that point I had only experienced the *you dump* scenario...And boy was I drowning in agonising internal conflict over it.

Now remember, I was that girl who spent her life daydreaming on a swing at the bottom of the garden, of a knight in shining armour riding up and declaring undying love before whisking her off to some far-off shore, meaning I'd spent my early teenage years trying to wriggle free from way too serious *mushy* teenage boyfriends. I was by far way too independent and restless for my own good (probably still am if truth be told), and needy teenage boys were an inconvenience to say the least. I also hated (and still do) the awkwardness of hurting someone or letting them down, so my strategy from early adolescence was avoid and retreat. I'd seem like I was physically present; my face would be smiling, but if you looked close enough into my eyes my soul was nowhere to be found. My friends would say I had an invisible shield around me saying *look but don't touch* - that invisible shield was my friend, it was my protection, my *safe place*, it allowed me to continue to live independently in my world of possibilities, a world without barriers, a world full of adventure, lots of sunshine and forever love.

Some habits formed in childhood, it appears, are difficult to break.

Anyway, back to boys and love. I had dated a boy for quite a long time when I was fifteen. He was actually a really great boy and everything was ticking along nicely until he made the whopping mistake of telling this fifteen-year-old girl that he wanted to marry her one day. *Woah,* red flags, red flags. That poor innocent boy had no idea that at that exact moment he'd just severed the only remaining cord that connected me to his future. *Better now,* I contemplated, than later when he'd be too attached for his own good. I tried to let him down gently, really I did, but then he went and cried... "Noooo" he sobbed desperately. *Dear Lord, you've got to be kidding me...* I palpitated and as if that wasn't bad enough, he then went on to beg, and when that didn't work, he wrote me letters and finally when none of those worked, he sent me a tape-recorded message on a cassette via my parents, verbally beseeching me not to dump him.

> Some habits formed in childhood, it appears, are difficult to break!

Well, it all came to a head one Sunday afternoon when he decided that as his former approaches hadn't proved successful, he'd have a go at being *Mr Angry,* and I caved. It was early that same Sunday evening, I can still see the chair in our living room where I sat curled up sobbing, the familiar sound of *Sing Something Simple* (the soundtrack to our Sunday afternoons growing up) playing on the radio in the background. For a good few hours my parents had humoured me by allowing the usual peaceful vibe of our Sunday afternoon to be disturbed by my *pity-party;* my mum awkwardly stoking my brow as she discretely pushed fresh tissues into my wet hand; my dad cracking one of his ridiculously daft jokes and poking me in the shoulder like a mischievous schoolboy trying to start a play-fight, as I tugged my shoulder away dramatically. But their compassion was waning.

As I remained, happily wallowing in self-pity, out of the blue the atmosphere dramatically changed. Suddenly, my dad, this man who had been my lifelong ally, my lifelong advocate and go-to-guy turned to me abruptly and said, "OK Kid, enough is enough". *What?...* clearly he hadn't grasped the enormity of what had just taken place in my life. The un-pleasantries, the anger, the harsh words – I'd just broken someone's heart and they were devastated, and I couldn't put it right (well not without sacrificing the amazing future that burned inside of me, to live instead a life of mediocracy).

"Oh, but Dad you don't understand" I declared insolently, "It was awful, he was so upset". Then came his prophetic words, words I didn't fully understand at the time, words which many years later would come back and haunt me. "One day, Kid" he said, "One day, someone will come along and break *your* heart and believe me, it's going to hurt a heck of a lot more than this."

Back then I couldn't imagine how anything could hurt as much as being the author of someone else's pain and not being able to do a thing to fix it?

Now, of course, I understand it all too well...

Wisdom is something you can't buy, it's bequeathed on us, a rare gift. My dad had that gift. Following his death, we grieved for a very long time, but in that grieving period we learned something special; love and wisdom don't die, they remain long after the physical man is gone. We lived in a home lovingly built by my dad's own hands. He himself had dug and laid the foundations, usually after a long hard day's work, whilst the rest of us slept. He oversaw a team of builders who came to help build the walls, he set the roof in place to secure it from the weather and then tirelessly, night after night, it was *he* who worked on the interior detail to create a perfect and unique home for our family.

As our family grew and we girls started to develop our own individual characters, he created a perfect space where he could spend time with us, one–on–one, intimately talking, quietly watching, curiously asking, but always learning, always growing and always loving.

After he'd gone, I would wander into his garage to talk to him, just as I always had. I'd tell him my problems, I'd ask for his advice and I'd run my fingers over his tools and workbench, lifting my nose in the air to breath in the lingering aroma of sawdust, whilst listening for the familiar squeal of the circular saw; replaying one of his daft jokes in my head. The evidence of him was everywhere, it was undeniable. As I did this, my heart would break all over again, remembering what I'd lost, what had once been, what I'd never have again, what my babies would never experience.

But one day I learned an important lesson...

It was late July and Dad had been gone just over four months. I stood in the garage as usual having my weekly fix, soaking in his memory in a way that had almost become a comfort blanket to me. Without warning, like a gift falling from heaven that suddenly tore back the veil from my eyes, enabling me to see clearly for the very first time, I caught a vision of the true inheritance he had left behind. The Carpenter had completed what he'd been sent to do – he had understood fully his ultimate purpose and by the time he left this world, his work here was complete. He'd taught us girls all he could in the short time he'd had with us, he'd shaped us with great skill, loved us unconditionally and nurtured in us our individual *unique* characteristics that he'd recognised and known would serve us well over time; he'd worked tirelessly to provide for our every need and imparted great wisdom and correction on us and though I had never fully understood the true intent of this man's heart until that very moment, standing there in my dad's garage, surrounded by the tangible and intangible evidence of all that he was, I was overcome by love. Love and the realisation that he'd

A goal driven by the love of a father for his daughters, a goal focussed on setting us up for greatness.

only ever had one goal – a goal driven by the love of a father for his daughters, a goal focussed on setting us up for greatness.

As I remained there, in the quiet and still of *My Father's* workshop, grasping for the very first time the reality of *that* truth, I heard a familiar voice gently remind me, you've *got this Kid, you can do it.*

Standing a few inches taller, shoulders pushed back, my head held a little higher, I smiled, wiped away the tears and took one long last lingering gaze around the seeds of my inheritance. Then, with a deep sense of peace and identity, I stepped boldly out into the sunshine, knowing I would never be without him again – I was my father's daughter and I would carry him with me always; I was strong, I was courageous, I was equipped and I was loved.

I was ready now to face the next chapter, a chapter, as it turned out, that had already started to grow inside of me...

Rasha'

Tut tut tut, you're slipping Y'shua, if only your rescue party had arrived in time, perhaps you could have saved her and her sweet little Mama.

Y'shua

You under estimate me, Rasha'. You always have.

Hang on baby girl, this stuff they're pumping into your Momma might be making you a little bit queasy right now and it might sound a bit noisy and chaotic out there for a while; the room is full, but between us and the doctors, we've got you both covered.

They don't see me like you do. They don't know they hear me either, but they do. I have a whole team guiding them. This isn't negotiable.

I know you sense her, don't you?

(watching her gaze upwards nervously, towards the narrow passage, from where she started her journey)

It's not her time yet, but don't be sad, you still have a little while here. And then she will be with you again soon enough - being a big sister means sometimes you have to do things first, so you can help *her* later.

We will deal with *him* later, the great creator of chaos – how he trembles at the thought of your precious little feet touching my earth. (loud chuckle)

And I will establish my covenant between me and thee and thy seed after thee, in their generations, for an everlasting covenant; to be a God unto thee, and to thy seed after thee. **Genesis 17:7 KJV**

2

Who Defined *Normal* Anyway?

She's a paradox.

She is faithful and yet detached. She is committed and yet relaxed.

She loves everyone, and yet no one. She is sociable and also a loner.

She is gentle and yet tough. She is passionate but also platonic.

In short, she is predictable in her own unpredictability.

AUTHOR UNKNOWN

My teenage years and twenties seemed to have no more gravity than my childhood.

Teachers have a lot to answer for.

At the tender age of fifteen, picture this, Mum and Dad rock up to my last ever parents evening; the one where all your subject teachers manage your parents' expectations about how well (or not) you're likely to do in your final exams and whether all their blood, sweat and threats over the previous five years have been worth it. Remember, I was a *good girl,* so behaviour was always 10/10; academically, yeah, I did OK. And, as already evidenced, I was a *word girl,* and a ponderer who loved to create beautiful things, so History, English Literature and Needlework were my absolute favourite subjects. I think my history teacher, Mr. Willoughby, in particular, had a soft spot for me. Enthusiastic, homework always thorough and done on time, fully engaged in class with lots of curious questions and an A* pupil; what's not to like...?

Anyway, there we were at parents evening, with Mr. Willoughby saying all the right things until he took the great liberty of suggesting that a career in banking would be the perfect thing for their sweet, well-behaved daughter. To be honest, I really hadn't given much thought to what I wanted to do with the rest of my life. I knew I didn't want to continue studying like many of my friends planned to do, and the things that really appealed to me; interior design and journalism/story writing; required me to do that.

The next thing on my list was travelling - though I wasn't quite sure how to build travel and sunshine into a career. But *banking,* come on, seriously? "I've always seen you as a career girl, a Businesswoman" my dad said encouragingly later that evening at home; always the encourager my dad, always the voice of reason, letting me have the final say, whilst also knowing how much his opinion mattered to me. My mum on the other hand treasured tradition, stability and certainty and imagined me marrying a local boy, living close by, having 2.2 children and leading a *normal* life - she had already made up her mind.

"What a great opportunity" - it was a statement, not a suggestion. "What a fantastic career and it pays really well."

Well, if it pays well... I thought sarcastically, as she proceeded to make it perfectly clear that Mr. Willoughby (and they) knew what was best for me, much more than I did myself.

Of course, they did, the good girl concluded with surprisingly little resistance or much of a fight. And not wishing to disappoint my amazing parents by exposing my reckless imaginings, within weeks, my applications were in and just one interview later I had my first *very good job* in the bag, with four months still to spare before my final exams. At just fifteen-years-old, my life was sorted. #result

The next five years were torturous. I realised very quickly that banking was definitely not for me. Deep down this intense yearning to wander and be free and to live barefooted in the sunshine just about anywhere in the world would not go away. This rebellious inner voice felt so familiar and comforting, yet I knew I had no right to give ear to it. Every day I would dread going into work and most Friday evenings I'd sit up late with my dad sobbing about how unhappy I was, trying to help him understand that I simply had to do something different with my life. Just as he'd been when I was a little girl, he brought wisdom and balance.

He never told me *no,* or that I was foolish to walk away from such a good job (though I'm sure that's what he thought), instead he would say "OK, so what do you want to do instead Kid?" Boy that was a stinger. I had absolutely no idea, I just had this all-consuming need for freedom, sunshine, wind in my hair, a cute little shack on the beach *somewhere,* a clapped-out open top car to get me to the local store for essentials and then... I hadn't given any thought to what I would live off, but oh how that picture felt like home in my heart. I could see It all so clearly - one day I would spot him, *the one,* the prince I always knew would eventually come for me, walking along the beach with his tanned face and leather flip flops and, as his eye caught a glimpse of me, he'd casually smile and say "Hi" and we'd both grin. And in that single moment, that once in a lifetime moment, we'd both know that we had finally found each other, the one for whom our hearts had been forever searching.

Of course, it would have been completely irresponsible and dumb of me to share that with my dad in these highly charged father-daughter moments; certainly, if I'd wanted to retain a single shred of credibility and support. Instead, I would hang my head, brush my tears and snotty nose on the part of my sleeve now tightly stretched over the back of my knuckles, shrug my shoulders and simply say "I dunno, Dad?"

And I really didn't. The job I had did pay well, I seemed to be good at it too and had been promoted several times, so there were great prospects, I'd bought myself a cute new little car, which most of my friends could not; yet there was this girl in me who didn't fit the clothes she was wearing, a girl who was slowly dying inside.

During this period, my dad who had some good business connections produced a number of what were honestly fantastic opportunities for a career change. When I look back now at some of these, I realise just how amazing they really were, but then all I could see was *safe, bondage, boring,* and *ordinary.* Why move from one prison cell to another? my heart would think deflated. Oh how I wanted to make my parents proud of me, oh how I wanted to be the sweet, funny perfect *angel* as Mum called me. There was this battle going on inside that was starting to make me wonder if there was actually something wrong with me - if I had been wired wrongly in the womb - if I had an inherent inability to be happy and satisfied. Was that imaginary world I pictured just some random piece of nonsense I'd created in my head to escape reality?

I'd run scenarios through my head of just going into work the next day and handing in my notice, then coming home and excitedly mapping out all the places I'd go and how I'd support myself. Grape picking in France was always high on my list, as that seemed practical and doable. When I reached the part about telling Mum and Dad, my chest would grow tight, my enthusiasm would waiver and hope would begin to retreat. How could I ever disappoint them like this?

Around seven years earlier, my elder sister, Angie, who would have been fourteen or fifteen at the time, went away on a school trip for a week and came back really *weird.* She started talking about Jesus all the time and telling everyone how they needed to give their life to the Lord. It was the end of the 60s and early 70s and at the same time she started to wear all these strange long clothes. We'd exchange glances with people when she'd walk in the room and smile and say under out

46

breaths, "she's a Christian" and they'd nod their head and say "ahhh" in an understanding and sympathetic way; as if that now made sense.

We were a church going catholic family, but this was a whole different ball game and let's just say, this newfound *Jesus stuff* put her at significant odds with my parents. She had an urgency and passion to share what she'd discovered and they..., they had their own thoughts on the matter. In fairness, I think they were hurt. From where they stood, I think it felt like everything they believed in, stood for, had raised us up on, was being challenged. And from my sister's side, well, she loved them, loved us all, way too much to loosen her *push*.

Moment of Impact

Things changed. There was a sadness and tension that appeared in our family after that and somehow I learned to be the neutraliser - the one who didn't judge, who didn't take sides, who still loved everyone, who wanted to check everyone was actually OK, who smiled angelically, quickly perceiving the emotional air around her and making herself inconspicuous when the moment demanded it. I became a master of harmony and the world remained calm. More than ever, I found self-sufficiency and joy outside in solitary open spaces, making dens, climbing the huge apple tree in our back garden, all the way to the top where the branches would get bendy and *questionably* safe; but from where I could see for miles, feel the wind on my face, close my eyes and imagine. It was like recharging my batteries. Inside I'd sit in my room with its yellow painted walls and write secret notes to my future self, before folding them up and hiding them under the loose floorboards in the hallway outside. It was just me and my day dreams, hoping that one day everything would go back to normal and everybody would be OK and jolly again.

She, my big sis, was amazing and I loved her to bits, but honestly, I didn't really get all this Jesus business. When she wasn't having any success with Mum and Dad, she'd come into my room and lean against my bed on the floor next to me, put her arm around me and say "it's real you know Cath, all of this. You've got to take it seriously."

47

She put so much effort into *getting me,* she really did, but honestly, I was OK with who I was. I said my prayers most nights before bed and I was a really *good girl* most of the time, so I was fairly sure God was pretty pleased with me and as much as I loved her, I had no desire to be in her gang and even more than that, I had no desire to become the disappointment to my parents that she obviously now was. I couldn't have handled that.

And things were about to get much worse.

When she was about eighteen, she met a boy - well a man really! She fell in love and announced they were getting married. He knew Jesus too (though my mum was quite sure he did *not*). He had one heck of a back story and as far as my parents were concerned, he was just about the most unsuitable husband imaginable for their clever, naïve, gentle catholic daughter - *even if she did need to repent and get to confession.* I actually liked him, he was funny, but I kept that to myself; especially in front of Mum. To be fair to my mum, I could kind of understand her thinking. Still, I did secretly like him. Even though he talked about Jesus a lot too, he was more worldly and objective. I remember he once told me that he understood how much harder it is for *good* girls to know Jesus than for *bad* girls, because, well...we're nice and kind and we don't swear and all that stuff. So well, *yep, that's* me off the hook, I thought. Maybe one day I'll become a bad girl and get to know this Jesus properly - LOL

Things got pretty unbearable for a time and I made myself scarce as much as I could, until finally one day she was gone, married and then overseas. There was a part of me that was really sad to see her go, but another part of me thought: phew at least I don't have to keep having these deep unsettling conversations anymore and at least there will be a resemblance of amnesty back in the house.

What I hadn't bargained for back then was the fact that she was relentless in her petitioning of heaven on my behalf;

What I hadn't bargained for back then was the fact that she was relentless in her petitioning of heaven on my behalf.

48

but more of that later; for now, let's get back my current dilemma – high heels or flip flops; favourite daughter or major disappointment?

Around this time, many of my friends were starting to date steady and my mum was counting on the fact that I would join them, but I found the thought loathsome. To me it seemed like there was this standard model for life that everyone was expected to follow and now I'd hit the *time to settle down and get married* stage. I hadn't even begun the *explore the world* stage, so how could I possibly be at the next one? Plus, my prince was never going to find me here. I knew I had to act quickly to find a compromise between drowning in the routine of banking and being a prospect-less beach bum; so I began earnestly to apply for new jobs. My main criteria were sunshine, travel and a good element of independence and / or freedom. But all this needed to be dressed up as a meaningful job.

I knocked on the door of some crazy things; Nurse training in South Africa (I hated blood, still do); Air hostess (I was too short); Air Force (the only thing to which my dad completely put his foot down); Au pair to a wealthy French family living in Belgravia London with holidays in South of France (I wasn't a fan of small children and my French was limited to a B at O'level, but vacationing on the Riviera...) I could write a whole separate book on my experience when I went for this interview, but that's one for another day.

As much as I love nice things (and I really do love nice things), money and career prospects and titles have never been much of a driver for me. The extent to which I valued and still do value my bank balance, is based on its ability to facilitate a longed for way of *doing* life, mostly determined by my five senses and my heart - the feel of the wind in my hair as I drive with the roof down, or the sun on my face; the emotional connection with a building or room as I enter; the smell of freshly picked vine-ripened tomatoes or cinnamon candles; the first few intermittent tweets of the dawn chorus as you roll over and snuggle back

I didn't want to be put in a box or to fit a standard model, I wanted to do life differently!

beneath a big quilt realising you still have a few more hours, or a love song being played on a saxophone with the lights turned down beside a crackling log fire; the taste of olives, feta cheese, sundried tomatoes and basil drizzled in olive oil and balsamic; people - who's with me, who's championing me, opportunities to champion and encourage someone else; and of course that elusive sense of freedom and antici- pation. I've never wanted to be put in a box or to fit a standard model, I want to do life differently.

As I secretly scoured the *vacancy* pages, that nagging voice continued to scream, *what the heck is wrong you.* But the pull was simply too strong and finally, I happened across an ad for an au pair, working for a wealthy family in Athens, Greece, looking after their five-year-old son. The position came with all accommodation, meals and bills paid, plus a small weekly allowance - all I had to do was get there. Navigating the remaining obstacles; my heart pounding with childlike excitement (plus a little wonder and nervous trepidation), realising that *finally,* I was actually going to do this. I emptied my savings account, booked a flight, handed in my notice and broke my mum's heart.

And with that, I began to breathe life into all those girlish daydreams, pushing down the barriers and casting off the world's expectations of what my life should look like, and it was wonderful.

Oh, the fun I had that summer, making new friend from all over the world, island hopping on my family's yacht (albeit with an under-five-year-old in tow and sleeping down below in the servant's quarters), learning a new language along with many life lessons, lying in the sun until my skin turned so dark I was barely recognisable; but more than that, developing a sense of early identity. It reminded me of those crit- ical lessons from my dad that *anything is possible,* and even more, it grew my courage and a gentle determination to be *me,* whoever the heck that was. In many ways it was just six months of reckless wander- ings, but it felt like sunshine to my soul and affirmation to my spirit.

At the beginning of autumn, with no comprehension that I would never again return to Athens, I made a surprise visit home to reassure my parents that I was alive and well. In an instant, as if someone had smuggled *her* in through the back door, *normality* came calling.

It seems to me, even now looking back, no real thought or conscious decision was ever made, yet despite having tried so hard to escape it, I found myself back in the bank and also back in a relationship in which I'd previously placed little weight. Before the final evidence of that glorious summer had vanished from my sun kissed face, my career was back on track and I had quietly moved from Miss to Mrs - safely married and living a few miles up the road from my family home. On the surface it appeared I'd got all the foolish nonsense out of my system once and for all and Mum and Dad could not have been happier.

Moment of Impact

My big girl burst into the world a few years later with all the drama that I eventually would come to realise was part of Gods great plan for her life.

Six months into my pregnancy I was busy nesting and getting the house ready for the new arrival. On that ominous day; the memory of which still causes me to grip tight the handrail of every staircase I descend; I was creating an arrangement of dried flowers and had run up the stairs to quickly grab the scissor I'd left in the bedroom earlier. As I started back down, somehow the heel of one of my shoes became entangled in the turn up of my other trouser leg and in *slow-motion* I found myself floating through the air in a downward spiral. I can still hear the strange sound that came out of my lungs via my mouth as I hit the hall floor below, my body; subconsciously knowing it had to protect the precious cargo it was carrying; twisting efficaciously, ready for landing.

I can still see the blood-streaked wall where I tried to steady myself as I crawled to the telephone to ring for help. And as I drifted into unconsciousness, I can still hear the doctors muted tones questioning my husband.

"We can probably save either your wife *or* the baby?"

THE SECRET PLACE

†

What I didn't catch, through the oxygen and meds and confusion, was the sweet sound of beautiful voices singing over me. Nor was I aware of the comforting breath that dusted my cheek as it hovered just above my head, keeping a close eye on proceedings, whilst dipping intermittently to utter words of reassurance.

It's a lie precious girl, just another silly lie. We're fixing you up nicely. And *She* - *She*'s beautiful and quite perfect. You're going to have to wait just a few more months to hold her, but then you'll begin to understand.

†

"This is the one" my consultant says, as the group of eager junior doctors gather around, prodding the messy and tender train wreckage across my abdomen; their eyes flickering backwards and forwards between the clipboard retrieved from the bottom of my bed and the patchwork of well-crafted stitches and vulnerable scar tissue, tentatively holding together the now excessively stretched skin ; their whispers too low for me to pick up much of the conversation, but their intonations making it clear I was providing great interest and curiosity.

"Well, aren't you the miracle mummy?" He smiles at me and they all chuckle in agreement, "how are you feeling? And how's our miracle baby?

One by one, they each take turns pressing their stethoscopes onto the undamaged side of my very large bump to listen to the *fighter* inside of me, giving me a reassuring smile as they do, then thanking me for the inconvenience.

And then, just as quickly, they're gone; leaving me to ponder *my miracle,* as the doctors had called it, and the fact that I would most likely never don a bikini again.

A few weeks later, with one final tug, my drama queen exploded into the world.

I had traded a spleen for the most exquisite thing I'd ever seen and I would have done it ten times over in a heartbeat. Without any understanding of the extent to which God would use her, I stared at her beautiful face and knew she'd have my heart forever - she was here, she was safe and she was Momma's girl.

It's quite amazing how God pieces together all the small, seemingly unconnected, pieces of our lives into a perfect jigsaw puzzle, every fragment important to our story. With my survival and her safe arrival, apart from the tell-tale scar and the slightly impaired immune system, as far as I was concerned, the spleen incident was *history*. How could I have known that He would use my now missing spleen to shelter me thirty years later in order to mobilise my calling.

My littler bubba arrived a few years after that. Oh, my baby girl, my TFBB (*Tara Fatty Bum Bum*) – she was a joy to behold. The sweetest, most contented, most funny mini-me ever.

> God pieces together all the small, seemingly unconnected, pieces of our lives into a perfect jigsaw puzzle, every fragment important to our story.

Not one to do things simply, with her feet first and refusing to turn, my scrummy girl was cut out of her slumber a few weeks early and as she was placed on my chest, though I had no comprehension of the significance, the #original3 was complete. Divine perfection. My seed. My legacy.

She was a funny looking treasure in those first few weeks, with no eyelashes or eyebrows (due to her early arrival), and her little round belly which protruded over her nappy, *plus* chubby little bottom, became her trademark. TFBB was a term of endearment, a secret love language between us. Still to this day TFBB

> the #original3 was complete. Divine perfection. My seed. My legacy.

translates into I love you *baby girl*. Everything about her was delicious and scrummy and everyday I'd gaze at this gorgeous bundle of contentment in my arms and wonder how I got to be so lucky.

At this stage our family were still four, but two and half years later that would change and with it, redirect the course of all our lives forever.

I choose not to speak too much about my first marriage. I can say I loved marriage and I loved being a home maker. I loved being a *Momma* and shaping these precious human beings, whilst nurturing their individual characters, quirkiness and gifts. As people we are all broken in some way, defined not only by the perfectly unique design of our heavenly father, but also by a damaged world – sometimes (often) a generational legacy, always the nature of our own childhood and upbringing. Thankfully, for most of us, we hold on tight to all the precious memories, allowing the more difficult things to slumber. And *slumber* they graciously do..., until that slumber is disturbed, until we're triggered - when their awakening takes on many different forms – forms that are neither helpful to us, *nor*, to those we love.

God has revealed so much about this to me over the past few years, I understand it much more clearly now. Back then, I was less wise, pretty bewildered and my heart took quite a battering. My husband was a good man with a big heart, but one who carried his brokenness in a way that left me desperate and worn down. For almost ten years I tried so very hard to fix it all. The burden

> As people we are all broken in some way, defined not only by the perfectly unique design of our heavenly father, but also by a damaged world – sometimes (often) a generational legacy, always the nature of our own childhood and upbringing.

between keeping my family together and preserving my babies and myself was almost too heavy to bear. Finally, having sold our home to relocate our little family to The States; imagining that location could maybe do what was needed; the dilemma was taken out of my hands and I found myself in a situation I never dreamed I'd be in – Divorced, living in a foreign country and a single mum.

I have no doubt that when we look to ourselves for answers, God does a little bit of meddling and somehow His meddling had planted the three of us in Montgomery Alabama, living in a trailer on my big sister's land, surrounded by cotton fields as far as the eye could see, never ending sunshine and most importantly, in a wonderful Christian environment. Well, she had been praying for this since I was seven years old, hadn't she? I'm sure not under these circumstances, but who are we to tell God the method by which He should answer our prayers?

I was broken, confused, scared, ashamed, carrying a huge sense of failure and disappointment – and yet, for the first time in a very, very long time, peace visited my soul and my world felt safe. Hope stirred – I could at last allow myself to dare; dare to hope for our future, dare to hope for me and my girls.

Moment of Impact

On 5th November 1995, just a week after my husband had left to go back to the UK; during a visit to a high security women's prison in Alabama, where I'd gone with my sister to speak to incarcerated mothers about the work the ministry was doing to help their children; I finally met Jesus. Without me realising when I'd stepped out of bed that morning, the Lord had orchestrated an appointment with me in that place. And there, inside the impenetrable walls of a prison chapel, amongst the Father's broken and hurting and shame-filled girls, I... *we*, gave Him our hearts.

We; this disappointed good girl and *they,* His lost, His let-down, His abused, His desperate; we were no different to Him, we were *all* his much-loved daughters; unique, perfectly formed, called with a purpose, cherished, cried over, and steadfastly pursued. We all carried His DNA, as we'd done our very best to navigat-

We; this disappointed good girl and *they,* His lost, His let-down, his abused, His desperate; we were no different to Him, we were *all* his **much-loved daughters; unique, perfectly formed, called** with a **purpose, cherished,** cried over, steadfastly **pursued**.

ing the snares of this world. But now, arms around each other, tears streaming down our faces, we were saved, washed clean, made pure; a new creation - beauty from ashes. Black, White, Hispanic, tall, short, thin, fat, blue eyed, brown eyed, green eyes, British, American, Mexican – sisters, standing together in their father's house as the angels sang and played the loudest victory chorus in heaven, and tears of unmatched joy rolled down our Father's face.

That night as I lay in the dark, reliving the events of the day, it dawned on me that finally, twenty-five years after my sister had begun to pray for me, I'd made it into the *gang*. And it felt great.

I started to read the bible for the very first time and though, initially, it didn't make a huge amount of sense to me, every now and then something would jump out and I'd ponder on it and then go chat it over with others wiser than I. So many crazy things happened during those early weeks, as the three of us adjusted to our new normal, as I grew in my understanding of Him, as I worked through my tangled emotions. And as the ministry that my sister and her husband would ultimately lead into a global organisation, was just being seeded. God used us and tested and stretched my heart and my imagination in incredible ways.

The first thing that happened was quite simply, a miracle. An outpouring of His glory and favour. A bit of divine showing-off to draw up and propagate the baby shoots of faith that had begun to push their way up from deep inside my belly.

During a late night panicked visit to the doctors with TFBB, a conversation about our *funny English accents* led to a discussion about why we were in Bama and about the ministry work that my Brother in Law and sister were involved in. I didn't know it then, but God was already working out His plans and purposes through this new, raw, inexperienced, unproven vessel, giving her a peek into the wonderment of life in the gang. A few days later and totally out of the blue, the doctor who had treated my sick baby girl, pulled his car into my sister's driveway. Carefully taking stock of the simple makeshift ministry operations, his eyes first examining the small mobile homes parked in what was essentially the back yard of their family home, before shifting to the group of small children boisterously bouncing on the large trampoline close by and then to the two young volunteers who were lovingly gesturing to the fearless pre-schoolers to slow down. I watched searchingly from inside the front window of one of the mobile homes, studying his face and curious about the large envelope clutched in his hand as he stepped confidently from his car and wandered across to the main house.

An hour later, I would discover in amazement and disbelief just what had been inside that envelope.

The title deeds to twenty acres of woodland and prime construction land.

By some crazy miracle, on that otherwise unremarkable day, a plot of land *practically perfect in every way* was spontaneously donated for the work of the ministry, sparked by a spontaneous decision to visit to the doctors. **Phase 1** of the vision for **NCO** could now be mobilised, Building work could begin. The promise of provision had been fulfilled.

And on my establishing shoots of faith, buds had begun to appear.

Not long after, the workers began to mysteriously show up, one after the other; random conversations, unusual meetings; people just came from nowhere. With their finances, with their expertise, with their creativity, with their passion and love. Who else but Jesus?

On another occasion I had been so moved by the message of a visiting preacher in church one Sunday morning speaking about his work with Romanian orphans, that I felt called to donate half of all the money I'd set aside to finance the deposit on a home for the girls and me. *It was going to an orphanage after all,* I thought, *and for now we could live rent free in this trailer.* I felt God needed to know I wasn't playing at this. When we left the UK we had sold our house, so when we separated we simply split what we had down the middle. I had $20 000, which ultimately was to be the deposit on a home for the three of us. All afternoon my head was telling me giving away $10 000 was a crazy idea, but I couldn't shift this need to show Jesus I was *all in*. Eventually and with total peace, I wrote a cheque for *Ten Thousand Dollars*, scribbled a note which read 'please don't say anything about this' (the preacher was a friend of my sister and I wanted to keep it under the radar), popped them both in the envelope and feeling happy with my decision, went to get the girls ready for the evening service.

The message that evening was no less compelling and confirmed to me that these children needed the money much more than I did and with great ease, as I walked out of the church, I dropped my sealed envelope into the bucket.

The following morning, my sister called me into her office awkwardly. She said she didn't know how to say this, but the preacher had called her in a state of panic. He knew my current situation and whilst blown away by what he'd found in the envelope, felt he couldn't take what was critically the only means of securing our own home. She said he had pinned the cheque to his office notice board as a reminder of my significant act of faith and generosity. I had mixed feelings at the time, but looking back I often wonder if maybe it was an *Abraham and Isaac* moment? Maybe, maybe not? But I can tell you that though I have had many vulnerable and uncertain moments since, the Lord has always provided ridiculously for me, in fact there have been times where I have felt like He has literally poured out the storehouses of Heaven over me in ways I could never have imagined.

Faith is a beautiful mystery.

Christmas was fast approaching and as the first one with just *us*, I made a huge effort to make everything perfect. I bought a *ginormous* Christmas tree and put up hundreds of fairy light around the decking outside; it looked magical. As strange as it was, it was also joy-filled and things seemed to be getting better at last.

As New Year arrived, with a successful and relatively happy *holiday season* under my belt, it didn't take long for that independent streak to start fighting back and feeling stronger in myself, I was sure I was ready to step out of this cocoon and take on the real world again.

Moment of Impact.

I decided it was time to head back home to England and start to build a new life for me and my girls. My sis and brother-in-law were terrified about me going home as a single mum and a brand-new Christian, but I was confident and raring to go and began to apply for jobs in the UK. One morning I was awoken to my phone ringing. I looked at my watch, it was 6.30am. Clearing my throat, "urggg Hello" I croaked, sitting upright and pulling my pillow behind me. It was already 12.30pm at home.

"Hi there" a male voice replied, "I have your CV here and would love it if you'd come in to see us as soon as you get back to the UK."

It was a bank. Not the same one I'd worked for previously, but they'd read my résumé and liked what they saw. Not going to lie, banking again.... *Hmmmm,* but getting this job would mean I could secure a mortgage to put a roof over our heads, so I couldn't be too choosy; plus, I already had a very specific roof in mind and I didn't want to lose it. It was going to be our little sanctuary; in the same lane I'd grown up and close to my mum and I would make it look beautiful. All the pieces of the jigsaw were coming together.

I can remember as clear as if it was yesterday, sitting in the departure lounge in Atlanta airport in March 1996 with all my worldly goods and these two little girls clinging to me as my brother-in-law turned and said "promise me two things:

1. Promise me you'll find yourself a good church as soon as you get home, and

2. Promise me you'll pray with those girls every day."

I had no hesitation in promising both of those.

As our flight was called, hugs done, tears wiped, goodbyes said; the three of us (plus blankie, Geggy and Sam) bound so tightly together by heart *and* by necessity - began our journey back home.

WASTELANDS

Rasha'

Bullseye. So, she'll never be mine hey? Watch and learn oh great Deliverer. This is my kingdom; these are my people. They are like little puppets in my hands. All I need to do is find their weak spot or *hearts-desire*... (chuckle)...she's been waiting for this moment her whole life - you forget, I've been watching her closely. And him... (loud laugh)

Y'shua (frown)

NO Rasha'. You're playing with fire - There will be consequences.

Rasha'

Oh dear (fake sad face)

Y'shua

Do your worst oh fallen star of the morning. Deceit and lies become you. The one who once shone so brightly, now scurrying around in dark places - playing with them as if it were pawns in your crooked game of chess - how the mighty fall...(shakes head reflectively)

You forget the leash I have around your neck, Rasha', mine to tighten and mine to loosen as I choose.

You think I didn't foresee this? You think I didn't make plans? Your haughtiness blinds you. Her; her seed; I have made provision. More than that, even. That light you saw, that was me - she's been set apart. Her journey has only just begun. (loud victory laugh)

And... (lowers eyes, slow deep breath)

...the other may take a little longer. The unbinding is a delicate process; but you should know, they carry my DNA, they are mine and no thief, even one as cunning as you, can take them from me. When it's time.... well, you'll just have to wait and see (peaceful smile).

Enjoy your small triumphs Rasha', the final battle draws nigh and I think we both know how that will end.

Be well balanced and always alert, because your enemy,

the devil, roams around incessantly, like a roaring lion

looking for its prey to devour. **1 Peter 5:8 TPT**

3

Under Royal Protection

By the window to the woods where the deer and creatures play,
there is a girl – a dreamer of dreams with a sore heart. She lives
there among her books and tea and a measure of heartbreak, loving
illustration, pretty things and falling asleep far, far into the night.

AUTHOR UNKNOWN

I remember the first time I saw his face. Of course, I see it with slightly different eyes now, but oh how that moment is etched in my heart. It was very brief and formal – a welcome introduction, as he reached out to shake my hand: "Hello" he said, "so you're the one."

Moment of Impact

He had this cute, crooked smile and a confident but endearing swagger, resting his hands casually on his hips as he spoke. He recounted how an old work flyer from my previous job had been passed round the office ahead of me starting and whilst I felt a little unnerved at the image of that, the way his blue eyes smiled into the deepest part of my soul, was more unnerving still.

I had arrived home just two months earlier and, in that time, had secured a good job with the bank, bought a lovely two-bedroom house and begun to gather lots of ideas for its renovation, starting with the girls' bedroom. To keep my promises, I'd pulled out the yellow pages (*Google* on paper for those under thirty), trying to find a suitable church. Every night I'd sit between the girls' beds and we'd hold hands and pray together. And each mealtime, we'd hold hands around the kitchen table and give thanks. I was feeling relatively proud of myself, that finally I had done this and that my girls were shielded from this big cruel world... and I could speak life and joy and hope into them.

My big girl danced and sang her way around the house with the confidence of a twenty-year-old, whilst TFBB, who has been a *Mommas girl* from day one, spent hours off somewhere chattering to herself, blankie draped over one arm, *Geggy* in the other and her *dodie,* hanging out of the corner of her mouth like an old man's pipe; leaving legions of *I love you notes* around the house for everyone. Then every single night without fail, just like clockwork, she would inch her way into my bedroom.

Standing on her tippy toes; bleary eyed, with her crazy long hair hanging loose across her face; the tips of her fingers would strain to turn the wobbly old wooden knob on my bedroom door. Having managed that, in complete silence and with a certain knowing, she'd reach up into the darkness and expanse of my big old brass bed, confident that I would sense her there and tenderly grasp her wrist to pull her the rest of the way. Then she'd find her place alongside me, her nose positioned tip-to-tip with mine; her right leg strategically thrown over my left hip; her hands clasped together inside mine and wedged securely underneath my chin; and there we would both lay, face to face until morning, like each other's invisible comfort blanket. Sometimes it seemed impossible to know where I ended and she began.

Sometimes it seemed impossible to know where I ended and she began...

Often my sleep would not be as peaceful as hers, but she never knew. I'd lie awake listening to the clock ticking on the wall, loving the comfort of her gentle breath against my cheek and the closeness of her tiny body; yet vulnerable and almost childlike myself – wondering what the future would hold, wondering if anyone would ever wrap their arms around me again and tell me it was all going to be OK? Sometimes I'd whisper quietly into the darkness: *I'm a little scared too.* It wasn't for anyone, just me speaking out my fears to the night, but somehow it made me feel heard.

By daybreak (never before) my big girl would come alongside us. She always loved sleep and her own bed, but the mornings were about the three of us, snuggled up together *as one*, chattering, before the craziness of the day. The little girl that had stirred within me and battled the shadows of the night was long gone by then; once more the fearless, strong, silly Mummy; the sorter of problems, the encourager of dreams, the giver of love, food, correction and everything in between.

> The reality was, I was their world and they were each half of mine and it was so much more glorious than I fully understood.

If we are not careful, we can let the total wonder of the moment give way to worry and thoughts of what will be – I did that a lot back then. The reality was, I was their world and they were each half of mine and it was so much more glorious than I fully understood.

Even with a job, money was tight, so many evenings we'd stroll across the road to Mum who was on her own by then and she would bless us with our evening meal. She also helped me with all the practicalities of getting the girls to and from school - it was a real team effort and a great blessing.

Finding a church was a whole different story. Our three-strong team walked sheepishly into several of the churches I'd circled over the course of the first few months. *They* clung to me and I to them, as quietly and discretely, we slipped into the back pews (always, just as the service was due to start), a mix of anxiousness and courage flooding my soul. I'd worked out that if we didn't arrive too early and slipped away again just before the end, no one would get a chance to ask too many questions.

"Which church are you from?" would be the usual one.

"Where's your Daddy?" was the one I always imagined coming next.

Of course, they wouldn't ask that, but they would think it, I knew they would think it. I didn't want to have to spill my shame to a bunch of strangers. I didn't want to tell these people who knew nothing about me that I was a failure, that my girls were now a statistic because I couldn't make my marriage work, that I was someone to be pitied now instead of applauded, that I could no longer be classed as a *good girl*, but a bad girl who had failed at life and was now *divorced*.

And most of all I didn't want to admit that I was a *newbie* – yes, I guess you could have called me a Christian, but I wasn't a *proper* one, was I? I didn't know all the right words to use or what to say at what time. I couldn't quote bible verses; crikey, I didn't even know what was really in the bible.

Suffocation would roll over me in waves and nausea lay heavy in my stomach. *Time to get out of here* would reliably ring in my head like an alarm clock at the set moment when the pastor began to wind up his message and the worship team (made up of people all over the aged of fifty) began their ascent back onto the platform. Ready to make our escape, I'd scan the people in the rows in front of us to gauge the optimum moment to make a dash for it. Always, it seemed to me, they would intuitively sense what was going on and frustratingly turn a second too soon, smiling sweetly at us; the two extremely cute faces either side of me acting as a magnet.

They are well-meaning, I'd acknowledge to myself, but as much as I knew I ought to need this and that I'd made a promise, I felt absolutely no affinity with any of these kind people; they weren't like me; I would never hang out with them socially - and with each visit I was increasingly reminded that it was us against the world. We were on our own, we were strong and we could do this together; me, them and Jesus.

Moment of Impact.

"Let's go home girls" I smiled down, giving their hands a reassuring squeezing, as the final heartfelt attempt ended in much the same way as the other two had. It all seemed futile and awkward and... lonely. And so it was, the #original3 gave up the search, heading home together, satisfied that they'd genuinely tried and been true to their commitments. Certain they could do *this* on their own.

My faith was as steadfast as ever, though I struggled massively to pray for my own life, because I felt so much shame about being divorced and guilt about not being in church. Many nights I'd sit on the living room floor, my back against the radiator, uncontrollably sobbing. How could this be my life? I'd wonder how God could possibly ever answer my prayers when I'd split my family up.

By the time we had arrived back from the States, just a month after the divorce was complete (it is very quick there), their Daddy's life had already moved on. The girls would be picked up for the weekend and come back with stories about horse-riding with Daddy and....? The adrenaline rushing through my body would turn my legs to jelly and my heart would beat so fast I felt sure they could hear it. "How lovely", I'd reply with a half-hearted smile. Nothing within me would allow myself to say anything bad to them about the situation or about their Daddy because I knew he adored them and it just wouldn't be wise. But inside, everything I knew to be right, to be lovely, to be precious was being destroyed piece by piece.

With the girls distracted by the TV, I'd retreat into the bathroom and sob; "Lord, help me – it's not supposed to be this way. I feel so alone and frightened and sad and without any hope. I've removed my girls from one situation only to have that replaced with another that's equally wrong. I don't know how to do this; or if I can do this."

"Mummy?" TFBB tugged on the edge of my T-Shirt as I slowly peeled vegetables for tea, my mind lost in a sea of despair –

"Mummy, are you OK?" she whispered quietly, "did we do something wrong?" The worried expression in her young, yet seriously discerning voice, stabbing at my heart. She strained her head around my waist to get a better look at my face, a concerned examination, from a little girl who doesn't want to make Mummy sad. My tears had been shed in secret, but my heartache, though placed back inside its box, was now betrayed by the tell-tale swell beneath my eyes.

"Should we not have gone on the horsies?" she asked timidly.

In that very moment, my heart tore open wide, as I scooped her up in my arms and squeezed her as tight as I possibly could, discretely wiping away the fresh tears trickling down, unseen, over her shoulder.

How on earth can I explain any of this to my precious, sweet girl Lord? is what I was thinking...

"No, of course you haven't done anything wrong, Sweetheart, Mummy is just feeling a bit poorly – I bet the horses were really exciting, what lucky girls you are, was it fun?" is what I replied.

The truth is, it really isn't supposed to be this way, but we live in a broken world, full of broken people, broken promises, broken dreams and stubborn independence. In my case I've tagged it as *Arrogant Independence*. It's an element of pride and self-reliance that says I can solve this; I know what I need to do; *I can take this into my own hands and sort it.* Sometimes I even go so far as to think I know what God must surely want me to do. And that's exactly what I did in this case. Not realising at the time, that God had actually removed the girls and I from of a bad situation, I attempted to single-handedly put my marriage back together.

> The truth was/is, it **really isn't supposed to be this way,** but we live in a broken world, full of broken people, broken promises, broken dreams and stubborn independence.

Excitedly I began to make plans for how this would go. Ignoring all the warning flags and facts, I knew that If I could bring about this *great reunion,* all of the pain, all of the shame, all of the *weekends at Daddy's* with the steady stream of girlfriends, all of the wrong life-lessons my girls were witnessing *(plus God's certain disappointment with me),* would all go away. I pushed to the back of my mind the past problems and painted this idyllic image in my mind. I was ready to make it all right again.

That is most definitely not how it played out.

And never have I been more grateful for God's correction and intervention.

I believe we all have an individual view of God and we make assumptions about what He thinks in different situations. We look through our own eyes or through the eyes of doctrine and religious law, overlooking how crazy tenderhearted He is, often forgetting His bigger picture, or all the other parts of the jigsaw puzzle. These days I know Him much better than I did then (though I'm still only scratching the surface), still I've found Him to be way more creative and mischievous than we give Him credit for. I think He laughs with us, cries with us, dreams with us – He wants the absolute best for us, but first He wants our hearts. He wants us to love Him, to trust Him, to talk to Him, to let go of all the broken pieces, let go of who we think we should be and allow Him (not us) to shape them into the masterpiece they were originally intended to be; perfectly imperfect; gloriously beautiful; called, known and loved.

> I've found Him to be way more creative and mischievous than we give Him credit for. I think he laughs with us, cries with us, dreams with us – he wants the absolute best for us, but first **he wants our hearts.**

So, despite my meddling, we remained #orignal3 and with my misjudged plan behind us, and with a renewed sense of hope, life in our amazing little home fell into a steady rhythm. Work was going well and I had been promoted twice and was now working as part of the business team. Socially my friend had been dragging me out to local pubs, but

I decided pretty quickly this wasn't for me and instead enjoyed cosy weekends snuggled up with my girlies in front of the TV, fire crackling, the scent of cinnamon candles filling the air. On the weekends when they were away, I'd put my *lights-off* playlist on in the background and work on something creative; writing, sewing or gathering ideas for my next decorating project – or just sitting in the quiet, dreaming. Life felt pretty good in the most part. I talked to God often and though I wasn't sure if I deserved it, I would ask Him to send someone special *for me*.

I desperately wanted someone who was similar to me in upbringing, who knew Jesus too, but not someone who was so far ahead of me in their walk with Him that I'd get left behind and feel out of my depth. I wanted to grow with someone together; in love and in faith. I told God it had to be *the one* next time. I wanted *the one* or none at all. I couldn't possibly go through any of this ever again, my heart would surely not survive and I certainly had no interest in testing the market.

The sound of the phone ringing brought me back from my mental wanderings. The girls were with their dad this weekend and the house was quiet.

"So", my friend said mischievously, "I wondered if you'd do me a favour?" She went on, "Someone who works with my mother-in-law is a Spiritualist and she's meant to be really good, will you come with me if I go, it's just at her house?" I'd vaguely remembered her saying something once about her mother-in-law having some sort of gift (as she put it), but I took that kind of stuff with a pinch of salt and didn't really believe any of it, so hadn't taken too much notice at the time.

"What do you think?" she pushed excitedly.

"Urggg, I don't think so," I sniggered back, "It's not my kind of thing, plus, I don't believe in that kind of stuff."

I knew that as a Christian I wasn't meant to entertain that kind of thing (though in all honesty, I didn't see how there could possibly be any practical risk?)

Besides the fact that I really

did think it was a bunch of nonsense, I knew that as a Christian I wasn't meant to entertain that kind of thing (though in all honesty, I didn't see how there could possibly be any practical risk....) – it was fake, made up *mumbo-jumbo*, trickery intended to bring fake hope to anyone naïve enough to think random strange women could really tell you your future. That was God's job and mostly He chose to keep it to Himself; I guess for our own good?

"Oh, pleaaaaase," she begged, "I really want to go and don't want to go on my own. Will you at least come with me?"

I put my head back, thinking for a second and sighed quietly, What's the worst? I reasoned with myself, a good old laugh at the ridiculousness of it later and a wasted few hours.

The small niggling discomfort of a good girl, a wise girl (of a Father) was doing its very best to snatch me back from the lair; *just say no, put the phone down, do it now,* it urged.

But the pleaser, the one who hated to disappoint, against her better judgement lamented 'OK.' Reluctantly shaking her head and smiling, almost bemoaning herself, "I'll come with you, but I'm staying outside, I'm not coming in."

Moment of Impact

We pulled up to a small terrace house, my friend's mother-in-law had come with us, to introduce the lady. The house was cosy and dimly lit with candles scattered around the main room. The lady who seemed pleasant enough took my friend into a back room and we waited on the sofa. We chatted generally for a while and time passed. My friend had been gone a good half-hour now and I wondered what on earth she was saying to her.

"I'm starting to get something." I looked up surprised and a little confused; "I'm picking up a man. It's like he's been waiting urgently to talk to you." I smiled politely, trying not to be rude, whilst wanting to make it clear that I wasn't interested and didn't believe in any of this rubbish.

"He's saying he watches your little girl chatting away to herself in her bedroom, with her pigtails, just like you used to do. He says she reminds him so much of you."

Straight face, my heart started to beat a little faster. *Don't give anything away, this is a trick, don't help her. Quick, quick, think, does this woman know anything about me.* My mind raced whilst trying to recall if there was any possibility that I had met her before, I didn't think so?

"I think it might be your dad," she announced much to my offence.

What a low punch, I was angry now, 'of all the low-down things to use, but how could she possibly know?

Before I could respond she began again: "he says he's watching you, you're not yourself at the moment. You're walking round with your head down. Lift it up, people are watching you. He said that you've lost your sparkle. When you were a little girl there was a light in you that drew everyone to you. You lit up the room when you walked in. You were always a happy little girl."

She then talked a bit about seeing me puff up cushions and loving making my house look nice.

Faster and faster my heart pounded. None of this made sense, yet all of it made sense. I was so confused. Every word coming out of her mouth was so specific and by now I knew that she couldn't possibly be taking pot-luck guesses.

"Prove it to me", I blurted out without thinking.

COMMAND HQ:

Unheard, in a place not far away at all, a loud contemptuous victory cheer went down.

Naively, "ask him something no one else would know," I challenged.

I knew I had her now. I didn't plan on being easy fodder for anyone anytime soon. But, as if in slow motion, she bent over and reached down to her leg and began stroking her shin up and down, as she asked, "did your dad have a problem, a sore on his leg here?" I froze. For as long as I could remember, my dad had a sore on his leg, right where her hand was currently caressing, that would not go away. He had some ointment that we all called his magic cream, which periodically did the trick, but back it would come time after time. I was transfixed.

Then, with the last throw of the dice, I knew for certain that whoever she was talking to knew my dad and knew me. She stood up from the sofa, spread her arms out to her side, lifted one foot off the ground in a balancing position and said, "I can see your dad stood on a car like this" – I had an old photograph of my Dad stood in the exact same position she was now, on the bonnet of a car he and my mum had when they were first married.

"Can I come and see you again?" I asked yearningly, as the door to the back room flung open and my friend walked out.

COMMAND HQ:

Simultaneously, out of sight, in a dark hidden place, a raucous narcissistic celebration had just got underway. The plan had worked to perfection.

Set apart indeed. He gloated as he raised his glass heavenwards. "Cheers your majesty, here's to the next challenge – I'd say that's ONE to me."

As the minions entertained themselves indulgently, he set about clearing places at the table for all of them. It would not be long now he boasted to himself, full of pride and conceit. Walking from the table he loitered as he passed the mirror, admiring the face of a victor, the face of a great strategist, acknowledging that he was more skilled and magnificent than even he had given himself credit for.

And *that's saying something,* he chuckled to himself, as he joined the after-party.

Now, a mere one week after that first heart pounding revelatory session, with pleasantries over and nerves settled, here I was sitting across *her* kitchen table, tape recorder switched on ready to capture every word.

It did not disappoint.

There was a *lot* that went on that tape, some things I choose not to share, but by the time she came on to the things that directly impact this part of my story, there was not a single doubt in my mind that wherever and however she was picking up this stuff, it was coming from a source that knew the intricate details of my life!

There was not a single doubt in my mind that *wherever* and *however* she was picking up this stuff, it was coming from a source that knew the intricate details of my life.

She told me lots about my dad again and how he remembered that light in me as a small girl, repeating that I needed to lift my head up, so I could see just how much people were watching me. Subtly, woven throughout these highly emotive statements, were 'leading' suggestions; hints about how my dad would like to see my future unfold; throw away comments regarding his thoughts and feelings on my past; 'fatherly' guidance (let's say for now), sprinkled with just enough *fairy-dust* to leave me fooled into thinking I honestly had some choice in the matter - for anyone that knew me, also knew, the huge value I placed on my dad's opinion.

She suggested that a new man was coming into my life - *someone with a lovely smiling face,* she insisted - *a really kind person;* enquiring if there was anyone around me like that, maybe at work? It seemed an odd thing to ask, but I humoured her briefly by speculating, then shrugging my shoulders, countered with, "Hmmm, not really." I was quite sure if there'd been anyone single in the office fitting that description I'd have spotted them by now.

"Well, watch this space", is all she came back with.

She then went on to say that she saw the brightest future ahead for me, one where everything would be wonderful; "In fact", she said, "I can't see any issues at all, everything looks perfect – there will be no more tears". Gosh, that felt like a pipe-dream. She slipped in that there would be lots of children and that whilst life would be busy, it wouldn't be a problem. Finally, casting her climactic-spell, she painted for me a picture-perfect scene; me, standing on the driveway of a large, detached house, smiling from ear to ear. *It had seemed like forever since I'd felt able to smile that way!*

For a good few weeks after the meeting, I'd drive around with the tape playing in my car; astounded by the accuracy of the factual and observational information within it. I knew it was something Christians are warned against, but I couldn't rationalise that warning against what I'd seen and heard. The stuff was so accurate, it was like someone had been shadowing me since I was a little girl and was now hanging out with my dad in heaven, to give me his encouraging words and advice and promises of things to come. I couldn't put any weight in it, nor could I deny it and because I felt I shouldn't have really given it the time of day, I couldn't I really ask anyone for advice. In the end, I dropped the tape in a box of old photographs and school books in my loft; the kind of box that gets lugged from house to house each time you move, but never gets sorted; and gave it no more thought, apart from on the rare occasion when some random conversation triggered a memory - when that happened the same conundrum would fleetingly drift through my mind - *Still don't get it, but it's irrelevant now anyway, so that's fine.*

Moment of Impact

After that first day in the office, I had very little to do with him, in fact, unless we passed on the stairs and said "Hi", we barely spoke. When the role came up in the Business Centre, he and the guy who would eventually become my boss interviewed me and I guess I must have impressed them, because I got the job. Once I started, he was *super* helpful; he was just *that* person in the office who went out of their way to lend a hand to anyone who needed it. Though he was quite private, over time, I learned our upbringings had been quite similar; both raised within a close family unit; both raised in church - I liked that. Regrettably, I learned too, that he'd been navigating the same torrid personal journey as me - I liked that far less.

I shared what little wisdom and encouragement I could, feeling sad and knowing all too well the reality and pain of what was ahead. Still, through our shared wrestles and scrapes, we became firm friends. Despite that, before the year was up, he'd left the team. He'd been offered a great role thirty miles away and whilst the dynamics in the office inevitably shifted and his absence definitely felt, the world kept revolving as it always does. Very occasionally we'd speak on the phone. I had received a promotion and he called to see how I was getting on.

Over time, his calls became more frequent, changing up a gear from quick five-minute chats, to longer, more meaningful conversations, and simultaneously, I began to notice small, subtle changes taking place in the empty places of my heart. I wondered, as these feelings grew, whether this might be God's answer to the many long nights of tear-filled prayers? Whether He might be about to take our two hurting, muddled lives and make something precious with them? There had been nothing but telephone conversations between us, nothing at all; yet something unspoken, something powerful, something beautiful had started to grow.

And with that, also grew confusion. I wanted to believe so badly that God was in *this*; that *this* was His gift, yet I wasn't sure with all we'd each walked through, whether that was even a possibility? And so I prayed; in fact, over the next few months I had non-stop conversations with God. To be honest, they were probably less of conversations and more like me firing questions at Him, hoping I'd get the answers I wanted. The real truth was, by now, my heart was so utterly invested that it would have taken a pretty radical act by God to untangle it.

By late the following year, *we* had quietly become *us*.

Despite the many sensitive issues that had to be navigated, I had never felt such joy. Though I had dreamed and prayed for this *once in a lifetime* love pretty much all my life, honestly, I hadn't really believed it actually existed. I'd often wondered if I had been the issue; if perhaps I simply didn't have the ability to love the way I imagined – the *all in,* forever, *till death do us part* kind of love – but here it was, everything I'd hoped for and more. We'd talked about family and faith and I dreamed that one day we would serve the Lord together in our local church, or perhaps in time even go to Africa and build a school or something – even though he worked in the corporate space, he was amazing with DIY projects. I had so much expectation, so much to be thankful for.

By spring, the children had hung out a few times.

He'd finally met my Mum, who was immediately smitten.

And already, TFBB had sent him five or six *I love you* notes – A sure sign of acceptance.

It seemed to me in that moment, life could not have been more perfect.

Rasha'

Such beautiful naivety. What a perfect picture of domestic destruction; just how I like it (laugh). They look so happy don't they Y'shua? Busy rebuilding Paradise; as if by resetting the compass of their lives they might somehow get it right this time. Well, we both know what happens in Paradise don't we, Y'Sssssssssssssshua?(sarcastic laugh)

Y'shua

Oh I remember Paradise you serpent of seduction. You crafty *ground dweller*. Though I prefer to talk about the three days we spent together in Jerusalem, right after...... Ahhh, perhaps your memory is hazy; or simply selective...............(shakes set of iron keys).

Soon there shall be a new covenant, bound in Heaven - Redeemed, bought-back. All that *you* meant for evil, I will turn for good. Out of this union will flourish fierce love, great purposes fulfilled for the Kingdom of Heaven. Many more holy covenants will come through each of the five seeds and their seeds. You see only your next move Rasha', I see the whole chessboard and out of this, shall the *King's glory* shine.

Rasha'

With great respect m'Lord, I believe you are mistaken - Tell me, I have never quite understood your design process? Of course, I'm incredibly honoured by the favour you bestow on me; time after time you make my work so easy; I barely have to lift a finger. Still, I am curious? You create this perfect *mini-me*, glowing with family resemblance; a real *piece de resistance*, then you tinker; adding a piece from this generation and a piece from that generation; knowing those pieces are already weakened and smeared with my mark; the whole process leaving deliciously exposed areas.

Even more curiously, after lovingly reinforcing and smoothing away any visible joins, you proceed to push your right finger through the middle, forming a great hole. I wonder, are you playing games with me my King? (a mocking reverence disguises quiet distrust and inquisitiveness).

No matter, I receive your gifts graciously (dramatic fake courtesy).

Y'shua

That hole that perplexes you so much, Rasha', is their birthright. It is their Father's seal. I carry every single missing piece here in my pocket. (opens pocket, emitting a blinding light that thrusts Rasha' to the ground). I am never without them. Sadly, there are many that never came, never knew; that struggled on alone. Oh, how I called to them (looks sad and reflective). But of course, you know that don't you, your grip unyielding.

Obviously, I don't have hers (smiles jubilantly), It radiates from her. But, the other...(pats pocket protectively), the other is right here.

This alone I have discovered, God made us plain and simple (upright), but we have made ourselves very complicated (pursuing many schemes) **Ecclesiastes 7:29 GNT**

4

Eyes That See Are Rare

Eye contact is such a wildly courageous, electrifying, adrenalizing
exchange between two naked souls.

In the first few *un-nerving* seconds, amidst the deafening absence
of words,

there comes an unmasking of the heart's true desire;

an unveiling of the mind's selfish intent.

In an instant and in a way that cannot be matched,

indisputable truth reveals itself involuntarily –

then, just as quickly, it's gone.

C.S.

April 2001

As the cotton fields swayed gently,
On a perfect day in spring,
In an old plantation 'home-stead'
We exchanged our wedding rings·
A more perfect place there could not be,

Nor a truer vow be made,
I felt sure I heard the angels sing,
As our friends and family prayed·
With the sun shining down on the red soil,
And the breeze sending flax through the air,
By, the small white painted chapels,
Where God's people bowed in prayer·
It's a place I will always hold close to my heart,
And I'll treasure those threads that have bound,
The worn fabric of two faded lives that were ours,
To the seamless love that we share now· X

I have always known that life flows out of my heart. If I love you, I love you hard. It's not a weakness, it's my superpower. I'm not talking about the way I love people generally; I do, I really love people in that *loving others, wanting the best for everyone* kind of way. Nor am I talking about infatuation or needy love. I'm talking spirit-filled, unconditional, supernatural, unexplainable love. The kind of love that is significant, that's part of your purpose, that tangible and exists in the very core of your being – the kind of love that requires everything from you, that cuts and bruises and challenges you in ways you never thought possible, the kind that suddenly stops fitting the pretty pictures you created in your head and shifts into reality and truth and revelation and growth; the kind that steers you ever closer to the person you were always meant to be and calls you to act in the complete opposite way to what the world expects.

> The kind of love that requires everything from you, that calls you to act in the complete opposite way to what the world expects.

I loved him that way. I can't say I fully understood what this meant at the beginning, how could I? I was caught up in those early fluttering's of raw emotion and expectancy. What started as a tiny seed had grown and blossomed very quickly into a glorious flower and it seemed we were living in an eternal summer. There was still so much I had to learn about him, layer after layer, I wanted to know where he had come from, what made him tick, who he had loved, who had broken his heart, his regrets, the things he really believed in, what he envisioned for his life and our life, and how he felt about Jesus. I had no idea what I was going to find as I peeled back those layers and I had no comprehension of the journey and hot coals this love would have to walk over, to come to the full realisation of the sheer unnaturalness of it all.

I loved the fact that he really *got me*, more than any other human being on the planet – that had never happened to me before - and whilst were really different in character and approach, in so many ways; in the important things; we thought alike (often, at the same time) and pulled together, standing united to support each other with the tricky stuff. He was naturally smart and I was in awe of his extremely logical brain, particularly when I was in one of my crazy, *thoughts all over the place/ idea generating* moments. Just like my dad had done, he brought balance, considerations, pros and cons; which at first drove my impulsive *let's-just-do-this* nature insane; but I quickly learned to massively value it and in return, I feel I brought him some street cred and *joie de vivre*.

We married in an old plantation house in America's Deep South. My niece was getting married and we were going over for the wedding so we planned a simple ceremony the week before. Out of respect, we kept the wedding fairly low key back home and only told my girls the night before we flew, they were so excited. It was hard not to have all the children with us, but it just hadn't been possible. My brother-in-law married us and we hired the house from a friend, it was like something from *Gone with the Wind*, with a sprawling central staircase descending to what would be our alter, unity candles erected, ready to symbolise the coming together of our two little families; outside, a large wraparound porch and wooden swing - a throwback to slower, simpler days gone by. The sun shone, the birds sang and it could not have been more perfect.

My girls gave me away and as we stood together at the top of the stairs squeezing each other's hands tightly, waiting for the music to start; knowing, but not saying, that this would be the very last time it would ever be just the three of us again; I caught a glimpse of him waiting for us down below and I gave thanks to God for this incredible day, for His faithfulness to us.

He met us at the bottom of the stairs, his smile reassuring me, and my heart leapt with joy as his eyes glistened with the hint of a tear. For the girls, this was an act of courage, of trust; for so long now it had just been the three of us against the world and now we were about to become seven; but by now they loved him too and as, *together,* they lifted my hand into his, we stepped forward to where our rings sat on the open pages of the bible in my brother-in-law's hands.

> For the girls, this was an **act of courage**, of trust; for so long now it had just been the three of us against the world...

Love is patient, love is kind. It does not envy, it does not boast, it is not proud. It does not dishonor others, it is not self-seeking, it is not easily angered, it keeps no record of wrongs. Love does not delight in evil but rejoices with the truth. It always protects, always trusts, always hopes, always perseveres

1 Corinthians 13:4-7 NIV

And now these three remain: faith, hope and love. But the greatest of these is love.

1 Corinthians 13:13 NIV

This was surely the happiest day of my life.

Home became a 400-year-old farmhouse that we bought to renovate soon after we married. This had always been *my* dream really, not his; I'd always imagined living in an old house in the country with chickens and ducks in the garden and a pair of green wellies standing proud at the door; so that's what we did. It took a lot of work and many late nights to complete, but it was an idyllic place for the children to grow up and call home. They all had such fun picking and naming their own hen and then collecting the eggs once they began to lay – it was quite an education for them.

We had been quite clear from the start that our priority would always be the children, making sure they never suffered because of any family dynamics, and so life evolved into a kind of *beautiful chaos*. There was always much to be fitted into family schedules, but we did all we could to love them hard, to shield them, to nurture and grow them and to (*perhaps*) overcompensate for the things by which we were both quietly burdened.

Despite this, we remained thankful for each other and our complementary gifts and skills, which together, albeit sometimes clumsily, helped us to balance the needs and the wants, the questions and the disappointments, the *conflicts of interest* and *conflicts of personalities*, the hurts and the tears and the social and spiritual shaping of five very different, but very amazing children.

Saturday nights were where the real treasure was found – Saturday nights were where the smelted particles of our blended lives poured out of the furnace like pure gold - Movies (frequently the Lizzie McGuire movie), popcorn, laughter, log burner, new dance moves; plus the occasional help with complicated homework or the odd arbitration of personality clashes.

No matter where my story ends, I will forever see this as one of the great gifts of my life.

Some of the most fun times were our annual summer holidays. Each year we would pack ourselves into *the bus,* as we'd call it; our seven-seater people carrier – two adults, five small to medium sized humans, suitcases, back-packs, tennis rackets, a football, copious amounts of reading material and maps, food and drink, games, a wholesale size box of giant cola bottles (candy) and chomps, nonstop chatter and debate and laughter. And of course, *Club Tropicana* by Wham blasting out of the CD player (always a holiday essential); as off we'd drive, down to the South of France. Preparing for these trips was always stressful - remember I was a barefoot, go with the flow, simple life sort of gal – these were military scale operations and a few weeks before I definitely did not feel like I was preparing for a relaxing summer holiday. But looking back on them now, they were glorious. They were (are) the things we all still talk about with fondness and laughter, and that makes me happy.

It was on the way back from one of these trips, having read the most amazing book and having all but forced two of the teenagers in my usual *overtly enthusiastic* way to read it too, I decided I had to write to Mel Gibson to try and influence him to make it into a movie. Though it was a Christian book, it was such a powerful love story that it had the potential to be turned into a mainstream blockbuster, which in turn, I was certain, would win souls for the Kingdom. I knew from all the trashy celeb magazines that Mel had a kind of *curious* faith. I didn't want this to be made by one of the gentle Christian film companies, those movies were only ever watched by Christians. No, I wanted this to be a huge, much anticipated, Hollywood, red carpet affair that totally caught people off-guard.

I think they all thought I was bonkers, as I shared my idea on the long drive home, but I wanted to inspire faith in them; I wanted them to expect the unimaginable; to live a life without walls. Eventually, I managed to catch their imagination, I knew I would in the end and we passed a good few hours

> I wanted to **inspire faith** in them; I wanted them to **expect the unimaginable**; to **live a life without walls**.

debating what I'd say to Mel, the day he called to invite me to the premier and which actors I thought should play the lead roles. We all had different ideas about that one. My boy just kept his eyes on the road and shook his head in despair. I entertained him and he mostly humoured me, but I always knew secretly he loved my quirkiness.

Once home, the double dose of faith in the impossible set to work.

What if, I thought, sitting down pen in hand, what if God does put my letter in front of him? *What if I could craft some clever words that might prick a vulnerable spot deep inside; crazier things have happened, right?*

I bought three copies of the book, spent ages looking for current addresses and then, asking God to do the rest, I dropped three bulky envelopes into the post box, express delivery; one to Mel's home address, one to his film company and one to his agent.

And then we waited...

Redeeming Love – Francine Rivers

1st November 2008

Dear Mel/Mr Gibson,

I have never done anything like this before. I'm a normal girl, living in a small English village, doing a normal kind of job. I have no idea whether you will even see this letter; however, having read the enclosed book a number of months ago, I felt an overwhelming need to share it with as many people as could. I pestered my children, my friends and other members of my family to read it and everyone who did reacted in the same way as I had... "WOW"

It seems that when a blockbuster is made, with high profile actors and actresses; publicised through every media possible, financed by big money - people flock to see it.

What if that wonderful story, had a profound message for a world in need of answers and *started to change lives?*

This is ultimately a beautiful love story, woven into some truly desperate events. Some of the messages are subtle, but they are there and they are profound: **Love, Forgiveness, Faith and Hope.**

Is it my desire to do this or God's? I don't know: However, I do know that if God wants to share His message, then He seeks out people who are prepared to respond to His requests. I read the book and knew that somehow its messages had to be passed on. I know that if I were to go to the movies to watch this story, I would be moved beyond measure and would talk about it long after I had left the cinema. Your name has been in my head since the day I read the last line.

My children and husband think I'm crazy, but I truly believe that if this book, by some miraculous event, lands in your hands and you have the time to read it, you too will feel a huge compulsion to turn it into something bigger.

Why you? Perhaps I see you as someone who has a strong faith; I read somewhere recently that you were the most powerful Christian in Hollywood - interesting? Perhaps it fits with the types of movies you've worked on in the past or perhaps you've had your own struggles - I don't know.

When I drop this into the post box I will have done what God has asked me to do and in many ways my job in this process is done. I will leave the rest up to Him, although I suspect my children will watch with excitement and anticipation to see whether their faith is justified.

*I pray this letter will find you and I pray you
too hear him and feel compelled to respond.*

With kind regards and hope

Cath

We didn't have to wait too long for the first reply - about ten days later
an envelope with a Californian post mark dropped through the letterbox and I tore open with awe and wonder;

ICON Productions

808 Wiltshire BLVD

Santa

Ca 90401

USA

6th Nov 2008

<u>*Request to make a movie based on a book*</u>

It went on to say;

*Thank you for your interest which is appreci-
ated, however, we are returning your letter and
book unread as it is our policy to return all
unsolicited submissions of any type.*

Ah well, I pondered, ever the optimist, there are still two more opportunities out there.

I would have to wait two more years before I received the second reply,
but the timing couldn't have been better as my faith was in need of a
boost by that stage.

The second reply was from Mel's agent who said pretty much the same thing; that it hadn't been read and they couldn't accept unsolicited mail. But this one was different. The spine of the book was well worn as if someone had read it and I couldn't help but wonder where on earth had it been for the past two years. I prayed that someone somewhere had found my book and been curious enough to read it and that somehow it had impacted their life - that's how God works sometimes. We don't always get to see the fruits of our obedience, but in this moment, I had a beautiful faith-filled picture in my head of what God had done with book two.

Sitting here writing all this down, I'm reminded of the supernatural power of God and I'm giggling to myself, that the third copy never came back. It's still out there somewhere. Our God is still a God of miracles.

> Oh, that one day **His glory** would be seen in a crazy girl's foolish **faith**.

Oh, that one day His glory would be seen in a crazy girl's foolish faith.

Outside of the children bubble, despite the endless supply of love, joy and shabby chic décor, life was packed with nonstop hurdles. We both had very demanding careers, requiring long working hours, on top of which, work on the house itself demanded much of our time, money and energy. As if that wasn't enough, we decided it might be a good idea to buy some small *doer-uppers,* houses that we could renovate and then rent and hopefully, in time, make a small profit. We

> His ways are cunning, his ways dump fault on one another, his ways are to encourage **contempt** and **self-righteousness**, his ways are to bring **accusations**, opposition, **false witness**; but mostly, with marriage as his number ONE target; his ways, indeed his expertise, is to bring dissatisfaction ('I deserve better than this'), **division** and *BOOM*......**temptation**.

did all the work ourselves, meaning we were squeezing more and more into what little spare time we had.

Unsurprisingly, the fairytale grew messy and complicated. They say don't they that the devil works hard to complicate our lives, to steal our joy? We cannot brush off responsibility for things just because we did not spot them. We cannot relinquish all obligation simply by acknowledging the shrewd and subtle ways of the great deceiver, the great destroyer. We have to wise up, we have to be ready, we have to be one step ahead. His ways are cunning, his ways dump fault on one another, his ways are to encourage contempt and self-righteousness, his ways are to bring accusations, opposition, false witness; mostly, with marriage as his number one target; his ways; indeed, his expertise is to bring dissatisfaction (*I deserve better than this*), division and *Boom*, temptation... and he is a master.

> *This iniquity of yours is like a breach about to fall, a*
>
> *bulge in a high wall, whose collapse will come suddenly—*
>
> *in an instant* **Isaiah 30:13**

Relationships aren't about rules; if you go looking for faults, you'll find them; we have to work with our own unique model and bring the best version of ourselves to the table. We are half of a whole and the more we view ourselves, inspect ourselves and consider ourselves independently of the other, the more we stop showing grace and begin competing for our individual needs. And boy doesn't *satan* just love to remind us of *our much-deserved* needs.

COMMAND HQ

He took a moment to appraise his notes...

Phase 1: Complicate – Enter pride and self-preservation ✔
Check. After all this time, he had this down to a fine art.

Phase 2: Divide – *Enter contempt* ✔

He smirked – Check. Her bewilderment had been providing him with hours of entertainment...and now it was almost time to bring out the grave-clothes - The burial was nigh.

His twisted face slowly released a vile leer, as he studied the widening breach between them. Against all the odds, his trickery had..., well...., done THE TRICK (he bellowed mischievously at his own joke). He had half expected this one to be more of a challenge than usual, but in the end, it was their good intentions and beautifully paired differences; the ones that Y'shua had coordinated so exquisitely to complement the other; that had paved the way for the execution of his plan.

He swung the axe again. With every chip, unvoiced expectations had crept out from their hiding places, triggering old wounds and sending each one into an emotional (and now physical) retreat.

He loved this part. It was a perfect storm.

Now there was just one final task left in this stage of the plan.

He stood upright, slowly unfastening the grimy black mantle that hung lifeless around his shoulders. Yanking it off ruthlessly, he stretched it wide and shook it out in readiness.

A putrid aroma of death filled the already rotten air around him.

Without a moment's hesitation, he leant across the invisible boundary, and with all the wizardry of the practiced magician that he was, he draped the mantle around all of their treasure, disguising its beauty and worth in one foul, double-cross, act of concealment.

All done, he scoffed, drawing himself back and dusting off his hands against each other in satisfaction. A master illusion, by the sleight hand of *yours truly*.

Dramatically, his gnarled body curtsied in a mocking grand-gesture, naively imagining anyone cared. To the visible eye, not a single morsel of value prevails, he laughed; a knowing laugh. A thrill ran through his entire being, as he glanced down at the remining task list.

THE SECRET PLACE

†

But someone did care.

Placing his foot on the serpent's head, Y'shua took the bottle from His Father and taking it in His right hand, delivered it carefully to Ruach, who hadn't once left their sides.

Had Rasha' already forgotten that burials paved the way for re-birth, for redemption, for deliverance? He shook His head, non-plussed... Was his memory so haughty and selective that he'd blotted out the truth; *that* the grave was... The Place of Consecration?

Ruach moved between them slowly and purposefully, His tender breath releasing the anointing oil. He felt their anguish, their unease, their alarm, their confusion (their hesitation), as if it were His own. He knew only too well, the potency of Rasha's venom and He ached for them both, knowing the journeys ahead. He would walk if for them if they'd let Him, but that would be a choice each would have to make for themselves.

He wanted their trust and their love, but He would never force them, it had to be a heart decision, otherwise it simply wouldn't sustain them.

He exhaled once more. Mercy, Peace, Love, Grace, Favour, Promise, Purpose, flowed out of every divine breath – How He loved them; how He prayed their hearts would catch hold of the remedy - of His life-line.

Y'shua turned to His left and shared a knowing smile with His Father.

In the darkness, within the covering, intended only to bring death and ruin, the holy work of re-building had begun.

†

COMMAND HQ

"Finally," he muttered, already bored and ready to get his teeth stuck into something (someone) new.

Phase 3: Value Hook (USP) – *Enter temptation*

He licked his cracked lips several times – In the business of temptation he remained *un-matched*.

The dictionary defines temptation as *an invitation; a decoy; to allure; a snare; bait; to seduce.*

For most, the word temptation summons up sinful images of lust and greed and deceit - a word that surely none of us would ever want to be associated with, yet virtually all of us live our lives flanked by daily temptation, subtly disguised in all manner of shapes and sizes.

Temptation it is the deliciously sweet, juicy and poisonous fruit of *a shining one, the Son of the Morning, fallen from heaven and* after the blood of each and every one of us. He doesn't show up dressed in scary clothing, breathing fire and roaring "Hey, fancy a walk with me down this dark and dangerous path today, it'll be fun..." No, he slips in discretely with a well advised strategy, slowly and subtly, dressed in charm, self-justification, promise and... lies, sweet, sweet lies. And he is relentless.

Temptation it is the **deliciously sweet**, juicy and poisonous fruit of *a shining one, **the Son of the Morning**, fallen from heaven and* after the blood of each and every one of us. He doesn't show up dressed in scary clothing, breathing fire and roaring "Hey, fancy a walk with me down this dark and dangerous path today, it'll be fun." No, he slips in discretely with a well advised strategy, slowly and subtly, dressed in charm, self-justification, promise and.....**lies**, sweet, sweet lies. And he is relentless.

None of it made sense to me, this happened to other people not us. But as much as I tried to fix things, nothing I did seemed to make any difference. Eventually, I understood. The only thing I had any real influence over was *me*. So, I turned to my Father, and I asked Him to help *me* work on me. He responded almost immediately, drawing me closer than ever before, but in the glow of His exuberant light and energy, I unexpectedly began to spot things that 'I' needed to deal with - Funny that isn't it!

For a good girl this was an unusual and highly disorientating experience and I hated how it made me feel. I wanted to be the *best* wife ever and so with renewed passion and faith I got busy cleaning up *my own* house. After all these years I still hadn't found a church, but my relationship with God was taking on a whole new meaning and it was about to go up another notch.

Moment of Impact

I sat down one night around the kitchen table with the girls, catching up with their day as they ate their tea. I always waited to eat with my boy when he got home from work, and that could get late, so the girls generally ate sooner. TFBB was about eleven and her big sis, fourteen. As we chatted and they ate, they began to casually throw into the conversation things about girls..., friends in-fact, at school. Girls and the things they were getting into with boys. I'm sure I don't need to paint a more graphic picture? I sensed a tension between how they thought they should feel about it; indifferent/cool; and an urgent need to get it off their chest, to unburden themselves.

Startled, I asked them to explain more - to lay it out for me.

My chest started to tighten and my stomach followed. I could not rationalise what they were telling me; we were talking about children, young children, and they were talking about things more shocking than I could get my head around. I knew deep down my girls were just as disturbed as I was, yet they weren't shocked.

"This is the norm, Mum; this is what everyone doing."

Those words went round and round and round my head all evening. I couldn't shake the *This is what everyone is doing*. I began to fear for my ability as a mum, to keep steering the girls in the right direction. *How can I protect them? How will I find the right things to say when the world is saying something different?* I'd never felt the burden of motherhood as heavy as I did that night, and never before had I ever doubted my ability to raise my girls the right way, as I did in that moment. I was scared. I was desperate. And I knew this evil, this filth, was real.

Our farmhouse was a long thin stone building and the upstairs was built into the upper roof of the original structure. All the bedrooms ran down one side and a long hallway ran the full length of the house. I always checked on the girls every night before going to bed, even when they grew older. I loved to watch them sleeping peacefully and thanked God for the huge blessing they were to me/to us. Sometimes they'd roll over, almost sensing I was standing there and through the smallest of cracks in their eyelids, smile involuntarily from that place between sleep and away, exchanging an unspoken "I love you too Momma," moment with me - before drifting back to dreamland. I could never tell if my big girl was asleep or awake; she had the longest eyelashes that meant her lids never fully closed. TFBB had a problem with her tonsils back then, which caused her to snore very loudly on occasion and we'd regularly tease her about it. It never seemed to disturb anyone's sleep, though I've sometimes wondered if the cracks in the old walls were caused by those loud vibrations rather than plain old age - LOL. How I loved those girls.

As I climbed the stairs that night, however, I was troubled.

I stopped and leant against the outside wall of her bedroom; my grown up beautiful outgoing gorgeous first born; her faith and her passion for life already so evident, despite the moments of typical teenage angsts – I had always sensed that she was never really mine, that God has simply leant her to me for a while, to nurture and to shape, until the moment he activated his purpose in her life. There was just something about her which everyone could see that suggested she was born for greatness. "I'm going to fail God", I murmured, feeling crushed, as I leant against the wall, my head down, my thoughts lost. I was already that Mum who said "NO." when everyone else's mum said "yes", how much longer can I hold onto that, I contemplated. They are so full of respect for me, but they will tire? They are in the world and this is such a vulnerable time for them, they will surely want to be of the world too, if only to simply fit in?

Fear gripped me. Without really knowing why, I turned around and laid both my hands flat against the plain magnolia painted wall and whispered "Lord, I'm scared. Lord, please take these girls back from me now, tonight. So... I don't mean take them away from me, as in, take their life Lord; just to be absolutely clear - OK? But I'm giving them back to you for you to do with their lives whatever you have planned for them – they are yours. Please let me share them with you and please give me the right skills and the right words I need to be able to deal with what's ahead and to deal with their questions and challenges, but from here on in, they're yours."

Slowly, I moved back down to the other wall. My TFBB, the cutest, funniest, bundle of scrumminess that ever walked planet earth, and almost a teenager. How was that even possible? She would always be my baby girl, my mini-me, the one comfy in her own skin, the home-maker and office manager in the making. The one who had already started a bottom drawer full of pink kitchen utensils for her very first apartment, the one who was so obsessed with paper and pens, who rushed to the door whenever she heard the post man's van pull up in the drive, begging to be the one who got to open the envelopes. "When I'm an executive assistant, I'll be able to do this every day" she'd declare with great excitement. She was a delight.

Placing both hands on the cold plaster of her bedroom wall I repeated my request to the only one in who's hands I felt the lives of my precious girls were safe.

As the veil between Heaven and earth was drawn back, a

As the **veil between Heaven and earth** was drawn back, a supernatural transaction took place between the *Mother Heart* and *Father Heart* of God!

supernatural transaction took place between the *Mother Heart* and *Father Heart* of God. The anointing oil dripped from the throne room, down through every principality, past every star and planet, through every cloud; down onto the rooftop of a 400-year-old farmhouse in the middle of the English countryside; seeping through its thick mis-shapen walls onto the foreheads of my beautiful sleeping babies; His girls, His chosen, His anointed.

And as I climbed into bed that night, I knew I had done all I could to protect my babies.

Two really significant events happened next. Through a number of coincidences, the girls and I happened across an amazing church. By now my big girl was eighteen and dating a boy from the church and I was back in touch with an old work colleague who was at the same church. God's clever isn't he? ☺ I'd been spending a fair amount of time in the bible and journaling and for the very first time had a number of clear *words* from God. I was hungry for His word on my *situation* and it seemed like a new light had been switched on inside of me, as my CRAZY BONKERS faith began to grow legs. Finally, I had something to work with, to trust, to rebuild my hope on and I was ready and willing to do all that God asked of me. And better still, now I had community, a church where I, (*we* - the girls and I) felt at home – like-minded, Christ-centered, family.

At the same time, my boy changed jobs, so he was busy with that, as I dug deeper into Jesus.

Moment of Impact

God's medicine always tastes bitter. Trusting and yielding to God almost always costs us something and we have to be sure we're ready to do whatever He asks; to walk whatever path He lays before us

Trusting and **yielding to God almost always costs us something** and we have to be sure we're ready to do whatever He asks; to walk whatever path He lays before us when we offer our circumstances up to Him for redemption.

when we offer our circumstances up to Him for redemption. We have to lay the good, the bad and the ugly of our situations and ourselves at His feet and surrender it all to Him.

1 Peter 1:6 says So be truly glad. There is wonderful joy ahead, even though you must endure many trials for a little while, these trials will show that your faith is genuine. It is being tested as fire tests and purifies gold, though your faith is far more precious than mere gold. — Jesus is being revealed.

When we get to heaven, we are all going to be tested in the fire. That fire is *LOVE*. How well did we love? How real was that love? Was it a word or was it a decision - an action? Did it end up a noun or a verb?

I was just about to find out.

Those precious to God become important to satan – Something had started to bother me. The thought of it made me shiver and I frequently pushed it as far away as I could. It's almost too ridiculous to contemplate, I'd chastise myself for even allowing a thought like that to sneak into my head. But it wouldn't go away. More and more the signs were there, more and more things just didn't add up, more and more my spirit became unsettled, crushed; more and more the light in me began to fade.

Often hiding the truth is not an outright lie, often it's just a slight distortion of the truth, but one-by-one satan swings his axe. And blow, by blow, by blow the craftsman of destruction does his stuff.

"Lord, help me," I cried out wearily, in hopeless desperation. The good girl wanted to handle this well, the problem solver wanted it sorted and the carpenter's daughter had simply forgotten who she used to be.

It was late, I was home alone, catching up on some work. I reached into a case to grab something, but what I found delivered a trauma so severe to my entire being that I was

> Often **hiding the truth** is not an **outright lie**, often it's just a **slight distortion** of the truth, but one by one-by-one satan swings his axe. And blow, by blow, by blow the does his stuff.

sure I would never survive. The light, that for most of my life had burned so brightly and so vibrantly, the light that had just about remained flickering in recent months, in one moment of truth, one moment of excruciatingly painful answered prayer, one moment of grace; its last embers, wriggling, popping, gasping for any remaining oxygen it could find; was extinguished. My world. in an acute moment of impact, went dark.

Moment of Impact

Sin is not a person; sin is a *thing* and its satan's thing and how he delights to bring it to our door; it's his currency of choice and it's the only thing he has to bargain (tempt) with. He dresses up his counterfeit gift as our hearts desire, wafting it under our nose, smelling and looking delicious, like the best thing we never had, like the thing we surely deserve, like a gift from God - A friendly wager we can't afford, new shoes we hide at the back of the wardrobe, a chocolate bar that will make us feel loved again only it never does, rebellious freedom to do whatever we want, just one little peek at the explicit screen in front of me, just one little drink (just one), a little white lie that won't hurt anyone, a lush new field to graze in where the grass is sure to be greener. Oh yep, he's studied this foolish, broken, self-centred human nature of ours for thousands of years. He sure knows how to play us. Having resisted for a little while, he gloats as he watches our resolve weaken (*as of course he knew it would*), dancing an arrogant victory jig as we tentatively and secretly are seduced by this *thing* in front of us, convinced by now that it is surely no more than we deserve. There isn't a single one of us immune to his games.

> Sin is not a person; sin is a *thing* and its **satan's** *thing* and how he delights to bring it to our door; it's his currency of choice and it's the only thing he has to bargain with. He dresses up his **counterfeit gift** as our hearts desire, wafting it under our nose, smelling and looking delicious, like **the best thing we never had**, like the thing **we surely deserve**, like a gift from God.

COMMAND HQ

Tick, tick, tick.

Rasha's irritation is starting to show – "*Come on you idiot, be quick*" – he knows he's working on borrowed time.

He's heard her prayers, the ones she speaks out loud; the ones she writes in that stupid book and he'll be damned if he's going to have this one snatched back at the last minute.

He leans in and presses each tender place to remind them.

"OUCH"

THE SECRET PLACE

†

Wavering for just a second, a still small voice (long since pushed away but still familiar, still soothing), quietly stirs up a knowing of what is true, what is real, what is right.

Up ahead, they see a small light. It feels good

"Yes, son"; that still small voice, just a little louder than before, "here I am, take my hand."

They lean forward, only slightly, but they lean; tempted to loosen the arms that remain folded rigidly across their chest. The warmth of the light feels so good on their face. They tentatively pull their right hand out from beneath the elbow of the left.

"Well done my son, you're doing great. I know this is so hard for you, I understand why. Just a few more steps, you're nearly there."

It was a nice voice, they liked it.

†

COMAND HQ

"Ouch."

They stumble; tripping over something left out on the path in front of them, something that should have long since been put away. Dazed and a little shaken, they quickly tuck their right hand back in position and secure it tightly, their gaze once again transfixed on the *thing* that has just caused their fall. Even in this fading light they can see it's still as special as they remember; still as desirable; still has their name on the label.

"The daddy of all evil is back boys," Rasha' boasts, thrusting his fist into the air, as his feigned promises reassure the *now limping* heart of the empty space this 'thing' is about to fill.

THE LIE

"Yes", they are sure of it now. "This will make everything right again..."

"Gotcha", satan sniggers, as our hands reach out and take hold of the dazzling gift in front of us and before we have a chance to pull them back, the stain from the outside of the package bleeds onto our fingertips. Now we're actually holding it, we can see the warning label, previously hidden, that says; **HANDLE WITH CAUTION – PERMANENT INK** (a lie of course).

As we stand there with our stained fingers, momentarily wondering if we may have made a mistake, he slings a chain of iron around our neck, fastening it firmly with a giant padlock. Then taking out his faithful box of tricks he selects more of his lies carefully and secures them to the links of the chain, making sure they're knotted nice and tightly so they won't fall off: **SINNER, FAILURE, LOOSER, GUILTY, UNLOVED, ADDICT, REJECTED, ADULTERER, NOT GOOD ENOUGH, HOPELESS, CRIMINAL, ALONE, TOO LATE, SHAME, NOT WANTED, DISAPOINTMENT, UGLY, FAT, UNIMPORTANT, STUPID, MISSFIT, WEAK.**

He leaves us with our prize of course, it was counterfeit anyway, the pretty wrapping paper and ribbon now torn off and cast aside like a game of pass the parcel, and what we find inside after we tear open the final layer is never quite as exciting as we hoped it would be. Nevertheless, we still smile and shake our hands in the air like a winner; *for surely that's what we are.*

By now he's convinced us that this is the best our life will ever be, it's all we deserve and that empty space within us... well, that's part of the deal. He sticks that *thing,* that sin, on us in such a way that we can almost feel it, like a mole on our face; it starts to become part of us, to identify us; that, by our very sinful nature and our stain covered hands; it's who we are.

But it's a lie, a big fat *lie.* Sin is wrong no doubt about that one, and we all suffer from a sinful nature (even good girls surprisingly; I know who knew?), but that sin has been justified; nailed to the cross in total victory, Jesus paid the price of all our sin so we don't have to continually drag it around everywhere with us. **Ephesians 1:4** tells us that *before the foundation of the earth was even laid and because of His great love,* **Christ chose us,** *that* **in Him,** *we would be* **holy & blameless** *before Him.*

> We all suffer from a sinful nature but that sin has been **justified**; nailed to the cross in total **victory, Jesus paid the price** of all our sin so we don't have to continually drag it around everywhere with us.

There is a bigger picture at work here, with decisions made outside of time that involve each and every one of us. We're all part of a plan over which God has control. Because of His nature He's chosen us to join Him, to be beside Him in this battle, to be useful and play our part alongside Him in the good fight. There's no incentive or competition, it isn't based on how good we are or what we do, we're chosen, he sees us *without fault.* I'm certain that our Father is saddened and weeps over our poor choices like any dad would, but

> Here's a family secret that satan doesn't want us to know – as soon as we run our dirty hands under Jesus' pure clean, living water, that stain washes right off! Yup, **that stain isn't permanent** after all. How cool is that!

he most certainly doesn't define us by them, that's something we do to ourselves. He sees satan's game and He isn't about to let his kids go easily. As dusk falls, He's out looking for us, calling us, telling us it's not safe to be out alone, willing us to come home before it gets too dark. You think by now satan would have worked out all his strategising and scheming and plotting to grow his team is in vain, for; no *one can snatch them out of my hands.* **John 10:28.** We're His, we all have His DNA, we all have royal blood in our veins and unless we consciously choose to ignore our Dad's voice and stay out all night, love always conquers sin. We may not choose Him, but He has already chosen us.

And here's a family secret that satan doesn't want us to know – as soon as we run our dirty hands under God's pure, clean, living water, that stain washes right off. Yup, that stain isn't permanent after all. How cool is that ☺

Have you ever blown out a candle on your way up to bed at night only to be woken by a wonderful aroma the following morning? When you get downstairs you discover that the candle has been burning all night long - somehow, even though you blew it out, the tiniest remnant of energy had survived, continuing to smoulder just long enough for a faint waft of air to catch it (perhaps the breath of an angel); and fan the all but invisible flame *whoosh* back into life - small at first, but then a little taller; mischievously dancing unseen through the night, forming beautiful patterns against the otherwise darkened wall of a sleeping house.

THE SECRET PLACE

†

As I dared to open my eyes, terrified of what I might find, the tiniest of embers; barely noticeable to anyone but Him; were holding on to His promises, deep within my secret places.

I'm here sweet girl, take your time, a gentle breath holding me, just holding me; *it's going to be OK,* a soft hand stroking my forehead, just soothing me. *Take your time, I'm here,* that soft breath again, catching the tinniest of flickers, almost willing it back to life.

We'll do this together precious one, you and me, you know you can trust me, right? We'll sort it out together when you're feeling a bit better. One day at a time, there's no rush, we're right on schedule. I knew what he was up to all along, I always know and I'm always one step ahead. It would be so much easier if he realised and gave up. Ah well my wonderful girl, no matter, let's see to these small cuts first. I fear we may have a slightly bigger repair job down the line but for now, let's get you back on your feet and equip you with some things you might need for the next few years.

Somewhere, in the inner chambers of her soul an atom of light wrestled free, sparking upwards and outwards, its brilliance delighting the one who watched on, the one who gave it life, the one who was life. It was so tiny she wouldn't even know it was there, but it was. He knew it would be a very long time before that flame danced again, but He would be with her every step of the way and oh how bright it would finally shine, pure and strong. He smiled as He pictured the victory; *I wish I could tell you now, sweet girl, of the days ahead, of how gloriously bright that light in you will shine; but I can't, it will be better to do it my way.*

With words that could have been uttered by her own dad, the carpenter's daughter stirred - Hope glimmered and He was pleased.

†

In my pain, I chose to hang onto love and Love chose me. Some days it felt like someone had thrust a knife into my stomach so deep that it had embedded itself there and now they were twisting and rotating it round and round. Other days, I basked in crazy bonkers faith and this steadfast love I could not fathom; pleading before the Father day after day after day for my heart, for my family, for my boy, for my life.

You can stay awake night and day and never be able to
understand what God is doing.

Ecclesiastes 8:16-17 GNT

God's ways are not our ways – I had seen God do some miraculous things and He had been teaching me so much about relying on Him and not myself. One night He woke me up in the middle of the night and I saw a picture in big bold capital letters simply saying **MATTHEW 10.** I made a mental note and drifted back off to sleep and by the morning I had forgotten all about it. I was in the middle of a period of prayer and fasting and so a few different things had been happening. God clearly frustrated at my poor memory woke me up the following night with the same picture: **MATTHEW 10.** "OK, OK God I hear you" - I picked up my bible and read.

There is so much in that chapter *now* that God was speaking to me, but at that moment my spirit immediately settled on *What I am telling you in the dark you must repeat in broad daylight and what you have heard in private must be announced from the housetops* **Matthew 10:27.** The Lord was asking me to share all that He had been teaching me about depending on Him rather than ourselves. I felt sure of it. We had a women's meeting coming up at church and feeling a very strong prompting, I asked if I could just have five minutes to share what God had put on my heart. I decided I would share a little of how I had been growing in my understanding of self-abandonment and how God had been teaching me to let go of things I couldn't influence and let Him do His thing. Clearly, I couldn't share any of the things I'd been going through personally, so I would just make up a scenario and use the example of a friendship where I'd had some challenges and had been praying for that friend, yep that would work fine.

All that week, unusual things began to take place and a courage and assurance that had been missing for so long seemed peculiarly to come back in full might. I was excited to be able to share with the ladies and our girls were going to be there too.

HOLY MOMENTS

Set apart for God

Will always leave you with a choice

Will always feel uncomfortable at first

Will always lead to change – *Go, I'm sending you.*

Sometimes God allows what looks like bad stuff to put you on the path to the palace. Remember Joseph? God allowed his brothers to throw him into a pit and sell him into slavery. That action, began a series of events that ultimately saw him in a position of significance; a position that allowed him to redeem his whole family during the famine in Egypt many years later. It definitely wouldn't have felt *good* to Joseph as he landed at the bottom of the pit, wondering what he'd done to make his brothers want to get rid of him so badly, but he had no idea what was ahead.

> *My thoughts are not your thoughts, neither are your*
> *ways my ways, declares the LORD.*
>
> *For as the heavens are higher than the earth, so are my*
> *ways higher than your ways and my thoughts, higher*
> *than your thoughts.*

Isaiah 55:8-9

Would I have spoken that night had I realised the chain of events that were to follow... I believe I would? For I had come to recognise The Lords voice well by that stage and he had given me an instruction and when The Lord asks us to do something, our answer must always be, YES.

...and when The Lord asks us to do something, our answer must always be YES!

Still, in my wildest dreams, I could never have imagined what my *yes* would cost me.

RUINED HOUSES, BROKEN WALLS, TORN TENTS

Rasha'

Seems your girl's not so precious and desirable now is she. What a terrible shame.

Y'shua

She's more precious to me than she has ever been.

Rasha'

Hmmmm, that's awkward - It's not really you she's lying on the floor pining for now is it? (mock awkward face). How it irritated me when she gave you all the credit at the beginning, stupid girl – that was *MY* victory. Well, enjoy all the condemnation which she's about to throw your way now. How tormented and wretched she looks.

Conversely, (both cast a sideways glance)

Y'shua

You know; I know; we all know the flaw in that statement. Look a little closer Rasha'.

Oh, I forgot, you can only see what I allow you to see; what any of them allow you to see.

That was her problem; her burden; her gift. She *could* see it, see what was true. You hated that didn't you; her, ignoring all your junk. She saw right through your schemes in the end. She's always seen much more than most; but of course, you know that Rasha' don't you, since you've been shadowing her for so long.

She will fight for him – And I will fight for her.

I will fight for them both; for all of them.

People are watching her, watching how she walks in faith; in grace, in courage – her story will be a lifeline to others. No, she won't blame me, Rasha', she will glorify me.

In his shelter in the day of trouble,

that's where you'll find me,

for he hides me there in his holiness.

He has smuggled me into his secret place,

where I'm kept safe and secure—

out of reach from all my enemies. **Psalm 27:5 TPT**

5

The Light in The Valley

It wasn't grief, it was love. Love with no place to go. Love that just kept bubbling up uncontrollably, stronger and more powerful than ever. Gathering first in the pit of her belly, then the hollow of her chest.

And then her throat, *where*; consuming every tiny atom of oxygen; it forced her to rasp suddenly inwards,

until finally, it found its way to the corners of her eyes.

And there, unmet, all that love simply emptied itself out across the ravaged flood-plains of her heart.

C.S.

When God gives us a life changing promise, he generally leaves out the detail. Instead, He asks

"Would you trust me?" Then, often without warning, He sets into motion a course of events that attack the very heart of who you believe He is. Events

And if we're brave enough, He will take us on the most amazing journey of our lives, lovingly **pruning** squeezing and **shaping** our entire inner being into something truly beautiful & bold; making us ready and equipping us for **our greatest mission**; the one He designed us for, the one only we can fulfil, the one that not only our story, but the stories of so many others rests on.

that uproot and remove the very things you define your identity by. The very things you measure the success of your life thus far by. And as He takes apart your life piece by piece, He gently whispers "come and hang out with me for a while, just you and me." If we're brave enough and desperate enough to step into the unknown, He will take us on the most amazing journey of our lives, lovingly pruning squeezing and shaping our entire inner being into something truly beautiful and bold; making us ready and equipping us for our greatest mission; the one He designed us for, the one only we can fulfil, the one that not only our story, but the stories of so many others, rests on.

I've tried to imagine what happens up in the Heavenlies as we walk this journey with God and slowly but surely, through day-to-day trials and experiences, we learn to trust God more and His confidence in us grows. Is there a moment of truth where He looks around to the hosts of heavenly armies and says "OK guys, it's time – she's ready for the biggie." – Is He excited, serious, concerned, relieved when that moment arrives? Is He thinking this is going to be a bit rough for a while for her, but *I've got her back and I know how it ends.* I like to think He does. Perhaps this is just my crazy imagination getting the better of me, but honestly; I'm just not sure we get how real God and Heaven are? I didn't back then – I mean I did, but I *really didn't.*

No matter how He chooses to initiate His plans, I eventually came to see that it's in these *defining moments,* that if we stop fighting against Him and work with Him, if we allow Him to lead us purposefully through places, emotions and situations we never intended to visit, and trust

> Then, we get to partner with the creator of the entire universe to fulfil **the plans of heaven!**

that when we've exhausted all the things a daughter can do to *fix stuff,* He will take over and do what only a Dad can do (and as you know, my *dad* was the best fixer in the world.); then we get to partner with the creator of the entire universe to fulfil the plans of heaven. Only then, when we look back, are we able to declare *now I get it,* because up to this point it's been about theoretical faith, but in these defining moment *everything* becomes real, in all its glorious colour, pain, excitement, amazement... Like we've just put on the best pair of glasses we've ever worn and now things have just become big and bold and serious.

> *They said to Him 'What shall we do,*
>
> *that we may work the works of God?*
>
> *Jesus answered, 'This is the work of God,*
>
> *that you believe.*

John 6:28-29

God instructs us to be his hands and feet and do 'good deeds' for others, but much of what we do in the *natural* comes from a place of simple, good honest decency that requires us to draw on our human talent and abilities and that's wonderful. However, fulfilling our unique purpose requires supernatural cooperation and a whole load of childlike dependency and faith. Recently, I've been hit with a simple but very powerful and exciting truth that comes down to two words, **JUST BELIEVE** – Smith Wigglesworth built a powerful *miraculous* ministry on it. Sounds obvious doesn't it, but if we truly grasped the enormity of the power within us and the fact that our lack of faith is often the only thing blocking the miracle we're praying into, we'd all be changing the world on a daily basis. Self-reliance has a habit of getting in the path of faith and moving us further away from God. Just to make sure He knows what He's doing, we try really hard to second guess Him because we want to work out how He's going to achieve the outcome were trusting Him for, but we could never understand the mind of God no matter how hard we try and when we do try, boy does the enemy know how to plant doubt in our mind. Because, defining moments typically lead to an eternal outcome that the devil is desperate to derail.

As I found myself smack bang in the middle of the most savage and

> Fulfilling our **unique purpose** requires supernatural **cooperation** and a whole load of **childlike dependency** and **faith**!

defining moment of my life; broken, powerless, clinging to the tiniest thread of hope; there was literally nowhere for me to go but to the feet of Jesus and I simply took up residence there. The throne room was always open to me. It was never like a royal residence when I was there, at least if it was, I never noticed – It seemed simple... safe, a place I didn't have to talk, to think, to remember, a place where I could just be with my Dad (so to speak). I never had to tell Him anything because He knew. I was so tired of talking, explaining, thinking, crying. Here, just the little girl again, sitting in yesterday's messy clothes, shoes missing, knees scuffed, face stained from tears that had been trickling down my unwashed face; a little girl who had been out to play and taken a nasty tumble. It hurt, it really hurt and I needed my Dad to rub it better, to make it better, to tell me it was all going to be OK.

I'd sit on the top step alongside His throne, He in it, my shoulder leant gently against His right side, my head down on His lap.

From this position, just beyond His bare feet, I could see an old wooden cupboard built into the plain white wall opposite. The doors of it looked like something I might have picked up myself from a reclamation yard to restore for the farmhouse. I vaguely wondered what was inside that cupboard, but not so much to ignite any serious curiosity; it was more of a passing thought as the tender caresses of His hand soothed the upside of my weary head. This was my resting place and the only source of oxygen and peace I could find these days. I needed intensive care and survival was the only thing that mattered in this moment. If I made it through, perhaps He would show me one day what was in that cupboard, but for now I had no words, no thoughts.

THE SECRET PLACE

†

"Father, Father," the spirit groaned with sounds I could neither fathom nor hear. No matter, the Father heard, "Help me Dad, help me, help me... help me... help me."

As she lay there in His lap, He pondered the order... 'There were some obvious ones that he gave to everyone first, but her mission required a specific combination; now, which ones first?' Satisfied with His decision He nodded and smiled a comforting smile to himself, 'Yes', He concluded, as he leant forward to the wooden cupboard, opening the door just wide enough to reach inside and take what He needed and lifting them out he gently pushed the doors closed again. He was excited to picture His girl with these, she'd had the smaller versions for many years, but with these full-sized versions she was going to look glorious.

Of course most that see her in them won't get it; she'll confuse them and she'll probably confuse herself – 'Ha Ha,' He chuckled out loud, only louder this time, 'oh how she'll wonder why she isn't more angry, she'll be so frustrated with herself, thinking perhaps that she is being foolish, being weak, but she won't be able to help herself' – 'Ha Ha', a real belly laugh echoed across the walls of the throne room, all three of them amused by the wonder of it all, all three of them looking with adoring eyes at the precious head asleep on His lap, on their lap – 'she had always been a force to be reckoned with, but now...now was her time, everything before had been leading to this – Oh how Rasha' was going to be enraged'.

"*Stay close baby girl*' He said as He stooped to kiss her head and with that, she opened her eyes.

†

Sitting on the floor of the spare bedroom of the small terraced house TFBB had been renting for a while now; her first attempt of *adulting* and flying the nest; I gazed around at the woodchip walls and damp patch in the corner of the ceiling, listening to the angry screams coming from the house next door and the cries of the children. My stomach knotted imagining their little hearts beating fast, scared of what would come next; wondering to myself if this was a daily occurrence. I hadn't been too keen for her to live here, but like me she had always dreamed of her own place and a taste of independence and I'd always encouraged them in that. I wanted them to seek out adventure and travel and to work out who they were, but I hadn't imagined this, she was not used to this type of environment and neither was I.

We'd freshened it up for her and added some nice touches, but *those sounds, tho*se vicious accusations coming through the thin walls again, the name calling that would stay with those babies for the rest of their precious lives; those were the things I didn't want her exposed to. How I wanted to envelope those little angels in my arms and rock them, rubbing my nose along their soft cheeks, telling them how much they were loved the way I'd done with mine; with ours - but I could not. I wasn't so sure I understood what love was anymore, or if I was even loved – I thought I was, but it no longer felt that way, it hadn't for a very long time.

At least I no longer had to carry the weight of pretence, the burden of secrecy, it was uncovered now; well in my very small circle it was, but despite the smallest relief of not carrying it alone and having the ability to speak out some of the hurt, it had come at a cost; a shockwave no one saw coming, a shockwave that splintered my precious family into a million tiny pieces. For a very brief moment, there was a sense of relief; I was tired of justifying who I was, tired of not being good enough, tired of the loneliness, tired of the half-truths, of never quite being sure. I didn't have to lock myself in a room to hide the tears anymore, yet here I was, willing myself to hold them in, to not let her hear; she'll be asleep soon, I reassured myself, knowing that wasn't true, but praying she would be spared another night of lying awake anxiously listening to her always strong and wise Momma sobbing into her pillow; "Lord please spare her that tonight," I begged. There had been years of held back tears and now it seemed as if with every spoken word they came spilling out, like a tap that could not be switched off.

I caught a glimpse of myself in the small space at the bottom of the mirror leant against the wall in the corner of the room. Black bin liners full of clothes and shoes filled up the entire floor space around it, my work suit hanging precariously on the corner to keep it from creasing, my 4" heels neatly stood to attention below. Makeup and toiletries spilling out of the wicker basket I'd used to transport them only seven days earlier. He was clear we were done. I'd tried to change his mind but it was made up. I wanted to keep him there, I knew this would all get sorted, it had to, it was crazy to imagine any other outcome, so I agreed to come here, just for a while, until we figured it all out. I looked old, tired....and my eyes looked dead. I gasped the air, my chest rising and tightening as the memories of those last conversations came flooding back and my teeth clenched, no, no, don't start again, the inner responsibility of a Momma who desperately wanted to protect her baby girl - who was so embarrassed to be in this role-reversal position, who had spoken such powerful life giving godly words over them and into them their whole lives, now a mere shadow of the strong oak tree they'd always seen her as.

She's in there, her bed head just millimetres away, listening to every movement, every sob, desperately wondering what she can do to help her Momma, but having no idea what to do. Crying herself to sleep for you – you must hold those cries in at all costs, you must be strong, don't let her hear you, don't make her even more sad than she already is, pull yourself together.

Satan is so predictable, you think he'd make up new straplines for each situation, but I guess if the old ones still work why change them. I chuckle now when I hear them because I recognise his game, but then it was different; round and round he turned that knife of bewilderment and disorientation in my abdomen, pushing and twisting and thrusting;

'We're two different people, you deserve to be happy, I can't give you what you want', are just a few of the common ones.

COMAND HQ

I figure he must have a specific tin for every situation full of little black straplines that he opens and whispers convincingly into our ears, tailored uniquely to the current campaign and target. Pulling out

Pulling out the age-old folded, grubby, well-handled, well tested evil parchment, he bends down and **mutters its trickery** into our vulnerable, unsuspecting ears...

118

the age-old folded, grubby, well-handled, well tested evil parchment, he bends down and mutters its trickery into our vulnerable, unsuspecting ears.

In my head these boxes are strategically stacked on five shelves:

<u>**On the top shelf**</u> sit the **SUBJECT** boxes, labelled **Parents - Children - Teens - Men - Women - Marriage - Family - Grandparents - Church - Business - Government - Royalty - Education - Healthcare - Agriculture - Media -...**

<u>**On the second shelf**</u> are the boxes that hold his overarching **OBJECTIVES: Derailed Calling - Crushed human spirit - Disunity - Broken relationships - Hate - Idolatry - Prideful nature - Parental disrespect - Lawlessness - Wickedness - Death & Destruction - Disease - Addiction - Immorality - Greed - Generational bondage - Chaos -...**

<u>**The third shelf**</u> are the 5 boxes that hold the secrets to manipulating the **TRANSACTION AREAS** (In business we call these the **CHANNELS.**) It's where his dirty work takes place. Where his filth, corrupt hands reach in, intent on plundering all the good stuff.

Our HEARTS (desires - false gods - hobbies - lifestyle),

Our MINDS (where he'll make you doubt God's love - provision - even existence)

Our SPEECH (critical words - complaints - gossip)

EVERYDAY THINKING (to make you just like the world)

Our BODIES (so it no longer glorifies God; food - alcohol - dress)

<u>**Then on the fourth shelf**</u> are the boxes that hold his tried and tested **METHODS; Sickness - Lust - Comparison - Self (image - importance - reliance - preservation) - Deceit - Wrath & Discord - Jealousy & Envy - Procrastination - Fear - Hardening of heart - False Responsibility - Ambition - Material & Financial excess - Busyness - Addiction (sugar - drugs - alcohol - porn - computer games - gambling - shopping) - Religion - Poverty - Diversity - Complacency - Communication -...**

The fifth shelf houses his sophisticated **PROFILING** – his **COUNTER-IN-TELLIGENCE DATA BASE**. It's a much deeper shelf than all the others and is where the real treasure hides. This shelf holds our individual **VALUE PROPOSITION** box, one for every child of God, containing all the records he has been keeping since the day we were born.

According to *Google,* the way to conduct *counterintelligence* is to get together your best team, choosing people who are likely to be clever and persistent in finding and testing vulnerable areas. Once in place, instruct the team to pretend it's working for your biggest competitor and try to gather information from outside the physical perimeter of your organisation.

> **Counterintelligence** is to get together your best team, choosing people who are likely to be clever and persistent in finding and **testing vulnerable areas**. Once in place, instruct the team to pretend it's working for your biggest competitor and try to **gather information** from outside the physical perimeter of your organisation.

Displayed on the lid of this box, our name, our date of birth and our family heritage. Inside, an eclectic mix of calculated and concluded facts about us; observed details from years of monitoring our every move, moods, mistakes and victories; a perfect instruction manual to *me*. Note I say *observed* for he cannot read our minds, but he is a master of drawing strong assumptions from his diligent and patient stake-outs and years of expertise and experience, plus the looseness of our emotions and tongues generally make it ridiculously easy for him to fill in the blanks. Within this instruction manual is the secret coding to our value system, our moral code and how we operate; a fusion of our personality, our gifts and skills, of how we were raised, the type of relationship we had (or have) with our parents and how that still affects us. Of our triumphs and losses, our mistakes and our weaknesses. Of our dreams and our fears, of the things others love about us and the secret things that others never see us do. Of the things we admire in others and the prideful things we quietly admire in ourselves; the things in others that repulse us and the personal self-loathing we carry that often gives way to shame. Our view of religion, our experience in church, our politics, our world view.

This untold, thus far, secret coding shapes his strategy to reap destruction on our lives, steal our birth right, derail our calling and smash our hearts into tiny pieces.

And he had just played a blinder.

Drained I looked down at the bible open on the floor between

This untold, thus far, secret coding shapes his strategy to reap destruction on our lives, **steal our birth right**, derail our calling and smash our hearts into tiny pieces.

my bare feet, illuminated by the small lamp standing on the floor next to me, the one I'd grabbed hurriedly as I gathered together the last of the knotted black bin-bags from our bedroom floor. I'd thrown into them, without any clear thinking, those bits I thought I'd need for a few nights, a few weeks perhaps; my mind in a fog, the adrenaline making my heart race so fast it caused the most nauseating sickness in my throat and stomach; the tears of unbelief and terror dripping off my chin onto my shoes and then the bedroom carpet. He'd helped me into the car with my stuff, he'd hugged me tight, his tears finally joining mine.

This is crazy, my heart screamed, we love each other so much.' I did not repeat this to him, we had already covered every bit of ground there was to cover earlier, and he was clear where he stood. "we are just too different as people to make this work," he said, his head down, not looking me in the eye. And he was unyielding.

"Is there someone else?" I would look straight at him, even if he did not return the favour. For months we had very little eye contact, but here, now, I wanted to read his face. I almost willed him to say yes, then it would all make more sense to me, but of course I knew he wouldn't - still I had to at least ask.

"Nope", he replied dismissively.

And then, with my bags squashed into my little car, I backed slowly *off* the drive, as he stood on the doorstep waving me goodbye, like it was just another regular day.

I was sure she was asleep now; it was late. The frightened whimpers from the house next door had long since died down and the world slept.

"Lord, give them sweet dreams tonight", I prayed silently, wondering how many more were living this way; angry, broken parents, mums trying to buffer the onslaught, taking the hits, as she shuffled their little ones off to bed and out of the way, children trying to be invisible, trying to be good, crying themselves to sleep, pulling the covers over their head to block out the sounds of the insults and accusations downstairs and the occasional slap and broken plate. I wondered what made a man so angry, so out of control, so unable to love his wife and his children well. Maybe he loved them in his own way, in the only way he knew, in the only way he'd seen – I wondered what it had been like for him; who had hurt him, how many nights of his childhood he'd lay in bed frightened, desperate for a loving pair of arms, I wondered what brokenness there was deep within his soul. I couldn't help but hurt for him too now, as well as for his babies.

Lord, what a broken world we live in, my body had little energy left, but my heart ached for their hearts, it just wasn't fair, they deserved so much more; if only we as parents could see clearly, if there was a way to teach us all how to grow a human being well, how to love well, how to nurture and shape your way Lord. Maybe almost all the world's problems would be solved just like that.

In that moment, I felt the pain in His heart and was certain that somewhere in the gift of *parenting* sat the hidden key to the entire brokenness of this world.

My heart ached with His. I pictured a set of dominos falling, each one knocking down the next; each generation passing on its demons – I wanted to put out my finger and stop just one domino from falling, that's all it would take, stop one, change one and the sequence would be broken, the curse would be lifted.

Not today, I chuckled to myself, knowing all too well the overzealous nature of my imagination and my inherent appetite to fix thing, but even I was amused by the simplicity and naivety of my conclusion.

As I ached for the broken people in the house next door, I remembered the broken people in this house and in *my* house. I wondered how peacefully my boy was sleeping, I tried to picture him there curled up in our bed, our quilt wrapped tightly around his body. I wanted to be there wrapped around him, I wanted to snuggle into his back, my nose up into his neck where the lingering smell of aftershave that he'd put on in the morning still hung. I wanted to tuck my cold toes between his calves as he gave his usual gasp at the shock of how cold they were, but still let me keep them there, pressing his legs together to speed up the heating process. Maybe he was restless like me. I hoped he was, but then I also hoped he'd get enough sleep for his busy day tomorrow. Was he missing me? I had no idea, perhaps it was a relief for him to have the house to himself, to finally be on his own, to be single again. Was he on his own? – There was that doubt again, that nagging, horrid, life sucking doubt. I rebuked myself for the hundredth time, I couldn't keep carrying this weight around, it was crippling me. Yes of course he was.

I looked down again at the well-worn pages of my bible, so many highlighted passages; promises. I could not get over how much God had spoken to me in this past week; word after word of promise. Word after word of instruction.

† Go where I send you... **Jeremiah 29:7**

† Pray for the people where I send you for when they prosper so too will you prosper. **Jeremiah 29:7**

† Rebuild; building again on the old foundations. **Isaiah 58:12**

† I will break the yoke around his neck. **Jeremiah 30:8**

† I will put my instructions deep within them, and write it on their hearts. **Jeremiah 31:33**

† You will be known as the people who rebuilt the city walls, who restored the ruined houses. **Isaiah 58:12**

† You will be called the city that God did not forsake. **Isaiah 62:12**

† Write it down in a book, for the time is coming when I will restore...**Jeremiah 30:2-3**

† I will rebuild them just as they were before. **Jeremiah 33:7**

† I will restore David's fallen tent, restoring its torn places. **Amos 9:11**

† I will keep my promise to bring you back home. **Jeremiah 29:10**

† I will heal this city and its people and restore them to health. **Jeremiah 33:6**

† You will hear shouts of gladness and joy and the happy sounds of wedding feasts. **Jeremiah 33:10-11**

† He will come to me when I invite him for who would dare to come uninvited. **Isaiah 30:22**

† Everyone my father gives me will come to me. **John 6:37**

† (& *the one who comes to me I will never turn away*) **John 6:37**

† Remove every obstacle from their path (build the road and make it ready). **Isaiah 57:14**

† No longer will you be called the forsaken wife, your land will be called *Happily Married*. **Isaiah 62:4**

† Your new name will be *God is pleased with her*. **Isaiah 62:4**

† My words will not fail to achieve the purpose for which I sent it. **Isaiah 55:11**

† I will be to her a wall of fire all around and I will be the glory in her midst. **Zech 2:5**

† There is hope for your future, your children will come back home. **Jeremiah 31:17**

† I will lead them back, I will guide them by streams of water,

on a smooth road where they will not stumble. **Jeremiah 31:9**

† I will not be silent until she is saved, And her victory shines like a torch in the night. **Isaiah 62:1**

† The moon will be as bright as the sun, and the sun will be seven times brighter than usual, like....... the light of seven days in one. **Isaiah 30:26**

† (*when the Lord bandages and heals the wounds He has given His people*) **Isaiah 30:26**

† Is anything too difficult for me? **Jeremiah 32:27**

† Nations will be drawn to your light. **Isaiah 60:3**

I could go on...

Every Word the Lord gave me in that first week became the foundation of everything that came after. It became a platform for strong *illogical* faith, it became the yardstick that I would go back to in my darkest moments to remind myself that He was a God of truth who didn't go back on His promises, it was the Word I checked myself against when I wondered if my faith was built around my own desires rather than His Word, His will. It was the Word I went back to when I desperately wanted it to say something different, when I willed it to be my interpretation and not His so that I could free myself at last and move on with my life. It was the Word that randomly stirred inside me again and caught me off-guard after His most profound revelation several years later that had finally and unconditionally released me from my promise, liberated me from my (false) responsibility. All the while, fanning into flames the mischievous crazy stupid what if ponderings of an abandoned *all-in* Daughter of a king.

> It became a platform for **strong illogical faith**, it became the yardstick that I would go back to in my darkest moments to remind myself that He was a God of truth who didn't go back on His promises!

But I had a long way to go before then and it was going to be the hardest walk of my life.

Ecclesiastes 7:3 GNT says *Sorrow is better than laughter; it may sadden your face but it sharpens your understanding* and over the next few years, what I would come to know and understand, would be life-changing and *me*-changing, but as the early weeks dragged by and my boy moved on with absolute certitude, I could not see the way ahead.

I eventually moved into Mum's spare room. It wasn't great for my heart - moving back to your parents age fifty isn't how life is meant to roll, but I could no longer bear for my girl to see me as I was and to carry such terrible anguish. I had grown used to carting my bin bags of clothes and toiletries from one spare bedroom to another and going through the daily motions, willing the night to come quickly so that I could retreat back into that bedroom to protect everyone around me from my *sad germs*. Everyone wanted to help me somehow, but they couldn't; no one could. My world had crashed around me for the second time, but this time was so much worse. I feared I would never recover.

I'd been working as a freelance consultant when things fell apart and now that contract had come to an end. So here I was, with no home, no job, no husband and half of what had been my family, my children, stripped away in one foul swoop of the enemy. People I loved deeply, people that had loved me, unable to be part of my world anymore; too awkward, too painful, too everything. I couldn't do this again, I had turned fifty, how could I start again for a *third* time. How could I find the energy and determination I'd had twenty years ago to rebuild a new life, make a new home?

He was home to me. I had never loved anyone the way I'd loved him and I was sure I never would again. He was my heart; he had been my anchor. I never imagined I'd ever find a love like that, as much as I created romantic notions in my head, I didn't really expect it to come; but it had. It had been undeniable, unshakeable, it had been one of those relationships that others measured theirs against. And now it was gone, *he* was gone. But he wasn't *really* gone – he was just gone from me, from the life we'd so lovingly and sensitively woven together, from the imaginary back porch we'd chuckled about growing old on together.

I carried the *potential* to do great things; *to change the world*, he had told me; I was an amazing wife, an amazing Momma, an amazing homemaker. It wasn't me at all, it was a combination of things it turned out, but mostly and most surprisingly, my growing faith and my increasing dependence on prayer had created a chasm between us that was just too wide to bridge.

I had no defence for that one, no clever come-back lines, it was non-negotiable.

Something inside gently fluttered, as if agreeing with the thoughts I was now wistfully lost in. Yes. This was fixing to be a very different kind of battle season. And I was going to have to learn to fight it in an altogether different way!

This was fixing to be a very different kind of **battle season**. And I was going to have to learn to **fight it** in an **altogether different way**!

I realised for the very first time that I had to let him go; that I had to *let go*. Whatever was going on here, whatever was playing out in the background, unseen in the heavenlies, I had to find a fresh battle strategy. So, I backed away; my heart reluctantly accepting for the first time that (for now, at least) God had different paths for each of us to walk. I didn't know if somewhere, one day in the future, those paths would cross again; but I had to believe they would. If only to look deep into his eyes and finally get to say: *there you are.*

I won't lie, death would have been so much easier at this point, indeed for the many, many months that were to follow. Death would have been final, it would have released me; but my boy wasn't dead, he hadn't died, he was simply *starting over* someplace else - the way *we* had once started over - the way so many of us blindly and naively and exhaustedly try to 'start over'. Amateurishly, picking up the broken pieces of our lives, salvaging what seems salvageable, discarding what seems ruined or surplus to requirements. Then, instead of rebuilding a more robust, beautiful and far more valuable version of the thing those broken pieces belong to, we try our best to make those pieces fit into something different; something they were never designed to fit.

It struck me that we were all part of the same story, part of the same plot line – like the Hallmark Christmas movies that have the exact same theme, characters, storyline and ending; the movies we can't help but watch because they make us feel all warm and gooey inside, the ones we already know the ending to before they even start, the ones we watch anyway, because, for a while, they make us feel good.

> Day after day, month after month, year after year; that *great deceiver* has the same story on repeat. And all over the world identities, marriages, families, destinies, are being pillaged right under our noses.

Only *these* stories, *our* stories, rarely have the guaranteed Hallmark 'happy-ever-after' ending.

My heart hurt for all of us. Day after day, month after month, year after year; that *great deceiver* has the same story on repeat. And all over the world identities, marriages, families, destinies, are being pillaged right under our noses.

Quite unexpectedly, I felt an overwhelming sense of love, of concern, of holy anger. A need to fight back on behalf of us all. A need to say *this stops here*, a need for restoration, for redemption, beyond what was imaginable to a watching world.

And so, with every ounce of courage I could muster, I cast off the black cloak of rejection, of accusation, of hopelessness that was trying its very best to attach itself to me.

I mourned for the boy I loved, for the life I'd lost, the life we'd all lost and then, in one fierce act of genuine abandonment, I released myself unconditionally into the hands of my Father, the redeemer of all things.

I wondered why it hurt so darned much, to let go of this completely; but then I realised... it was because it was real. No matter where it had started, no matter the strategy that may have orchestrated it in the beginning, the same strategy that had finally brought it tumbling back down again, no matter what the ultimate ending looked like, no matter the things that had taken place in the middle, no matter where my boy stood now; for me it was real, more real than even I had truly understood.

God has the ability to fulfil His plans through and in our lives, no matter what the circumstance or how totally unlikely it seems, we just have to believe and trust Him and then, stand – Total abandonment to His will and direction was the first step for me. In the early days, really well-meaning church family would encourage me by saying "well, you just have to let go of it all, abandon yourself to The Lord. Just trust him with it, He's got so much better for you."

I bet most of us have heard that at some time or another?

To abandon means *to cut loose,* to see what happens next, to refuse to plan, to live without concern, to have no thought of the consequences, to relinquish responsibility. Woahhh. Sounds like a great idea doesn't it? Oh what we would give, even pay for that kind of *get out of jail free card* when our hearts are bleeding all over the sofa and the bed and the dinner table and... just about everything else we come into contact with.

Let me just put a few things straight for those of you my friends who've wrestled with that line as I have. Let me reassure you here, as a meddler and a fixer, 'leaving everything to the Lord' isn't some superpower that really holy and righteous Christians seem to skilfully possess; in-fact, I would take a guess that fewer have it that we might imagine? Indeed, this supernatural power is a gift, that on our own, none of us can learn, practice or adopt. So, when you're wrestling like I was, big time, don't be too hard on yourself.

Heaven truly knows the extent to which I tried to 'make myself' *abandoned* and failed. But the one thing I never failed at in this season, was taking everything to my Father in prayer. I had nowhere else to go, so when it was hard, when it felt *impossible,* when I had difficult decisions to make, when I was angry, when I saw the tiniest flicker of light, when I felt rejected and unwanted; up I'd go and sit beside Him and lay my head in His lap and wait. Sometimes His answers, His peace would be immediate, sometimes it seemed forever, but always I felt better for being with Him, always He delighted in loving on me and spending time with me, always I could be my authentic self no matter how I was feeling and always He would gather each and every one of my tears as if they were the most precious of jewels.

Father, will you help me?

It had been a really hard day. Mum had left for the States to visit my sisters for a month, so at least I had the house to myself and didn't need to feel embarrassed that I wasn't bouncing back the way everyone was used to seeing me do. I'd sit around on the sofa all day in my PJs watching the odd bit of TV, snoozing here and there, having the odd conversation with friends who'd call to check on me, making endless cups of coffee that I never finished, building an ever-taller pile of crumpled tissues on the floor – I felt exhausted most of the time these days, I was sure I would never get back to being *the old enthusiastic me.* It felt like God had pruned every single thing from my life, like *everything* and there was nothing left, just this, a body sitting on a sofa in the bottom of a deep dark valley, with nothing to do, no purpose, no reason to even try.

God had given me quite a few nudges to write down what I was learning and the things He was revealing to me so I'd been reading and scribbling bits and pieces here and there and my highlighter had become my new best friend, but the days seemed even harder than the nights, still, in faith and for the benefit of others, I'd go through the motions. I had my girls of course, my most precious blessings, but they now had their own lives, own partners and I felt that my sadness was casting a dark shadow over them, which distressed me greatly. The three of us were so attached by heart that it was impossible for it to be any other way but I could hardly bear it. Sometimes after a particularly bad day I'd find myself contemplating if it would be better if I just didn't wake up the next morning. After all, nothing depended on me anymore. Nothing would stop turning if I didn't show up, I had no job to go to, I wasn't running a house, my girls were independent, I had no *significant other* that would miss me. By default, my presence alone became a *super-spreader* of sad germs to friends and family. And my own pain - well that was almost unsurpassable...

Truly, these were just passing thoughts, attacks on my mind by the one who was irritated that I kept on getting up each day and putting two feet firmly on the floor. Even in these early compass-less days he could see that I was already starting to understand things I hadn't before; with a growing wisdom and hunger and he wasn't best pleased. Never once did I believe his lies and his taunts, but pain makes us super-vulnerable and a sitting target.

Father, your word says that I have to cast all my cares on you, that you have plans for me that you will bring all things together for my good, that you will restore what has long since been in ruin, that you will be the glory in my midst. I don't know how to let go, I don't know how to stop my brain from thinking or my hands from interfering. I feel like I'm alone at the bottom of a deep valley and I don't know how to climb out, but I know you don't want me left here. Will you help me, please?

THE SECRET PLACE

†

I think I heard a shuffling noise and the squeaking of what sounded like the hinge on an old cupboard door, I can't be sure, but when I opened my eyes and had given them time to become readjusted to the familiar dark, cold, damp environment of the valley floor, He was sitting there, opposite me on a rock, gazing on me as if I was the most beautiful thing he'd ever seen. The light radiating off Him onto me was such a welcome relief from the vast darkness of this place and for a moment I tried to grasp the fact that he had left the comfort of the throne room to follow me here. The King of Heaven, here in this awful place with me and He looked happy to be here?

"Hey", I whispered with a sort of, *thank you – you came*, half smile.

"Hey" He whispered back lovingly with an unspoken, *yes of course I did*, type grin.

At His feet were six boxes, carefully stacked and gift wrapped beautifully. Like a small child on Christmas morning catching that first glance of the presents under the tree, a tiny flutter of excitement tickled the inside of my tummy. Ordinarily my eyes wouldn't have been able to see anything, but His presence cast a light that made thing a little more visible; the place even seemed half bearable. Beside the six boxes was a plain unwrapped cardboard box. The box was open and seemed empty.

I guess He must have had a spare one left over after He finished wrapping, I thought fleetingly, paying little regard to it. As if He sensed me eyeing the pretty boxes, with their gold shining paper and purple satin ribbons, He looked from me to them and back to me, "We'll open those later", He teased, "let's just sit and talk for a while."

He exhaled as if He was just really happy; that *Sunday afternoon* kind of exhale when, lunch is done, the pots are washed, the fire is roaring, the family is snoozing or otherwise occupied and Momma sinks into the sofa with an *ahhhhhh*, counting her blessings, *all is well in the world* moment.

Honestly, I'm not going to lie, I genuinely didn't understand why He would want to hang out with me so much, especially with this dreaded *sadness bug;* or why He stooped to get down and dirty right next to me on the floor; but He seemed to just love being with me and talking to me and, let's face it, I'm a girl with lots to say. We talked for hours, well mostly I talked and He was happy to let me, then, when He did offer up a response it kind of made my ramblings seem a little less hopeless, like there was a reason for it all. He laughed at me a lot too – I think He found me funny (or crazy) or both.

I drifted off to sleep a few times, waking to find my head in His lap, His hand stroking back the hair from my face, His gaze still transfixed on me. He made me feel like I was the most precious thing in the whole of the universe, like He wanted soak me up and never leave me, like He would do almost anything for me – No-one had ever loved me quite that way before. It was as if he'd finally got me all to himself and He wasn't about to share me with anyone anytime soon. "Did you sleep well?" He asked.

"I did thank you," I smiled, "I can't remember the last time I slept like that."

†

A valley is a place between two mountains, it's basin the lowest point, so for obvious reasons getting down into the valley is generally a lot more fun and a lot less work than climbing back out again. Trees and vegetation along the slopes will typically shield the valley from sunlight, making it dark, cold and uninviting. Most people fear *their* valley; they see what others go through, they stand with them, pray with them, cheer them on from the sidelines, trying if they can to pull them out; all the while hoping they never find themselves there. But I was just about to discover that the valley, much like my

> **The valley**, much like my dad's garage, is a **sacred space**, where all the stripping back and skilful repair work gets done in secret. Shielded from the distractions of the world; skills are gained, knowledge is shared, questions are encouraged, mistakes are anticipated, patience is requested, love expands, trust grows, tender correction ushers in a desire to do it better next time, character is shaped and **stories are birthed**.

133

dad's garage, is a sacred space, where all the stripping back and skilful repair work gets done in secret. Shielded from the distractions of the world; skills are gained, knowledge is shared, questions are encouraged, mistakes are anticipated, patience is requested, love expands, trust grows, tender correction ushers in a desire to do it better next time, character is shaped and stories are birthed.

When fresh rain falls onto the mountain top from above, it's drawn downwards by gravity, through the landscape, merging with other pockets of water along the way, becoming a stream. This stream of fresh water, meanders slowly, collecting nutrients and oxygen from the existing flora and rock formations as it flows; whilst all the time the clay, sand, rock particles and soil hold on to any impurities within it; meaning that by the time it reaches the floor of the valley, only the purest, freshest, nutrient rich water remains - flooding the thirsty plants that grow in this unique terrain with manna from heaven, in a way that the plants and trees that grow along the mountain side and mountain top cannot experience.

THE SECRET PLACE

†

"Shall we?" He asked mischievously, His eyes glinting, one eyebrow raised slightly higher than the other as he glanced sideways over to the boxes; sitting untouched, unopened, in the same place He'd left them several weeks earlier and looking just as enticing. I'd been sick with excitement the whole time, wondering what was inside, but refusing to let Him see my interest. A foolish concept I know as He knew it all anyway, still I tried to play it cool. Though He hadn't said as much, I was fairly sure what was in those boxes was for me and it was so nice to have something to look forward to, even if that would only last momentarily.

I'd thought at first His visit was just to check on me, kind of the way I usually visited Him in His place, just the other way around, yet here He was, it had been weeks now and He'd never left. I felt sure he would go soon, but He was showing no signs of it, in fact

He seemed like He'd moved in permanently and was loving every moment of it and for sure, everything felt better when He was around. He had been showing me new things and getting me to look at things in totally different ways and I felt like I was learning so much and beginning to come alive again. Perhaps I did have some purpose after all? I still had really sad days, but He always found a way to lift the sadness off me and help me to find the truth.

"Well?" He was teasing me again, revelling in my childlike delight, knowing full well I'd been desperate to know what was inside those boxes. "Come", he sat down crossed legged beside the boxes and patted the floor next to Him with His right hand, "Come sit here with me."

Coyly I sat down beside him on the floor as he took the first box in both hands and passed it to me.

"Some of these are going to be new to you, others are larger sizes of what you have already, but have outgrown."

I sat quietly, but alert, hanging on His every word; in the stillness I was aware of every rise and every fall of my chest as my breath slowed in reverence, sensing this was a holy moment. I took the box, placed it down on the floor and lifted the label to read.

"This is something you've always had," He said before I had time to read, 'but for the journey ahead you're going to need the largest size and this is going to look wonderful on you. It's going to do something to your heart that neither you or anyone else will understand, but I know how much you're going to love wearing it; I picked this one myself, especially for you, it's perfect."

I read the label curiously **GARMENT OF GRACE - Size L -** Slowly un-bowing the ribbon and peeling away the paper I reached into the box and found a dazzling white velvet cloak. I lifted it out carefully, the touch of the fabric so soft to my fingers, the intricate needlework perfectly finished. Slowly and nervously, I swung it around my shoulders, tying the white silk fastener across my chest. It hung beautifully and I felt almost regal as it draped elegantly down to the floor. An amazing sense of deep, deep love filled my entire being, accompanied with a great calm and holy power I'd never experienced before.

"This is your staff my darling. Don't be discouraged by those who scoff at how you use it, remember those who have gone before, trusting my word and the power of their staff."

Wow, no pressure, I thought nervously. "Is it OK if I leave it on, it feels so lovely?" I asked, genuinely unsure what I was meant to do now. He let out a loud roar of laughter, "Sweet girl, you never have to take it off." He chuckled, delighted by my enthusiasm.

Next, He slid two more boxes across the floor to me. I read the labels, said **DISCERNMENT – Size M/L** and **FAITH – Size XL.**

"You'll be familiar with what's in these boxes," He exclaimed, "you've had the previous versions since you were a little girl, but this mission you're on requires something extra. When I created you I always knew this time would come, so I made sure your imagination was quite lively and your curiosity very, well....curious; otherwise all of this might have been too overwhelming for you, so I think you're gonna handle the upgrade just brilliantly."

I put my head down, my cheeks suddenly flushing a pale pink and chuckled bashfully, slightly embarrassed that that the King of Heaven had spotted my gypsy soul and fanciful head – but, like He'd just told me, He made me this way – wow, I wasn't weird after all, this was me and He made me this way, wow... Wow...

"Well that has to be the cue for this one," He said handing me the fourth box. "This isn't for opening now. What's in there is significant, but it's not for today, you will know when the time comes to unwrap. You won't fully understand it at first as there's a bigger picture that I can't give just yet, but I think you'll enjoy what you find. Plus, by way of a of bonus, I'm sending someone to help you work through it. They will be my gift to you and you will be my gift to them."

He had that playful look on His face again, "and by the way, that previous one, the one where you just realised I made that crazy wonderful girl on purpose; you can have that for free – Foolishly I'd assumed you'd always known that." I looked down at the label which read **REVELATION No 1.**

The fifth box was already at my feet.

"Sorry but this is another one you can't open right now. There is a set time for this to be opened and again, you will know. You must take great care with this box, as I can't stress enough just how important the contents are and just how much you'll be using them. Don't let them out of your sight. There is one who will try his hardest to get them away from you."

A little shaken I flipped the label over, **BATTLE CLOTHES – FULL SET: Heavy Duty.**

"Huh?" I looked at Him confused, my mouth slightly open, my eyebrows pulled together enquiringly.

"Don't worry, you've got this, we've got this; you'll understand soon enough."

My dad's voice echoed through my mind and my heart; *you've got this Kid* – he had prepared me so well. I looked across at my Father and then again into the deepest recesses of my soul where all my love and happiest memories were stored, *Yes I got this Dad... Father,* I thought, quietly determined that 'whatever *this* is, I'm in, and with that, I placed the box alongside the revelation box and reached to grab the sixth and final box.

"Not so quick," He scolded me as I startled back, wondering if this last gift was for someone else.

I hadn't been aware of anyone being in the valley with us, but maybe He was leaving soon and taking this last gift to someone else. Well, He'd been ridiculously generous to me so I was fine if that was it? As if He heard my thought, He slowly pushed to empty box in my direction.

"Yes, that is for you and no I'm not going anywhere, I won't ever leave you, I never have, but that last gift comes with a condition." He looked straight into my eyes as if He was studying my thoughts; "well....don't you want to read the label to decide whether what's inside is something worth a trade?" He was looking really serious now, like He was waiting to see my next move, waiting to see if I was willing to give as well as receive.

What am I going to have to give up; I started to wonder and to worry a little. He has been so generous and gosh how life with Him was so much more wonderful than without Him, but I have been believing Him for so much, for miracles so huge they seemed ridiculous - what If He's about to ask me to trade all my hopes, all my dreams for whatever is in that sixth box. Would I do it, could I do it? – should I check what's in the box first before answering?

I'd been through so much and I'd had to make so many huge decisions over the past few months that my decision-making brain was exhausted. Everywhere I looked there was uncertainty and decisions that needed to be made that I just wasn't ready to make yet. My mind raced: could I really trust Him, would He really stay with me, did He really love me as much as He says or is it just all in my crazy imagination?

He turned rapidly, a look of anger covered His face in a way I hadn't seen before,

"How did you get in here?" he spat out.

I looked around trying to see who he was talking to. By now he had stood up and moved over to where light that had been radiating from Him ended and He spoke into the darkness.

"Get out, leave now, I already told you, you'll never get her."

I heard the most chilling howling sound, almost a mix of arrogant laughter and rage that gradually faded into the darkness.

I studied His expression as He turn back toward me - a look of ferocious love and concern coming from His face - and in a split second I was sure. Every single doubt that had float-ed through my mind only a few seconds early had gone; replaced by an absolute certainty that whatever lay ahead, whatever mission He may send me on, whatever my ultimate purpose was, whatever I may have to give up, not for one single second of it did I want to do it without Him by my side. Him who had just faced off to the evil lurking in the darkness close by and told Satan in no uncertain terms that I was HIS girl. What kind of love is that.

> *Him*, who had just faced off to the evil lurking in the darkness close by and told Satan in no uncertain terms that I was *HIS* girl.
> **What kind of love is that!**

"So," He said, exhaling and calmly gathering Himself, acting like nothing had just happened, "are we going to play that game of swapsies?" I turned the label over on the remaining wrapped box, it read **PEACE & FREEDOM - exchange only.**

"Well," he said, kicking the plain empty box toward me, "do you want to trade?"

I looked at him blankly, like a pupil looks back at a teacher who's waiting to be given the answer the pupil clearly doesn't have. Again, he watched me, "there's a price to pay for peace and free-dom," he paused, willing me catch up. "Come on, you already know this, you've been asking me about it a lot lately, remember?"

I tried to think, what had I been asking for, *think... think...* and almost simultaneously it came to me as he heard my thoughts, *abandon-*

ment. I squealed. This was starting to feel like a good game now.

"Abandonment, yes," He said, acknowledging my heart and my thoughts and the now victorious declaration coming from my lips, "yes, yes; well done, but abandonment coverers a whole lot of ground. You are going to have to give me your cares and your dreams, you have to put into this box your whos', your whats', your hows', your whens'; you have to place them willingly inside and then trust me to take care of them. And once you've given them to me you don't get to come visit for a sneaky fiddle; once they're in here they're mine. You have to understand what that means."

I thought for a brief moment.

"I will surely treasure them and take the best possible care of them," He smiled empathetically, "and I'm really quite good with this kind of stuff."

Was that a wink? Now he was teasing me.

"Look", He said, His comforting eyes looking straight into mine, "I promise you won't be disappointed."

Once again, my mind drifted back to my dad, taking all the broken parts of my things into His garage, making me wait agonisingly until He was sure it was ready, delighting me every single time with the finished results.

Like a child, hurriedly trying to clean the mess from her bedroom floor so she could have her Mommas promised treat, I threw them in one after another; my hopes, my dreams, my ways, my timings, my expectations, my fears, my labels, my ideas – all of them went in the plain cardboard box and as He closed the lid and placed His hand reassuringly on my shoulder, something significant shifted in me and the strangest sense of peace and complete abandonment to the will and plans of my Father engulfed me in a way I had never experienced before. I had always been a free spirit, but this was way beyond that.

In the exhilaration of the moment, I impulsively wanted to give Him something back for all that He had just showered on me; "Father, what can I do?" I despaired, feeling small – let's face it, what can you give the one that owns it all anyway?

"Oh, darling girl, you must learn how to receive. You don't have to play that good girl game with me you know. There are no strings attached, I love to give to you, it makes me so happy. And besides, you have just given me more than you could ever imagine." He looked genuinely touched; "you've just put your heart in that box back there; you've given it to me freely and you're trusting me with it, I'd say that's a pretty huge gift. And some of the tough work we've been doing together these past few weeks, in time you're going to be bringing me boxes spilling over with fruit, just you wait and see."

†

Turns out the valley is one of God's best kept secrets. Like one of those super exclusive luxury spa resorts on the glossy pages of *Conde' Nast* with the heading *The world's Best Kept Secret*, half a million price tag for two-night B&B (joking obviously), but you know the kind of place I mean. Well, here I was, sitting in Heaven's spa, having the biggest detox of my life and starting to sense that something significant was taking place and it wasn't just the *abandonment* thing, I was becoming aware of this out of the ordinary level of grace that was on me and spilling out of me.

Despite the excruciating pain, the severe pruning and the fact that everyone around me saw things quite differently, this grace and deep love seemed to be super-naturally bubbling up inside of me. It made no sense at all; I should have been feeling very different; however, I could almost feel in real time God dig-

> Here, sheltered and hidden under the covering of His **sacred tent, in a time not too long ago, for a brief moment, the world supernaturally stood still and I partied with a King; my life forever changed.**

ging me up, dusting the old soil off my roots and repositioning me back in the same place, but bedded in with fresh soil, cool fresh water, some extra nutrients and a good strong stake to support growth. Without me realising, tiny green shoots of hope had begun to push through the bare space left by the severed branches and with these green shoots came the craziest, most unshakeable faith ever - I just knew that I knew that I knew.

Here, sheltered and hidden under the covering of His sacred tent, in a time not too long ago, for a brief moment, the world supernaturally stood still and I partied with a King; my life forever changed.

Even more, in the lowest and darkest of places, satan showed up and lost.

Now I had a mountain to climb. I wasn't sure what I'd find at the top, but I knew getting up there was going to be an adventure and with every small step the air was already getting cleaner, the sunlight brighter and my legs stronger. I was glad to finally be leaving the valley behind, but I would forever cherish the days I spent alone with my Father in His workshop.

If you ever find yourself alone, broken, lost, stuck in a pit, I urge you not to devise some clever plan to get yourself out. Instead look around, look for the light and when you see it just stand still, for He is on His way. He has left the comfort of Heaven just to be with you and He will stay as long as it takes, longer if you'll let Him. Believe me I know. One day you may find yourself back up on the mountain top, looking down longingly; your heart remembering the wonders of your Fathers workshop.

The Lord is close to the broken-hearted and saves those
who are crushed in spirit.

Psalm 34:18 NIV

Don't ever let anyone or anything steal that moment from you.

Rasha'

She really *is* important to you, isn't she, Y'shua?

Y'shua

They are *all* important to me, Rasha'. Every single one, I love the same. They are in me. My blood is in them.

Rasha'

Yes, but *she* really *is* important. Why is that, what am I missing? You meet her in secret places, you shower her with gift from that creaky old cupboard of yours, you make her foolish promises you can't possibly keep, you pass her private messages and tell her of great wonders (yes I heard her spilling it all out over those irritating girls of hers). She has no idea I'm listening to every conversation. And then she writes it all down (*Seriously.* - mocking look). You really ought to have left them a few extra pointers.

And now you bring the other one alongside her – the two of them together like cute *Sisters in Arms*. What's wrong Y'shua, your little sweethearts just too feeble to stand on their own; even *with* your sparkly gifts. They have form, the pair of them. I know what to press. And I know what to dangle.

All I have to do is remind *her* what a terrible mother she's become and she falls apart; right before my eyes. Such fun. (gloats) Who knew their little *triplicity* held a bigger chunk of her heart than he did. (shocked face)

So, remind me; what's the deal? (innocent face)

Y'shua

(loud laugh) You really expect me to feed any of my daughters or their anointed into your ravenous mouth, you *wolf*. You repulse me Rasha'. **STAY AWAY!** I've told you before; she; they are mine. You ask me if they are too weak alone. My answer is a resounding NO, they are both might-ier than you could ever imagine.

But together.... Ha Ha (loud roar of laughter) - Together they are Majestic.

For the wind (spirit) blows (breathes) as it chooses.

You can hear its sound (voice),

but you don't know where it came

from or where it's going.

So it is within the hearts of those who are Spirit-born.

John 3:8 TPT

6

A Call to Arms

Take that step.

Even when it feels like all you've got is a tip toe – so tip toe!

For who knows what wonders line the path of the brave one,
bold enough to take the
first uncertain step in the right direction.

C.S.

I began to expect the unexpected, without caring particularly how it would come about or when. I began to know that whatever would come; and it surely would; it would be the best my Father had for me and it would be wilder than my wildest dreams and that was saying something, for my dreams had always been a *little* on the wild side. I stopped having any real concern about my finances too – an alien thing to a money centric world and, even though money had never been my driver, my indifference to it made no sense at all to the banker and strategist in me.

Don't get me wrong, I was still relatively wise and considered about what I had and my future; particularly as there was just me now and as it stood, I wasn't working and no longer had a home (nor anyway to purchase one for that matter). The Lord began to provide for me in ways that allowed me to endure long spells of unemployment in order to do stuff for Him (and I might add to bless the socks off me in the process) and always just as things were getting a little bit scary, He'd show up with the goods, right on cue.

"Hey Mum, how do you fancy coming to this women's conference with me next month?" TFBB had mentioned it a few weeks ago and I'd tried not to get into too much of a discussion with her over it. I hadn't felt like *doing* anything that took me away from the security of that which was familiar and safe since everything had happened.

The girls had tried to get me dressed up and on a night out to celebrate one of their birthdays and to cheer me up a month earlier. We'd booked somewhere nice to eat and a place to stay over in the city so we could all relax and have fun, but it had been a disaster. I'd tried really hard to get into the spirit of it and to show them how thankful I was for their love and encouragement, but the whole evening had only rubbed my nose further into the truth of my situation. I didn't want to be *dressed up and single*, as it seemed the masses through which we had to squeeze our way in every place we ventured, appeared to be.

I didn't want to be looked up and down like a fresh piece of meat, by eyes that clearly had no good intention on their minds. I was married, I loved my husband - I wanted to be sitting at home, candles lit, the *lights-off playlist* creating a smooth vibe in the background, us chatting happily over a bottle of *Hardys* and a plate of basil and lemon pasta. Me subtly trying to float the idea of a family place in the sun somewhere hot, one day, much the same way I had for the past sixteen years - he always humoured me; I knew it probably wasn't as high on his bucket list as mine; still I hoped one day it would be an adventure we could perhaps embark on together.

I looked around at the short skirts and low-cut dresses, so much flesh revealed that nothing was left to the imagination. I observed the testosterone thick air conjugating around the small groups of men watching and sniggering in the corner with evil intent, wondering if they would all wake up the next morning with regret and a sore head; the same empty hole still aching for something real to fill it.

Noooo, here they came again, NO. I could feel them rushing up at an uncontrollable pace. *No Lord, not here, please not here. They've tried so hard to give me a happy evening, I don't want to hurt their hearts, but I have to get out of here now.* I leant over to the girls, "Hey please don't worry and I want you to stay here, but I'm just going to head back to the hotel. I've had a lovely evening, so thank you so much, but baby steps, hey?" – I smiled trying to reassure them.

"Is everything OK Mum?" my big girl asked, "we'll come with you" – I could see the concern and love in her eyes, but I wanted to escape alone; I needed a little time, I knew what was coming and I wanted to protect them from that, particularly as they had tried so hard.

"No honestly Sweetie, I'm all good, I'm just not ready for all this yet. The meal was delicious and I've had a wonderful time. You guys stay and have fun for a little while and I'll see you back at the hotel."

I didn't give them chance to object, there was little time to waste and I knew from experience I had to make my move right now. Quickly, I hugged them both, turning to push my way through the sea of cocktails, dry ice and folly; into the ornate brass Victorian rotating doors where more bodies were pushing their way in on the opposite side; finally making it out onto the pavement where I no longer needed to pretend....I no longer could pretend.

Pulling the collar of my jacket up tight around my neck, the cold night air a sharp contrast to the sweltering heat of the cocktail lounge, the tears that I'd so miraculously held back began to flood my face with black streaks from the carefully crafted mask I'd painted onto my face earlier that evening.

Barely able to breath, I ran; terrified to look up in case some random stranger caught a glimpse of my now savaged face; through the noisy, neon, party filled streets and narrow alleyways I fled to the safety and concealment of my hotel bedroom, where the horror of the past few months took what little life was left in my broken spirit, opened a dozen of those black boxes and screamed over and over and over again **REJECTED, UNWANTED, ALONE', PATHETIC, DISAPPOINTMENT, FAILURE, UNLOVED, BURDON, EMBARRASMENT, ITS OVER, WEAK, HOPELESS**, until I finally and inevitably fell asleep exhausted.

I decided that I would never put myself through that again, so when TFBB suggested the conference, fear gripped me. *Avoidance is surely the best policy,* I contemplated, hoping it had just been a casual question. However, here she was again; "what do you think Mum?" I knew I couldn't hide away forever, but I also didn't want to deal with lots of questions and there would be many of the girls and ladies from church there.

Up to now, I had been extremely careful who I shared the details of my situation with, selecting only a small handful of very close friends who I knew loved me and who I knew I could completely trust with my heart, my truth and my children. I was walking through a disaster zone and I had to have a few safe hands to hold as I spilled out and worked through my backstory, my *now* reality and my potential future. If I had any chance of making it out the other side, I needed steadfast encouraging friends who would stay the course; listening with non-judgmental ears, who I could speak completely openly with, knowing my words would not end up as gossip. I had to have strong powerful prayer partners to buy into my increasingly irrational faith and to petition heaven alongside me and for me (they needed to be able to see what I could see); and I needed wise council.

That said, I also had to shield the children (or adults as they now were), who were also navigating the same disaster zone, each of them from a slightly different perspective, each of them with their own unique wounds and questions; each of them, precious ore, being shaped and melted and refined in this torrid furnace.

Because we'd both been through broken marriages previously, I'd made it my mission over the years to pray consistently for godly partners and godly marriages for them all, spending many hours in my typical heart-outpouring style, instilling greater understanding around the importance of marriage and desolation of divorce. Which of course by default, they'd all experienced and developed their own narrative for.

One of my great worries was that all of the fervent prayer and effort might now, simply be extinguished.

"I don't know Sweetie," I said, "do you really want to go?" I knew there were going to be some awesome speakers there and to be honest, my cup was pretty empty and filling up on some strong encouraging messages really didn't seem like a bad idea, plus I could see she wanted to go. "Why don't all three of us go together?" I spurted out impulsively, "a nice girly few days – we can book a triple room and hang out and hopefully we'll all get something really positive from it? Yep, check with your sis, I'll pay and you sort the tickets and the hotel."

THE SECRET PLACE

†

"See you there precious girl", a voice whispered deep in my soul and though I barely heard it, the date was fixed.

†

Thousands of people were already excitedly waiting for the doors to open by the time we arrived; Starbucks coffee in one hand, their tickets in the other. For many this was an annual trip but I had never been. I wasn't a big fan of *Ra-Ra-Christianity* that whipped peoples' emotions up into a frenzy, but there was something special about women speaking *into* other women, a powerhouse of girls eager to learn and grow and share with each other. I had to admit it felt good. We would be here for two days and tonight the girls and I had booked to go for a lovely meal together.

Day 1 turned out fab, the speakers were good and I made loads of notes, feeling pretty proud of myself for not getting upset once. Privately, I declared this a great victory.

As we shuffled in to our row for Day 2, apologising to everyone having to stand up to let us by, trying desperately not to spill any of the coffee held precariously over the heads of the ladies in the row in front, something familiar caught my eye up ahead as the auditorium lights flashed on and off to the beat of the worship music, causing it to glisten.

THE SECRET PLACE

†

"Just put it on the floor for now, daughter," He breathed, "won't be long now."

Startled I looked down at the recognisable bright gold foil and purple ribbon sitting on my seat, the upturned label visible, **REVELATION No 1**. I looked back quickly at the girls to check if they could see it too.

"What?" TFBB enquired blankly.

"Oh nothing" I replied with a new understanding, as I carefully slipped the box onto the floor and underneath my seat, discretely just as He'd asked:

"I knew you were here yesterday" I said putting my head back, my eyes drifting upwards, a warm smile spreading across my face, my spirit drifting outwards, today's is going to be a good day *Pops...*

†

The music was loud and the conference centre dark, apart from the stunning lighting display that showered the entire space with shards of synchronised violet beams, creating a feeling of deep peace, whilst luminous tiny white flickering lights across the ceiling were a reminder of His wonderful creation and the beauty of the stars in the night sky. I looked around; there were probably ten thousand women standing side by side, worshiping their Father together, each one lost in their own thoughts, their own prayers, their own conversation with Him. It was a beautiful picture of love. I couldn't help but wonder how many other of His girls would leave here today with an unexpected gift; I hoped it would be many; I felt sure it would, I prayed it would.

"Ok, so we're just going to take it down a level now, to get into His presence and... "

The drum beat and the bass quieted, replaced by a much gentler sound that flooded the room with a holy presence. One by one, with hands outstretch and hearts open, we each closed our eyes and our mouth to allow the spirit within us speak. I felt honoured and humbled that I could stand side by side with my own girls, as well as all these others. God had been so faithful to me.

THE SECRET PLACE

†

"I gave you safe passage."

Woah, what was that? - my spirit and my heart raced. There had been a handful of times where God had made small statements to me in the past, but never so clearly and specifically as this, and then, just as quickly I started to get a vision.

"You were never his" - there it was again.

†

Moment of Impact

The Vision

I was standing at the front of a very large wooden rowing boat that had come to rest on a narrow stretch of beach; a vast ocean behind me. The tip of the boat was wedged on the sand, two thirds of it still in the water. In front of me was a large mountain – I was standing at the helm of the boat dressed in a long white garment, a tall staff clenched in my right hand; my posture like that of a warrior about to lead an army into battle. Though I did not turn around I was fully aware that my boy was stood directly behind me, so close I could almost sense his breath on my neck; one foot in the boat, the other lifted over the left-hand side, almost touching the water. I had a strong awareness that I was being called forward by God to an unknown but important mission.

As if it was time.

I had a choice, but also a deep realisation that I was not going to say no to Him. I also had a gut-wrenching awareness that my boy was waiting behind me for an opportune moment to slip out of the boat unnoticed, I picked up a brief hesitation, but still a knowing that ultimately he would go.

The sensation I had I can only compare to watching an epic romantic medieval battle-torn movie like Tristan and Isolde, where, twenty minutes before the end you start to sense that an undesired tragic ending is looming.

As the penny drops, you begin desperately willing it not to be so, willing this irritating instinct you've just had to be wrong, yet knowing deep down it's not going to be. You get that sinking feeling. Finally, when the sword has fallen on the ill-fated pair and the credits are rolling to the haunting echoes of the final score, you sit wretched for a few minutes, simply staring at the screen, trance-like, as the sadness of the final outcome sits like a heavy ache in your heart; as if, if you stare at the screen long enough you can re-write the ending. Then, with a sigh of acceptance and inevitability, you stand up, switch off the TV, gather the empty cups and bowls of popcorn and head in the direction of the kitchen.

Standing at the front of the boat, being called on, with my boy behind me about to leave; that is the emotion that sat on me. I was completely aware in the vision that this calling was about me alone, whilst also aware of feeling great sadness for my boy, as if he was going to miss out on an adventure; like he was losing something.

Just to my left, standing on the sand at the water's edge, were my two girls with their own boys; beyond them the beach trailed away to nothing and I could not see where the mountain met the land.

I had no visibility to my right.

The vision was so clear and God's initial explanation so clear cut that I instinctively leant to my girls, one at a time without hesitation, declaring in awe, "God's just spoken to me about us."

This was what he showed me:

- The expanse of water had been the last twenty years, the time from when the three of us left the States up until now.

- God had provided *safe passage;* He had protected us and provided for us throughout that time and throughout my marriage.

- He had been faithful to my prayers for the girls and they were now on their own journeys, with their own boys and my work was done there.

- Now, God was specifically calling me onwards, alone, but in a position of power to fulfil a specific mission(s). He was giving me no visibility of what was on the other side of the mountain, I had to follow blind, but I had a great sense that this must now be my priority, my service to Him and that it would be an adventure. I had a knowing that I was chosen and called in that moment. I had to leave my comfort zone.

- My boy had the option to join me on the mission, but he would slip away quietly in the other direction. God knew that, I knew that.

- In the vision I could not see where the beach, beyond the girls, led.

- Initially, I made some impulsive assumptions about the words, *you were never His;* which in time would be rectified.

In a dramatic revelation four years later, I would discover the real meaning behind some elements of this vision, but for now, with my limited understanding of Heavenly visions, He had given me all that I was able to presently digest. And I felt re-energised.

It had brought some joy and hope to the girls too – to see their Momma called by God. It felt good.

Back home I couldn't wait to sit down and offload the extraordinary events of the weekend with H. She was fast becoming my *go-to* prayer buddie - wise counsellor - tissue queen - story exchanger - truth bearer - spiritual partner, and actually, just a really great friend. As my world had unravelled God had quietly sent her into my life and though our personalities and approach to life were quite different, we had Him in common and we totally complemented each other and bounced off each other. The real truth is that we came into each other's lives at the moment when we both needed a really good friend; but what God brought to us was so much more than that. We were both already blessed with great friends in our lives, she (as a social being) more than I, but I had always had a small, but perfectly formed group of long-standing loyal friends, many from my school days. However, the nature of the conversations H and I shared would most likely leave our *normal* friends running for the hills, thinking we'd lost the plot or taken some sort of illegal substance.

The name of Jesus and the activity of the Holy Spirit have a habit of spooking people, hence why, with the particularly unique battle season that was upon us, there was a need for much more than good friend-ship – and though it was birthed out of a pile of ashes, from a place of desperation and the need for fierce prayer and wisdom, God was already transforming our bond into something lasting and beautiful – a steadfast friendship based on love, truth, challenge, trust, honesty, encouragement, growth, prayer, fun, laughter and ultimately, *travel buddies;* but more about that later.

"Close your eyes", she said to me as I sank back into her sofa making myself comfy, relaxing back into the remarkably clear shoreline seen.

I hadn't wasted any time calling H to arrange a catch up; this was a significant development and lying here with my eyes closed and mind tuned back in, I was amazed by how much of the detail I could still see and feel.

"Go back to that place and look around – tell me what you're seeing; hearing; feeling." She guided.

I walked through the scene again looking more closely this time, inspecting every area of the picture in case I'd missed anything the first time. I noted to myself how remarkable it was that in what had been only a split second in the arena, God had been able to impart so much information. Almost everything was as I had remembered it, apart from I could now see high up on the mountain what looked like a homemade rustic wooden beach sign that pointed back down the mountain off to the left.

We talked till late and chatted about what it might all mean?

"When you go home tonight, I want you to draw out the scene. It will help you get clarity on it; plus, it will be useful in the future to come back and refer to."

I liked that idea and said I would, we prayed together and I hopped in my car and drove back to my mum's where I sat snuggled in my single bed, the pillows piled up behind me, the quilt tucked tightly under my chin – its wasn't home, but I had sure been thankful of this resting place these past months – and into the wee small hours I sketched, making notes on all the things that came to mind.

Finally, tired, I dropped the A4 sheet of paper into my bag, open on the floor at the side of the bed and turned off the lamp exhausted.

And then it was morning.

And I remembered. I took a deep breath and slowly exhaled.

I showered quickly, grabbed a coffee, my keys and my phone and jumped in my car. Taking another deep and uneasy breath, I turned on the ignition, put the car into reverse and made my way along the familiar route.

Fighting heavy eyes and an even heavier heart, I looked around our kitchen in disbelief. This still didn't feel real to me. Forlornly, I began the painful task of bubble wrapping plates and glasses, carefully placing them into large cardboard boxes ready for storage. I'd driven over early, knowing my boy would have left for work hours ago. We'd arranged it so and, in some ways, I was thankful that there would be no awkward moments, yet deep down I was sad. The clock was ticking way too fast and my heart wanted to hold on to every small part of what was left of *us*.

As I'd turned the key in the front door, the door to *my* house, *my* home, the place I'd lovingly decorated and made beautiful; I'd felt like an intruder. Walking along the hallway, staring into each room one at a time, on the face of it they still looked the same; same coloured walls, same pictures hanging from them, same furniture; yet something was gone. Our home had been plundered by an invisible enemy. The air even smelt different. The tension between what I wanted to believe, what I wanted to be true - versus what the wisdom inside of me and all the physical evidence that seemed to fall from every crack was yelling at me, was merciless.

I wondered if I'd ever feel normal, happy, giddy, treasured again?

As if rescuing me from this fresh onslaught, my phone vibrated on the worktop. The hard marble surface made it unusually loud and I jumped.

"I was praying about your vision last night after you'd left", H had texted. "I think it's Psalm 121."

Taking a moment to lasso my thoughts and drag them back to the hope filled conversation from the night before, I flicked to Google and searched Psalm 121 and began to read. Immediately something jumped out at me.

The LORD is your shade at your right hand;

I went to grab my drawing from the bag I'd left by the front door. On the right-hand side of the A4 paper I had written the night before: *Cannot see anything to the right of me.*

Psalm 121 (NIV)

A Song of Ascents.

I lift up my eyes to the hills-- where does my help come from?
My help comes from the LORD, the Maker of heaven and earth.
He will not let your foot slip-- he who watches over you will not slumber;
Indeed, he who watches over Israel will neither slumber nor sleep.
The LORD watches over you--
the LORD is your shade at your right hand;
The sun will not harm you by day, nor the moon by night.
The LORD will keep you from all harm-- he will watch over your life;
The LORD will watch over your coming and going both now and forevermore.

It could not have been clearer; we were going on an adventure, The Lord and me.

I had no idea what that meant or what it might look like. I had no inkling what I'd find when I finally got to the top of that mountain, but I now had His word that He had my back. And I trusted Him.

Of course, the Lord doesn't often give us specifics, so we have to loosely make some kind of plans until He redirects us and I began to wonder what I should do next. I couldn't hide away from the world forever and I'd never been very good at playing the victim. Though we had not once spoken about divorce, my boy had already bought a new house and was busy renovating that, still clear our marriage was over. I resolutely stood in faith on the promises God had made me and the unshakeable love I had for him. I could not and would not accept that this was a done deal. I was certain that in time, when all the learning and transformation work was done my God would be true to His word and would restore everything; only this time it would be new, better, redeemed, cleaned up.

> I sensed that in His grace and goodness Jesus was sharing His own heart with me, letting me see through His eyes, letting me experience **The Mercy Seat** – what an incredible honour that was.

I found I had this unbelievable grace upon me. Often, it seemed like God had placed this supernatural *grace-cap* on my head; for despite everything, I simply felt no anger – it was as if none of it was important, that it was just the devil doing his stuff, so it wasn't real. Daily, I battled in the heavenlies and though some days it felt exhausting, there was this stubborn determination within me to keep going until I had breakthrough. And the more I understood, the bolder my prayers and declarations became. As many around me looked on, thinking (I'm sure) how weak and naive I was, I flourished in courage and strength and knowing. I would find myself praying earnestly in tears, with a deep, deep *no strings attached* love, that seemed anything but normal; sensing, that in His grace and goodness, Jesus was sharing His own heart with me, letting me see through His eyes, letting me experience The Mercy Seat – what an incredible honour that was.

And as I began to see through His eyes, I found I had no choice but to face my own part in the wider story. As the days passed and I pondered and prayed, I began to see my own failings. It is impossible to be so close to Jesus and not feel a little bit grubby. As I've said already, we can't wash

Sin is Sin; whether we recognise it at the time or not, whether intentional or not; Sin is sin. It involves a **choice** and it carries a **cost**. A cost to others, a cost to us.

our hands of stuff, simply by declaring we didn't see it for what it was. Sin is Sin; whether we recognise it at the time or not, whether intentional or not; Sin is sin. It involves a choice and it carries a cost. A cost to others, a cost to us. Though it didn't sit easy with me, I knew I couldn't move forward without asking myself some super tough questions and working them through, lovingly, with my Father. This good girl longed to clear things up with *her Dad.*

What I found was **unmerited mercy**, **favour** and **grace**. What I found was a Father who simply wanted the very best for me, who wanted me to understand, to see through His eyes, to choose well, to be on-guard. What I found was a Father who was giddy with excitement over my enhanced heart condition. And what I found, to my complete amazement and delight, was a Father pacing the side-lines, just waiting for the opportunity to rinse off the dirt, bandage the wounds and **restore** and **redeem** all the pieces of my broken dreams.

When I was a little girl, my own dad never really told me off – for one, I was generally pretty well behaved as you know, but secondly he was too smart to use anger, oh no, he'd look at me with loving eyes, then hit me with that line 'I'm really *disappointed* with you Catkins' – Urgggg, there it was like a punch in the stomach, disappointment, the hardest word I ever had to swallow. So now, here I was again, desperately needing to know how disappointed my Father was with me; whether I'd blown it, whether He planned to off-set the promises He'd given me against my failings, my poor judgements, my sin. What I found was unmerited mercy, favour and grace. What I found was a Father who simply wanted the very best for me, who wanted me to understand, to see through His eyes, to choose well, to be on-guard. What I found was a Father who was giddy with excitement over my enhanced heart condition. And what I found, to my complete amazement and delight, was a Father who was pacing the side-lines, just waiting for the opportunity to rinse off the dirt, bandage the wounds and restore and redeem all the pieces of my broken dreams.

On me this looked like crazy grace, freedom and an absolute assurance that despite the exposed foundations, despite the fact the walls lay in ruins, the houses and streets empty and desolate, the tent was torn; the ancient foundations would be re-established and the city rebuilt, restored. He would be the protection around it and His glory would hang over it as a sign for all to see.

Boys and girls, ladies and gentlemen, *dat light was gonna shine bright again.*

You see, there is a mystery about our wonderful creator and, as much as people have tried for thousands of years to fathom it, we never will. He tells us only as much as we need to know or can handle about His own character and heart, but one of the critical things that gave me a small window into this and helped me build a wild confidence and freedom around His feelings for me, despite my own mess-ups and flaws, was the story of David and Bathsheba. A story that incites many a debate. As we know, God called King David *a man after His own heart* – he slayed a giant, was anointed as King, led great battles, sought God for his every move, refused to kill his old boss, Saul (even though Saul was busy trying to kill him) simply because he'd been anointed by God. Instead, he chose to keep out of the way, up in the hills; what a righteous man, what a pure heart.

Yet... (drumroll)...enter stage left, the dark destroyer.

I often think hell sure must have had one heck of a party when this one went down. If you don't know the story, go read it in **2 Samuel 11.**

What struck me, was how well David understood the true heart and nature of God.

Most people know that his potential downfall began with a beautiful woman, another man's wife. Yup, I know, not very original, but remember, the old ones are the best. We know in the end this truly was a great love story, but we can't dodge the elephant in the room, that it definitely didn't start on very solid or righteous footings. It began with lust and proceeded with adultery, an out of marriage pregnancy, a murder and a tonne of lies.

After a great deal of monitoring and strategising, Satan must have tottered off to his war room, drawn up a detailed plan, wandered over to the shelves and his dirty little boxes and arrogantly picked out his tried and tested methods, along with the unique value hook - The most desirable woman he could find - Enter, Bathsheba who fortunately for satan took baths, naked on the rooftop opposite David's bedroom window and whose husband was away at war, busy fighting David's battles. Not sounding good is it?

Perfect, now let's see:

- **Shelf 1** - Royalty - Government

- **Shelf 2** - Immorality

- **Shelf 3** - HEART: Desire - SPEECH – Lie - BODY – Adultery and Murder

- **Shelf 4** - Lust - Envy - Deceit

- **Shelf 5** – David had been *one to watch* since he was a small boy tending sheep in his father's field, so his box was crammed full of treasure.

As we know, it all played out *perfectly*.

Yet, when David finally saw the error of his ways and had taken it to The Lord, repented, fasted and ultimately paid the cost (the life of their son), he was bold enough, confident enough and secure enough in the heart of *his Dad* to ask, "hmmm, would it be OK if I keep hold of Bathsheba because I love her a lot?" (my translation, obviously)

Not only did God say yes, redeeming the whole situation, He also blessed them with Solomon, who became the next King of Israel, got to build the temple, amassed great wealth and became the wisest man that ever lived. Why would God do that? David had other sons, but God anointed a son born from that relationship. It surely is a huge mystery.

It was quite clear from my vision that my own relationship was not going to be redeemed any time soon. I was out of work, with little heart or energy to rush back into consulting and my sister in the States had been pestering me to go out there to help them navigate the significant restructuring of the family led ministry. It had grown expeditiously over the years and now alongside the many volunteers, also had large numbers of paid staff, its own school and church, a thriving thrift store, plus dedicated homes for the babies, the boys and the girls. They were on the cusp of coming together with a separate organisation that rescued young people in Eastern Europe from the grip of human trafficking. On top of this, they had recently been asked to take over the running of an orphanage in Kenya. There was so much going on and I knew with my background and expertise that I could help practically.

It will keep me busy and buy me some time, I contemplated. I chatted with the girls who thought that a three months stint over there was a great idea, so I booked the flights and began to prepare.

"Hey, Momma, it's me, you OK?"; the sunny voice of my big girl danced down the phone line and my heart smiled. I was so blessed to see the wonderful kind wise women they had both grown in to.

"Hey Sweetie, I'm great thanks, how about you?"

"So, I was thinking, I have a little time available at work, why don't we take a short trip somewhere nice before you leave?"

I love doing things impromptu. I think it's something built deep into my being and it adds an element of excitement to thing. So here we were, one week later sitting on the tiny beach in Villefranche-sur-Mer on the French Riviera soaking up the scorching rays and looking out over the blue waters of the Mediterranean, that were gradually sneaking up to nibble the edges of our towels – it was spectacular and just what we had both needed. It was only a few days, but they would be special days and I was about to make a significant decision.

Moment of Impact

"I've got something to tell you."

Suddenly upright, I looked over at her, as she yanked out her earphones and raised herself alongside me.

"I'm going to write a book."

"Oh?" she replied enquiringly.

"It's going to be a love story; it's going to be my story, but more than that, it's going to be a story that shows the power and faithfulness of God. I'm going to write it in faith and write about my journey and all that God is showing me, but I'm going to write it believing that by the time I get to the final chapter God will have delivered my *Ta Daaa*; that God will have restored everything against all the odds and he will get all the glory. If He hasn't or if I've misunderstood what He has in mind, then the whole book will have been a waste of time, but I'm just going to stand in faith."

I paused, studying her face carefully to gauge her response, "what do you think?"

She was a wise one and generally thought about her answers before offering them. She had been really hurt in all that had gone on and I knew she was struggling to understand the level of grace I had been showing, however much she admired it. Indeed, engaging with the faith I was now standing in had been something she'd found she just couldn't do. She wasn't entirely sure what outcome she wanted and I understood and completely respected that. I had been more than aware that there was something rather *out of the ordinary* about the way I was walking through this. From a place of deep love, she was angry at what had happened and wanted better for me.

With each passing month, I'd started to see this role of protector grow in her spiritually. As I walked in grace and boldness, TFBB close behind, she became my (*our*) watchman, my (*our*) armorbearer. Whilst she would have preferred that I remain *unexposed*, my battle strategy was set, so she *scouted* ahead and cleared the ground of land mines, whilst I defiantly played hopscotch around them. We made a great team, but it meant we often looked at situations from our unique positions. Both with wisdom, both with discernment; just different lenses.

> With each passing month, I'd started to see this role of protector grow in her spiritually. As I walked in **grace** and **boldness**, she became my **watchman**, my **armorbearer**...

"Well, you've always wanted to write a book and it will take a good bit of time to do anyway. I think it's a great idea, Mum." She went on "I don't know what ending God will give you, but I do believe He'll give you your *Ta Daaa*."

And so it was, the seed was planted, the commitment made and faith dared.

As the plane landed back on the Manchester tarmac, I realised to my amusement that in less than a week's time I'd be back here boarding a flight to Bama. Three months seemed like forever to me right now, but at least it would keep me busy and maybe, just maybe......I dragged my thoughts back quickly refusing to let them hijack today's joy. The last five days had been such a gift; me and my girl soaking up the vitamin D, wandering along the ancient narrow streets, eating amazing food and sharing a pre-dinner bottle of Rosé from the spectacular viewpoint of the tiny harbour-side café, as the fishing boats bobbed up and down on the tail end of the currents caused by the odd jets ski and larger boats further out in the ocean. We were more like friends than mother and daughter. Yes, I concluded, sitting alongside my girl, our tanned skin glowing with health and vitality, it had been a precious five days and I was thankful.

The next week would be busy, packing and getting everything ready. The sale on our home was due to complete and I had some last-minute paper-work to sign. Piece by piece our life was being unravelled and by default our connection severed – *CHOP* - as if it had never happened. I hated it.

H was coming over during the week for a catch up before I left – the weather was looking good so we'd decided to BBQ.

"We'll call round to say bye, Momma, the day before you fly," she shouted as she pushed the car door closed, blowing me a kiss through the window and hurrying towards her handsome husband who by now was waiting on the front doorstep, a huge grin on his face. He'd missed her, but I was grateful he'd been happy for her to come. I waved to him, swinging my car round in the direction of Mums, my thoughts already tuned in to the following week's *to-do* list and the uncertainty of the next three months.

As predicted, the weather that week had been glorious and I had man-aged to race through all the last-minute things far quicker than I had expected and was now pretty much good to go. H was arriving around 7.30pm and I had the BBQ going and food prepared. She'd messaged to say she'd been held up with something urgent and was hoping to still make it but would be late, so I sat in the garden enjoying the still warm evening sunshine and the peace, nothing to hear but the occa-sional bird tweeting and the distant sound of a lawn mower, *someone working off the stress of a chaotic day in the office*, I thought with a smile. *None of that for me for a while* I mused, pondering as I often did how my life ended up so *un-normal*.

I seemed to have spent my working years immersed in long spells of business strategy, working extended periods in *grown up* stressful environments; sandwiched around random, salary-less wanderings or expeditions; an itinerant with *no fixed abode*. Secretly, I kind of loved it this way, it fed that gypsy soul of mine and that need not to fit in anyone's box; on the other hand, I couldn't help but worry that it just wasn't *normal*. Living out in the States when the girls where small, just the three of us, my sister had bought me a ceramic wall plaque of an old VW camper van which read *Home is where your Stuff is*, I still had it. These days it needed to read *home is where your black in bags are*, I chuckled sarcastically to myself. Somehow, I loved that plaque and despised it at the same time.

Just as I was nervously watching the time, thinking how I'd hate to head off to Bama for so long without saying bye to H, I heard her car pull onto the drive and jumped up to greet her.

"What a day" she exhaled, clambering out of her car flustered, her bag and a bunch of flowers in one hand, a bottle of raspberry lemonade in the other; "that bloomin devil didn't want me to come tonight, almost everything has gone wrong today, then I got stuck on a call with... anyway, I'll tell you about it later, let's get some food."

I chuckled; whenever we were together it was as if the clock was ticking way too fast for us to get through all the chatter and highly important exchanges we needed to share. I guess I was the worse, my curious brain full of information and newly acquired facts I just had to share, but she was used to me by now and always we would find ourselves looking at the clock at the end of the evening exclaiming *Wow is that the time?* We never wasted a moment. I was so glad she was here and knew it was going to be a great night.

I took the flowers inside, sat them in some water in the kitchen sink, grabbed some ice from the freezer, poured out two glasses of lemonade, then headed back outside. The garden furniture from my old life had proved useful on Mum's patio and H was already settled into the comfy grey sofa. As I started towards her the lowering sun seemed to catch something bright on the grass beside the sofa, sending a flash of light in my direction so that I needed to turn my head slightly and squint to avoid the glare.

THE SECRET PLACE

†

"It's time baby girl" He said, "this is going to change everything."

By now, I was getting used to these impromptu visits. As I handed her the glass and sat down, there at my feet was the final box, still as beautifully adorned in gold and purple, still holding on to its original label:

BATTLE CLOTHES – FULL SET: Heavy Duty

†

I don't think I'm going to be able to explain what went down in the garden that night, it was a holy moment. As we sat and talked and shared stories and battles and experiences, and as the fading evening sunlight gave way to the chilly deep blue hues of a clear July night sky, scattered with twinkling diamonds; as the hours passed by way too quickly and the call of our beds became louder; we sat huddled together, throws wrapped around our shoulders to keep out the cold – two friends, brought together with a common goal; to fight the good fight.

In those sacred hours, right before our eyes, God had completely **lifted the veil** between earth and heaven and the dark places that lined their borders and for the very first time I understood fully where the **real battle** was and who it was with and even more excitingly, I was being given the tools, the strategy, the faith and the passion to fight it. And that **changed everything**.

In those sacred hours, right before our eyes, God had completely lifted the veil between earth and heaven and the dark places that lined their

166

borders and for the very first time I understood fully where the real battle was and who it was with and even more excitingly, I was being given the tools, the strategy, the faith and the passion to fight it. And that changed everything. It was only the beginning of this great awakening, but already I was discerning the mischievous barriers H had faced earlier in the evening just getting here...

Tonight, was a problem for the assailants of Heaven, *we* were a problem for them.

Pfffff, I thought, you have no idea, *Battle On.*

As we stood in the darkness, almost dazed and bathed in wonder, unable to put a name or an explanation to what had taken place during the preceding few hours, we hugged, prayed for each other and said our last goodbyes, knowing that we were both forever changed.

"I think we are going to be life-long friends", she smiled climbing into her car. "I'll be praying for you Hun." And with that she was gone.

A tiny bit spooked and slightly amused to be standing outside in the dark in the wee small hours, having just declared war on satan, I hurried inside and locked the door. No pressure, Cath, I chuckled to myself as I drifted into a deep and peaceful sleep.

The kids were arriving at lunchtime to say their goodbyes. TFBB was hoping to follow me out for a two weeks holiday; she was dating now and it seemed serious. He was a good boy and I was pleased and she thought he might travel over with her. We'd planned to take a trip to the beach together before I got stuck into the real work, so I would see her soon enough, but for my big girl it would be a while. For some reason I was feeling anxious.

These days I had a growing need to hold on tight to the things that were really precious to me, as if they might also just slip away too if I took my eyes off them for very long. I knew that was all part of the fall-out from everything, but I sensed today was going to be a tough one. I navigated it the best I could, loving their company and hiding my apprehension for the most part, slipping away to the kitchen under the guise of washing the dishes when it got too much. I didn't want to embarrass myself or them for that matter with tears, especially in front of the boys. What must they think about me – what a predicament? How I wished I could still give them a proper family.

COMMAND HQ

There he was again, with his little black boxes of lies; I tried to cut him dead and right on cue.

"Mum", I turned around, swallowing hard and smiling, a look of concern on their faces. "Mum we've got you something." Together they each handed me a card. TFBB then pushed a handle, adorned with a big red ribbon, into my hand, attached to a cute pull-along cabin bag. It was perfect. "I know you've probably already packed your carry-on case for tomorrow, but it will be easy to swap over and I wanted you to start with something new and shiny and fitting for this next part of your journey. A cute case for a cute Momma." – She gave me a tight hug. I loved it and I loved the sentiment behind it even more.

My big girl then handed me a small package, carefully wrapped in crinkled tissue paper and tied with a pretty pink ribbon. "Mum, I'm so proud of you. I've never known anyone stronger or braver. You inspire me, both of us to love harder and to trust God more. Me & T are just so thankful for who you are. You'll always be home to us."

My heart summersaulted. If I never achieved anything in my life again, I thought, here is my legacy, here is my greatest achievement, here are my beautiful girls, all grown up and perfect in my eyes.

"Mum, I know it's been hard, but I know that God is going to do amazing things while you're away. It will be an adventure, so I though having a little journal would help you capture every moment."

I took the package, wrapped with so much more than the paper and ribbon around it, and opened it up. Inside was a duck egg blue journal, the words

168

TRAVEL JOURNAL printed across the top. It had a silk screen printed cover with images of mountains and valleys. In amongst the pages were secret storage pockets to file keepsakes. One by one I opened up the cards.

~~~~~~~~~~~~~~~~~~~~~~~~~~~~~~~

Beautiful Mummy Thank you for who you are,

Thank you for inspiring me to be a greater woman,

For inspiring me to love wholeheartedly, for inspiring me to be strong in all things.

You are a faithful, loving, genuine, hilarious, kind mother and I know that I wouldn't be the lady that I am without you. You have guided my steps and taken me on a journey many would only dream of. You are honestly Captivating and the bravest strongest woman I have ever set eyes on. I hope that I can learn from you even more and be as beautiful inside and out just like you.

"BLESSED is she who has believed that HE WILL fulfil His promises to her" Luke 1:45

Love you more than any words put down,

your little girl TFBB x

And then my big girl's.

~~~~~~~~~~~~~~~~~~~~~~~~~~~~~~~

Momma, thank you for an amazing little trip.

We are praying for you this next few months and want you to know we are ALWAYS thinking of you.

Genesis 9:13-15, I have placed my rainbow in the clouds. It is a sign of my covenant with you. When I send clouds over the earth the rainbow will appear in the clouds and I will remember my covenant with you. Never again will the flood waters destroy all life.

Catherine; Meaning Pure, Clear, Innocent

I wanted to remind you of your identity. You are pure, your heart and intentions are clear

and your soul is innocent because He first loved you.

You are fearfully and SO wonderfully made and He is well pleased with you.

He has made His face to shine upon you. I love you dearly, Catherine x

And I love you dearly too, Momma – L&K x

In that moment my heart exploded, I felt like the luckiest woman alive, with no words that could express the extent of my gratitude to God for His favour. Leaving wasn't what I really wanted, but it was the best option for now. I had prayerfully and wisely weighed everything up and made the decision to go. The rest of it was in God's hands.

Early tomorrow morning, with my new case and the content of the box we'd opened in the garden just a few nights before, I would set off on a new adventure, to who knows what. I still had a mountain to climb, but I had God and two of the most mighty and precious angels cheering me on.

And in amongst the pages of my lovely new journal the next part of my story would begin to unfold.

Journal

Thursday 18th August 2016

10:55 GMT

Well, my precious grown up girl...

REPAIRING THE BREACH

Rasha'

Secrets, secrets, secrets...

Why do you spend so much time down on that grubby carpet with her? That's no place for a King (the familiar tone of lofty temptation as he mimics the dusting off of his garish robe).

Y'shua

Isn't a father's place wherever his child is?

It is no place for her either, yet *YOU* drove her there with your meddling and obsession with her Ora. And still (pauses with a look of indescribable passion and ennoblement) she bears it for me. We bear it together.

See, even in the darkness, she mesmerises you, Rasha. How you despise the treasure she carries. I don't think you know if you hate her or covet her. Jealousy is crippling isn't it. If only your dark empty heart could forget how good that light felt when we walked together. Forget that you *chose* this (nods towards the endless darkness and wailing).

Perhaps you thought you could have both; the light and the dark? You see now, how impossible that is.

Rasha' (a momentary flash of wistful recollection is quickly replaced by the familiar game face)

Bears it for you.... PFFF. Look at her, she's a failed sample Yeshua, clutching at every ancient word you ever spoke, flattering you, drawing you in with her crazy hero worship that believes you're going to do something unimaginable for her. Be careful, *You,* who craves their love so fiercely; I fear your beloved bride may break your heart in the process of her sweet manipulation and vain desires.

Y'shua (smiles)

The time is coming close. It won't be long now, all that I have surely planned for her will come to pass. Finally, that which has held your curiosity hostage all these years will be revealed. And it is only the beginning. Others will follow. Out of the ashes of your mauling, slander and failed strategies my pure, my righteous, my vindicated, my redeemed, my power-filled warriors are rising and equipping.

For the LORD will comfort Zion;

He will comfort all her waste places,

and He will make her wilderness like Eden, and her

desert like the garden of the LORD.

Joy and gladness will be found in her,

thanksgiving and melodious song. **Isaiah 51:3 KJV**

7

Battle Cry

The devil caught me with my head down and got excited.

Until I looked up and said AMEN

UNKNOWN

It's hard to put into words exactly how I felt as I stepped off the plane into that familiar Georgia sunshine.

Everyone around me had been commenting on how brave, how courageous I was, but inside I felt anything but brave. I was surviving on the smallest shred of that *you can do it Kid* attitude that my Dad had meticulously woven into me and a hope (a belief) in the impossible, from an *I am possible* God.

Charles Spurgeon, the famous nineteenth century British preacher said in the PREFACE of Cheque Book of the Bank of Faith – Daily readings by CH Surgeon; 'God has given no pledge which He will not redeem, and encouraged no hope which He will not fulfil.'

'A PROMISE from God may very instructively be compared to a cheque payable to order. It is given to the believer with the view of bestowing upon him some good thing. It is not meant that he should read it over comfortably, and then have done with it. No, he is to treat the promise as a reality, as a man treats a cheque.

He is to take the promise and endorse it with his own name by personally receiving it as true. He is by faith to accept it as his own. He sets to his seal that God is true, and true as to this particular word of promise. He goes further and believes that he has the blessing in having the sure promise of it and therefore he puts his name to it to testify to the receipt of the blessing.

This done, he must believingly present the promise to the LORD, as a man presents a cheque at the counter of the Bank. He must plead it by prayer, expecting to have it fulfilled. If he has come to Heaven's bank at the right date, he will receive the promised amount at once. If the date should happen to be further on, he must patiently wait till its arrival; but meanwhile he may count the promise as money, for the Bank is sure to pay when the due time arrives.

Some fail to place the endorsement of faith upon the cheque, and so they get nothing; and others are slack in presenting it, and these also receive nothing. This is not the fault of the promise, but of those who do not act with it in a common-sense, business-like manner.'

In the months that had passed since that awful day; a day like no other I'd ever know; God had gifted me with such a steadfast and stubborn faith that I still cannot fathom it; even now. As I write these words, here in the middle of my story, there are things I am still believing of God that seem more unimaginable than they ever did. Even crazier, the fulfilment of these things have become

I had sensed that this crazy stupid faith (as I had come to refer to it) was gifted to me to help me fulfil the calling on my life. I was well aware that the unshakeable certainty I was carrying was neither logical nor typical, yet this only excited the extraordinary, the mischievous, the barrier basher in me more than ever.

no longer personally desirable to me. The evolution process has been nothing short of miraculous.

This promise; this cheque in my possession, which I endorsed in bold capital letters was so crystal clear to me, so etched into my soul, that I have been unable to perceive any outcome other than it being honored in full by the Governor of The Bank of Heaven. From my time in the valley with my Father, I had sensed that this *crazy stupid faith* (as I had come to refer to it) was gifted to me to help me fulfil the calling on my life. I was well aware that the unshakeable certainty I was carrying was neither logical nor typical, yet this only excited the *extraordinary*, the *mischievous*, the *barrier basher* in me more than ever.

Stubbornly standing in the gap alone, scuffing my knees till they bled, declaring truth and the breaking of chains till my voice was horse, carrying the weight of others on my back, gave me purpose and a focus. It gave me hope. It was keeping me alive. I possessed a Holy Secret; that, at His chosen time, God would reveal the might of His power and glory to the world and I would be able to say, *see, I told you.*

> I possessed a **Holy Secret**; that, at His chosen time, God would reveal the might of His power and glory to the world and I would be able to say, *see, I told you.*

Many would say to me, Yes, but everyone has a choice. God gives each of us free will. Yet, I could not shake two words. Two very *small words, never-the-less, words that kept leaping out to me over and over again. It was as if He was illuminating something to me that other were clearly missing:* **I WILL...**

It seemed to me that others were placing the right of free will, which God does give to His children, higher than His ultimate purposes and plans and His own supernatural power; as if; as long a man resisted, God was somehow stuck, drumming His fingers on the arm of His throne, all His plans, balancing on one mans, one woman's, decision?

I was having none of it.

Over and over again, off the pages of His word came this clear promise; *then, I will.*

I will *show my concern to you and keep my promises to bring you* *back home* **Jeremiah 29:10**

I will restore you to your land **Jeremiah 29:14**

I will rebuild them as they were before **Jeremiah 33:7**

I will heal this city and its people and restore them to health **Jeremiah 33:6**

I will put my breath in them and bring them back to life **Ezekiel 37:14**

I will put my spirit in you and see to it that you follow my laws and keep my commands **Ezekiel 36:27**

I will put my law within them and write it on their heart **Jeremiah 31:33**

I will forgive their sins and no longer remember their wrongs **Jeremiah 31:34**

I will lead them back; I will guide them to steams of water on a smooth road where they will not stumble **Jeremiah 31:9**

And this one...

Write down in a book all that I have told you, for a time is coming when I will restore you; I will bring my people back home to this land and they will take possession again. **Jeremiah 30:2-3.**

As much as I searched, I couldn't find anywhere where His word gave someone a promise that was dependent on *the other guy playing ball.*

Yes absolutely, there are some suggested *ifs* for the person receiving the promise; God loves us and wants to grow us into all that we were intended to be, so of course on the road to our promise our Dad is keen to gives us a few smart boundaries and *best-practice* guidelines to help us along the way. He'll lay down some *Fatherly Wisdom* through

His written Word or He'll meet with us in His secret place for one of His precious *Dad - Daughter chats*. Sometimes He will unexpectedly illuminate a thought or idea that represent the most efficient and prudent course of action – When we occasionally wander off-course, procrastinate (which I have a huge tendency to do) or simply get distracted, deep in our spirit we'll sense that something just doesn't feel right – that's Him, our Dad whispering "Hey baby girl, don't go there, it's not safe for you there, look, here, let me show you where the path is." Other times, help comes via an unexpected human encounter.

All of this protects us, but more importantly, gets us *ready*. If we messed up last time, how can we be sure we won't mess up again, unless we grow and learn? I don't know about you, but I don't want to keep messing up; I want to embrace the promise when it comes with all the readiness and boldness I can muster. I want to bask in His glory and be blown away by His faithfulness. If I've not been prepared and refined, when (if) I reach my destination I'm most likely going to hold back; or even shift into self-preservation mode and put up those old barriers. Even worse, I'll charge in full throttle and inflict havoc and chaos amongst the people and places I'm called to love and bless.

It's that old saying: *If you always do what you've always done, you'll always get what you've always got.*

Back to my dilemma. As much as I looked, nowhere could I see a single *if they* – The great I AM said to me consistently, I WILL, and I had no reason to doubt that He could and He would, regardless of any earthly resistance or lack of cooperation. I was sure that the person I'd hung out with

> The fire within me had been stoked and I was going to trust Him for every promise He had made me.

in the valley most definitely did not need His reputation protecting with some sort of *get-out* clause, just in case. – I was ready and willing to challenge anyone who felt they needed to manage my expectations. The fire within me had been stoked and I was going to trust Him for every promise He had made me.

Well today at least...

What was less certain, however, was how; when; my part in it all (or not); and His expectations of me in the meantime.

Oh, the joys of *The Meantime.*

I once heard an amazing message called Don't decorate the meantime – Don't pitch up your tent in somewhere you're not staying. Don't get comfortable in your waiting – yes get involved; get busy doing and helping; yes, get busy learning and gleaning and growing; but don't decorate that place and let it become home, because you're just passing through. Sometimes it feels like you missed your ride out of town and now you're stuck here, but that's a smokescreen by you know who, who wants you to think you blew it and God's forgotten you.

Are you spotting the pattern here?

God *sends* me. I am seeing that more and more. He has a habit of picking me up and pointing me in a new direction with the instruction 'Go.' One of the scriptures He gave me right before one of these *Go* moments was **Jeremiah 29:7** *Work for the good of the cities where I have made you go as prisoners. Pray to me on their behalf, because as they prosper, so will you prosper too.* Sometimes we are sent as the solution to His promises to others, yet in that obedience, we share in the harvest. And as we work and pray and watch; secretly, in *the meantime;* we are being sharpened and refined and made ready.

> God sends me. I am seeing that more and more. He has a habit of picking me up and pointing me in a new direction with the instruction GO!

And here I was...

Staring around at the familiar walls of my *Alabama meantime; the little wooden home from home;* so many emotions swishing around inside of me. I had stayed in here so often before. *We* had stayed here so often before - during holidays or visits for family weddings, it had been a perfect retreat, everything we needed and more.

Outside, from within the thick bracken, a timid dear poked out its head and once sure the way was clear, wandered over to the small patch of dry prickly grass in front of the duplex window. It was more just red soil than grass, but there, it tentatively grazed, its ears pricked up on high-alert, ready to detect any potential foe, unaware it was being admired from inside. Beside the porch steps stood the little golf cart, as always parked up ready to provide visitors with easy transportation up to the main house. Everything was just the same. Except that it wasn't the same at all...

A car horn beeped outside. I smiled a little anxiously, wandering over to the door, unlocking it and opening it politely as I waved back at the familiar face, now hanging out of the lowered truck window, gesticulating warmly.

"Call me if you need anything," my big sis had encouraged earlier, as she'd dropped me off; simultaneously plonking my heavy cases onto the decking and the front door keys into my hand. 'I will', I'd promised, thanking her and giving her a half-hearted smile. We really hadn't had chance to talk much on the drive back from Atlanta, but I knew tonight wasn't the night for that. Tonight, I just wanted to lock the door behind me, pull down the blinds, put on something comfy and steel myself. Take all of this in; adjust to this new season; pull out my journal and capture my thoughts. No, I would not need anything tonight, I'd concluded, but to be alone.

Lord, make this brief I thought; touched by the welcome, still desperately hoping the truck would pass on by without stopping. Tomorrow I will be ready for everyone, I assured myself, but not tonight, not yet.

Two gorgeous faces suddenly peered up over the side of the beaten-up truck, waving and giggling. I pulled a funny face back and waved with both hands and they giggled again, putting their hands over their mouths pretending to be shy and then bobbing back down to hide. "Hey Miss Cathy, glad you made it," the soft southern drawl called from behind the wheel, "did you have a good flight?"

Everyone here was like family; most had been involved in the ministry for years and so had become good friends. I wasn't sure how much people knew about my situation, but it was inevitable they would find out soon enough, when the usual 2/3 weeks passed and I was still here. The dirt road ran all the way around the perimeter of the land connecting all the main buildings and houses and it was common to hear people beep their horns in a welcoming tone as they sped by leaving a cloud of dust behind. With the house usually standing empty, inside lights were generally a signal that someone had arrived; a guest, a family member, an old friend; the house was always kept ready. And it was just good *plain ole southern hospitality* and manners to send out a *glad to have you back with us*, welcome honk.

How I loved this place. It somehow always felt safe and peaceful? There was this sense of *sleepy days gone by* about it, like you'd stepped off the conveyer belt of life for just a brief moment. Unsurprisingly, there was also an element of *home* about it too. 20 years ago, it had been home for a while and right now, I had to admit there was a real possibility it could become home again? If God decided not to restore my marriage, I could make a great life here and for sure, my sister was desperate for me to make this a permanent move. So many impossible decisions had to be made.

"I had a great flight thanks," I smiled back, "just ready for some sleep now." I tilted my head and closed my eyes animatedly.

He nodded in acknowledgement, "catch you tomorrow, get some rest, he called as the truck wheels spun and crunched forward on the gravel and the two squealing cheeky monkeys began to bump up and down in the back in unison with the chorus of *see you later* honks; barely visible through the now dusty air.

Smiling warmly, I stepped back inside and bolted the door. Well, this is it Kid, you're really here.' My thoughts wandering.

I looked around at its little kitchen, the washer, the fridge that had been so generously stocked for me, the comfy sofa and large TV; a true *home away from home*. I was thankful to have this place - somewhere I could retreat to, somewhere I could breathe and find quiet, somewhere I wouldn't have to put on a show. Honestly, I was blessed to have everything I could possibly need.

Yet, standing here in the quiet; my life, my girls, *my boy* over 4000 miles away across the Atlantic Ocean; I had never felt so alone in my entire life. This strange leftover puzzle piece that didn't quite fit anywhere anymore; that didn't know where home was anymore. I knew I was valuable; deep down I knew there was treasure in me; really rare treasure.... Or maybe not so valuable these days. Maybe I was fooling myself – perhaps I had been fooling myself all along? Perhaps that's why my life had turned out so fortuitous, so hap-hazzard, so changeable?

> Despite feeling like a leftover puzzle piece that didn't quite fit anywhere anymore, I knew I was valuable. Deep down, I **knew there was treasure in me, really** *rare* treasure...

THE SECRET PLACE

†

"Hush now my darling girl, hush. I'm right here, we all are. And you, my chosen one, are right where you are meant to be. I know, I know. I ache with you. Watching your pain is almost more than I can bear.

Come; let me take that weight from you for a while, for tonight at least; let me pour out my love on you. You are not being over-looked; you are being set apart. I am hiding you now to protect you and to develop you. Even when you are not visible to fickle eyes, when you feel invisible, you are valuable.

When it is your time, people will stand and wait for you to show up. You are treasured more than you could ever imagine; you are my shining star, my complete delight. You are on MY assignment now; I am so in awe of who you're becoming."

He leant forward, gently removing the small crystal stopper from the jar in His hand, careful not to miss a single one. She was trying so hard to be brave, but He could see that the overflow of elixir seeping out of her heart was already starting to well up. That huge heart, so full of love. He watched the first one slowly, without any drama, slip elegantly from the corner of her eye, slipping gracefully down her motionless face. He observed a numbness, as if the fight had left her.

Moments later the next one, running parallel, meandering their way across the contours of her cheeks, glistening in the light that radiated from within. He lent a little closer and held out the bottle in His hand, timing it perfectly – clink, clink. The sweet high-pitched sound as each one splashed and blended with the others was intoxicating. He waited as she stood there, allowing a third to fall uncontested. Clink. Every single one was precious to Him.

"There" He replaced the stopper securely. The jar of elixir glistened in His hand, 'her heart was so full of treasure'.

It was the internal boasting of a very proud Father.

He placed the jar inside His pocket and took out the other.

As she walked into the dark bedroom, slumping onto the floor between the foot of the bed and the large dark set of drawers, her face buried in the carpet, her body spread out in total defeat, He watched, never once taking His eyes off her.

"Father where are you? Where are you?"

She cried out, unaware of His nearness.

Her pain bore heavy on His shoulders. It was a pain He had felt so many times before as each had waited for their time, convinced He had forgotten them. Wondering how they got to this place. Not realizing He had brought them there. Sometimes He had to remind Himself how time felt to them. Waiting and wondering could make Man do foolish things.

His thoughts wandered to His friend, Abraham; He chuckled at how He'd tried to solve his own problem, to deliver his own promise. But in the end, He had trusted. And Joseph, how Joseph had clung to that early dream, year after year, waiting with expectation as things got worse, knowing his vision was from his Father, yet not quite understanding the full weight of what he'd seen. It had been hard to watch his confusion and weariness as each situation seemed only to get worse. But oh, what a mighty man and leader was being birthed in those hidden places.

He smiled with enormous pride remembering. Recounting the day Joseph fully understood the true meaning of the bowing sheaves of grain from his boyhood dream (**Gen 37**). The day he finally came face to face with destiny. By then he was ready.

He walked over and lowered himself down alongside her. She was led on her side now, her knees pulled up towards her face, both hands layered one on top of the other beneath her cheek - her eyes staring out into space.

Gently brushing her damp hair away from her face; "I'm right here, I'm right here."

He opened up the second jar and carefully tilting it, let a few drops of oil fall onto the fingers of His rights hand. With words of a heavenly language, he placed his fingers on her forehead and let the oil run down freely. It rested where it needed to and He smiled. Then, one by one, he took her hands from beneath her head and opened up her palms, touching each of them in turn. With the remnants he ran his finger lovingly over His own palm, slowly tracing each letter of her name that was etched there.

He could not love her more.

"Time to sleep now my anointed one," He whispered in her ear, "it's been a busy day."

†

By the time I finally opened my eyes I'm not sure how long I had been lying on the floor; it had gone dark outside, leaving the bedroom in pitch blackness. I felt exhausted, yet better somehow. I always felt a little better after tears, like I had let something go. The street lamp filtering in through the front window was casting a small beam of light across my unpacked case; still standing proudly in the centre of the living room floor where I'd deposited it earlier. From this angle it looked like a giant stood there and I concluded that, unlike David, this girl needed some sleep before going in for the kill - unpacking would be a *tomorrow* job. I pressed myself up off the floor with my elbow then wrist, wriggling my fingers to get rid of the pins and needles that were stabbing my hand and lower arm. Then, stretching out the creek between my shoulder and neck. Reaching to my face, I prised loose the crusty fringe that had somehow glued itself to my eyelids and upper-cheek and with a gesture of affection and self-care, I gently walked the cool tips of my fingers across the tender skin below my eyes.

The past few months had taken their toll; I looked tired, the lines had gotten a little deeper and weren't bouncing back so quickly; 'my battle scars' I mused. Using the edge of the bed frame to hoist myself up onto my feet, I slowly groped my way around the mattress in the darkness. With little thought, I tugged off my now crinkled travel clothes and dropped them onto the floor in a haphazard pile, before falling into the fresh cotton sheets.

Apart from the comforting hum of the ceiling fan above, the room fell silent.

As I drifted into a peaceful sleep something deep within reminded me that this was going to be an adventure, full of possibilities.

She was back.

There is something I want to say here, something that is important for anyone going through *stuff.*

Healing isn't linear; our journeys aren't linear.

Healing isn't linear; our journeys aren't linear.

At this stage in my story two contradictory things were taking place;

I was walking through the most painful thing I'd ever had to navigate; my whole world had just been deconstructed piece by piece (for the second time), my heart had taken a trauma so violent that as strong as I was, it consumed every waking moment; no different than if I'd been involved a car wreck, sustaining multiple injuries that required long term reconstruction and rehabilitation. Coming to the States, I'd taken a step of faith, to *GO,* to do something useful in the waiting, but in doing that I'd physically separated myself further from all that was familiar, all that my heart ached for and for the first time, it was just me – 'you're on your own here Kid' my Dad would have noted.

On the flip side, I was also going through the most incredible divine awakening. I was being fast-tracked in heavenly places and in heavenly things and this fierce roar was beginning to emerge from deep within my belly, releasing a bold declaration to the hordes of hell that I was coming for them. Jesus kept showing up and showing off and the little girl, *little Cath,*

I was being fast-tracked in heavenly places and in heavenly things and this **fierce roar** was beginning to emerge from deep within my belly, releasing a **bold declaration** to the hordes of hell that I was coming for them.

was like a child in a sweet shop, captivated by all the different flavours and shapes and colours; impatiently wanting to try them all to see which ones I'd like.

On top of that, what I didn't know then, what I couldn't have known, what no human ear could have possibly detected because it was not an earthly sound; far away, as if rallied by each divine roar, a duet of tiny bellows were echoing into the atmosphere, synchronising their war cry with *Momma* and with each other.

Far away, as if rallied by each **divine roar**, a duet of tiny bellows were echoing into the atmosphere, **synchronising their war cry** with **mine** and with **each other**.

I'd get up, I'd fall down, I'd get up, I'd trip, I'd crawl, I'd get up – My mind, my heart, my soul, my spirit (and probably parts of my body) had all taken a real pummelling and needed to heal, but my inherent gusto and passion and good girl courage were dressing to disguise the wounds. But unhealed wounds inevitably weep – it was bound to get messy.

Some days my life seemed as if it was done, finished, past its sell by date. I felt forsaken, looked over, gripped by a sense of hopelessness and loss. Still, on other days, I felt unstoppable, fearless, full of awe and wonder and anticipation. Full of mountain-moving, chain-breaking miracle-making power.

Crazy, right?

Healing, and more importantly, growing fully into *me*, into *you*, is disorderly, uneven, inconsistent and yes, very messy. But in the middle of the mess, I found a Comforter. ONE who was all-seeing and ever-present, one who was unlimited and excessively extravagant, one who was patient and gentle, one who was timely, yet more significantly, also *out-of-time*. He

He's was a *no-hurry* kind of **Comforter**; in spite of *my* urgency, He never once broke a sweat and was merely lovingly amused by mine.

was a *no-hurry* kind of Comforter; in spite of *my* urgency, He never once broke a sweat and was merely lovingly amused by mine. Eventually, I learned to be kind to myself, to treat myself gently; to cry when it hurt, to yell at the walls when I was angry and confused, to turn my face to Him when hopelessness came slithering out of the dark shadows, to find willing ears when I needed to just spill some stuff out, to sleep when I was tired, or even when I just fancied my duvet and a movie...

But always, when morning came, I learned to get back up, put on my battle clothes (and lipstick) and be today's best version of me.

On good days, I'd celebrate my victories and on tough days I'd reflect, take the learning and record it in my journal. The truth was, I was doing amazing.

I just didn't know it yet.

Once I got to work on the development and growth of the Ministry and underneath the operations and people challenges, I quickly realised just how much my professional knowledge and skills could help, and that somehow shifted my pity party for one. I realised that God wasn't just helping me out here, He was using the gifts and expertise that I had gained over the years to help this incredible ministry; who were supporting vulnerable children and young adults; to create and implement a new strategic vision for the future, with a sustainable and more global structure, operating model and leadership team. I knew from day one that they wanted me there permanently. That they hoped I would apply for my green card and stay as part of the team, but as much as I loved what they were doing and the whole environment, there was always this knowing that God had other plans for me. Aside from my girls, staying would have been easy, but I knew this wasn't my ride and I was believing God for other things. I had Christmas on my radar; yes, *that was my target date. That would allow me to serve here for three months, get home and everything would fall back into place.*

In the meantime, the work here, in the middle of Alabama's back-country, where life was slower and akin to simpler days gone by, was about to get very interesting. Existing, amongst these small deep-south, bible-belt, close-knit communities, where families have lived and churched and baked and crafted together for generations, are unspoken rules, unspoken hierarchies around how things get done. Though only small, this area had been of significant economic, judicial, political and tactical interests to the Confederate armies, the British, The French, the Creek Indians over the years and had played its part, alongside its State Capital in the Civil Rights movement of the 1950. As part of the work I was doing, we were exploring the acquisition of new bigger offices downtown and a wonderful opportunity had presented itself to us, but as we explored this in detail, it became apparent that we were shaking a hornet's nest, one that was about way more than just a building.

Drawing on my influencing and communication skills, honed over years working in the UK Financial Sector, along with much needed wisdom and discernment, together we cautiously manoeuvred the highly questionable process. Something that started off as too good to be true was morphing into something very unsettling. And as the passionate, problem solving, storytelling, wildly vivid imagination of little Cath bubbled up, I found myself in the midst of a thriller which in my head had walked straight off the pages of a John Grisham novel: bribes, backhanders, threats under the cover of night, covert telephone conversations, tip offs. And now the local newspaper was on to it and we'd been asked for our comments.

Sitting in the upstairs courthouse, waiting to hear our proposal and supporting arguments read aloud and voted on publicly; in an evening hearing that was called at very short notice (*most likely so that few people would make it*), my heart was pounding. I wasn't quite sure if it was terror or exhilaration; I suspected the latter. Looking around I chuckled to myself at the old wooden floors and long wooden benches; at the hand full of southern ladies scattered around the room, fanning themselves to keep cool, clearly curious having read the first newspaper article. At the Mayor, dressed meticulously – cavalier and intimidatingly seated in a position of eminence right at the front, leaving no doubt who was in charge. And at the rotund judge who was now shuffling his way through the side door towards the wooden rostrum where the American flag stood proud. 'All Rise' - Everyone in the room stood. It was like a scene out of To Kill a Mocking Bird.

The irony was, right underneath where I was standing, right below this heritage courtroom, was the room where my boy and I were legally married almost sixteen years prior. Before we could be married before God, we'd needed to be married before the law, so we'd driven excitedly up to this courthouse a few days before our wedding, dressed in just our jeans and t-shirts and giddily climbed the steps to this building, passports in hand. Everyone in reception had been busy making a fuss about our *cute* English accents (as they put it), curious about how this sweet British couple had ended up in Alabama, just as the judge had popped his head around the corner, ushering us into his very grand and patriotic office.

"This young couple are from *England*." he exclaimed to the police officer who, strangely, was stood in the back corner of his office hand-cuffed to two men. All three smiled back. He pulled out the chairs for us at the oversized desk, then went around to the back and sat down. Leaning back, in the most un-formal of formalities, he proceeded to asked a few questions and check over our documents; then, seemingly, without any awareness of how *off-the-wall* his request was, asked whether we'd mind if the two handcuffed strangers acted as witnesses. We didn't mind at all, and though we gave each other a look of *what the heck*, it actually added to the fun and joy and story-telling potential of the occasion – what an adventure it had been.

And now, here I was again.

I couldn't help but wonder about the extraordinarily unconventional life I'd led?

For legal reasons, plus a good dose of common sense, I am leaving this event in the courtroom. The outcome is neither relevant, nor signifi-cant to my story. I share it merely to highlight that God knows us, He always has a plan, and He uses all the little parts of each of our stories to interject at different points to bring Heaven's solutions to earth.

190

He knew my fears, He saw my empty places, He knew the future needs of the ministry and the children it supported; He knew what I was good at and what would make me feel useful and less like a victim. He amusingly knew I'm quite certain, what would enchant and ignite my playful love of adventure and mystery. And because He knew/knows every milestone and dateline to my story, whilst He couldn't deliver the outcome I wanted on demand, He delivered what was best. Best for me at that stage, best for others (at that stage), best for His bigger picture, bigger purpose; and best for His ultimate Glory.

And He was just about to bless me with the most perfect, beautiful picture of why.

It was to be the first of a number of specific visions that would mark my time in the States. It was the beginning of an awakening in my spirit and the arrival of yet another undeserved, yet much valued gift.

Since that first night, the space on the floor at the bottom of my bed had become my *snuggle place*, my *hope spot*, my *safe space*. It was where I'd lie and dream, where I'd prop myself against the bed frame and open my bible seeking His wisdom, it's where I would call out to Him in anguish, it's where I gave Him praise for victories of which there were many; it's where I was lying when H called to check on me, saying she'd just felt compelled to call. This small area of increasingly flattened carpet had become my portal to the feet of Jesus.

One Sunday morning I had got up earlier than normal for church. I made a coffee, checked my phone, then plonked myself down in my safe space; my back against the dark mahogany bed frame, my knees bent, my toes pushed back against the matching chest of draws facing me causing the knuckles to turn white. In much the same way I did most days, I said *Hey* to my Father, opening up my heart-space to Him so that He could simply listen to every emotion and ache and urgency and anxious thought that were stored up there.

Lord... I trust you, I know you are good and I know you love me. I know you don't make promises you can't keep and I'm sure I heard you right when you said to *write it down, make it plain so that there is a record, so that it may be read at a glance – so that it will testify about it at the end – Write down clearly on tablets what I reveal to you, so that it can be read at a glance; so that there is a record* – I've been doing that and I know you also said:

> *Put it in writing, because it is not yet time for it to come*
>
> *true. But the time is coming quickly,*
>
> *and what I show you will come true.*
>
> *It may seem slow in coming,*
>
> *but wait for it; it will certainly take place,*
>
> *and it will not be delayed.*

Habakkuk 2:2-3

Father I have waited and my heart grows sick. I don't understand what your *quick* looks like. I worry that I have misunderstood the promises I'm clinging to – what if I've misunderstood all of it? I don't think so, but this is all so new to me and my heart is so heavily invested......; Ohhh, I don't know, I'm so confused... Lord, please fix it soon.

As much as I had learned to be abandoned, the yearning in me for a swift resolution to this saga dominated so much of my time. I could not and would not imagine stepping into a future that looked different to what I believed He'd promised. The clock was ticking on my time here and my mind was already thinking about home and what might happen... and Christmas... I hardly dared imagine what Christmas would be like if this didn't get sorted quickly.

From where I was sitting, I could already see that it was going to be another beautiful day. It was early September and over the last few days as I'd driven along the backroads towards the offices, I'd marvelled at the fresh breeze in the air. Newly arrived, it was starting to nudge the first of the copper leaves from their branches, a sure sign that Fall was on its way; despite the fact that the sun was still shining and producing glorious temperatures of eighty degrees. For an English girl like me, this was a seriously hard thing to process. 80 degrees is usually a sign of a heat wave back home, not the start of the autumn season, still, here I was smiling at this beautiful scene in front of me, trying to work out how I got here.

It only seemed like yesterday that I was trimming the house for Christmas and preparing for the usual crazy family Boxing Day celebrations. Our home was the one where all the family came together at Christmas and now, not only the home was gone, but also it seemed, most of the family too. In the blink of an eye, *puff,* all gone and with it, my heart and every part of life as I knew it.

I was missing the sweet faces of my girls so much. I smiled just thinking about what an incredible blessing they were. It was my stepdaughter's birthday today, so as I'd sipped the final dregs of my coffee I'd been able to chat a little to her over social media. TFBB had posted some old pictures of them all in her 'happy birthday' post, which made my heart both smile and scream at the same time. My children, my life; it *was* real; how I poured my heart and love into them all and the life we all shared, but now it was gone, all gone and I knew that without God's miracle there was nothing I could do to make any sense of it all.

I forced myself into a standing position, wandered into the kitchen and turned on the tap. Pressed motionless against the kitchen cabinet, the onslaught for my mind began again. My seconds earlier expectant spirit was already buckling under the relentless pressure to look back; just like Lot's wife, the unsettling voice was willing me to cling to the past, was reminding me that what I'd lost was the best of me, that what was behind was comfortable and familiar, that my future (my purpose) was rooted in my past, that my life could never be better than that. Suddenly, the stream of boiling water coming from the open tap and intended for my coffee mug ran across my hand. I yanked it back, the sudden sting of realisation forcing me to drop the mug into the empty sink, smashing it into a million tiny pieces. *Perfect,* I thought looking down at the pile of broken porcelain, Yep, that's about the extent of it,

I lamented, *almost* forgetting who I'd just been talking to, *damaged beyond repair.*

COMMAND HQ

"That's my girl" he snarled as he moved his wizened lips away from her ear - How he hated the ease and frequency with which she chatted to Him and the increasing strength and knowledge she was displaying. This had just been a little child's play and though it had worked a treat this time, it was clear he was going to have to up his game.

Scooping the remnants of the broken mug into a piece of kitchen towel, I rinsed out the sink and headed back into the bedroom.

THE SECRET PLACE

✝

"Hey", He beamed up at me. He knew this was a surprise, a *good*, surprise. I looked down smiling, tears beginning to appear in the corners of my eyes.

"We'll have none of those now." He tilted His head and raised an eyebrow, half berating and half teasing. In His usual warm way, He patted the carpet next to Him, "Come, sit with me again, I want to show you something important."

I had missed this.

I lowered myself alongside Him, that familiar sense of warmth and love and safety and expectation that I had felt on each of the other occasions came flooding back. In His hands was an old wooden bat; one that looked just like the old *Rounders* bats from my days as captain of the school Rounders team. I guess here in the States they would say baseball bat, but this was much shorter. Tied around the neck of the bat was the familiar purple ribbon and at-

194

tached to that was the usual label. I tilted my head to read, notably bolder than on previous exchanges. I gave Him a mischievous grin, acknowledging the growing familiarity between us. He smiled back affectionately.

Lifting the label closer so that I could see it, it read **REVELATION No 2**

†

Over recent weeks I had been pondering more and more on **Ephesians 2:10,** and the concept of God preparing good works for each of us to do on earth *in advance*. That we each have a predetermined divine purpose. The more I thought about the *in advance* part, the more I tried to imagine what God's mind-map must look like... all the way back to creation and onwards until the end days, every single individual life having a predetermined divine purpose, that knits together perfectly with everyone else's to achieve His ultimate plan, *Heaven on Earth* – if it really was like that, it was mind blowing to me.

Though I felt certain God would have an adequate framework to coordinate all of this, what had been puzzling me most was the practical implications of just one of us either not knowing Him or choosing not to walk fully *leant in*, close enough to hear Him tell us who we are and what our purpose is; or at least directing us towards it step by step – what happens then? I became curious whether someone, somewhere, who we we're meant to *bump* into en-route would simply miss out on what God intended to do for them through us? And if so, what's the domino effect? Does God redirect someone else to do what we were meant to do for Him? I realised God did not need my help to solve this complex conundrum, but I had a personal reason for being curious and I guess in my dumb human way I was trying to apply Cath logic to an eternal mystery, so that I could make sense of how God might resolve my current dilemma.

I know.

THE SECRET PLACE

†

He smiled knowingly. "It's pretty awesome that you're thinking that way."

He was just letting me know the ground we were about to cover. "It's important stuff. But it's infinitely more complex than you could ever perceive. I know why this has been so heavy on your heart. I feel it too. But you have to trust what you can't even imagine. I know how to move every heart that I have created and I know the right time to do that. I've always had a plan for each and every one of them and my plans have never fail.

> But you have to **trust what you can't even imagine**. He knows how to move every heart that He has created and He knows the right time to do that. He's always had a plan for each and every one of us and **His plans never fail.**

I knew how Rasha' would tempt them and manipulate them and I knew how they would respond, but that is all part of the refining process; to the story they will eventually tell. Sometimes we have to go to a place to realise the truth about that place and I'm always there waiting, watching, covering, holding out my hand. Sometimes it's just me and them, that's the ones who already know how to recognise my voice; other times it's me in another and them. Like you, *you* carry me in. But the plan has never failed me or failed them. Don't get me wrong; the battle is fierce and the more he can smell their potential, the harder he makes it. But he never wins......and he never will."

As if he could sense my thoughts, He added, "Yes, prayer does change things, but I am out of time, I know the prayers that will be made, they were always

> *Yes, prayer does change things, but I am out of time, I know the prayers that will be made, they were always factored in – plus* **prayer changes you**, *changes everyone who risks letting go, risks humbling themselves. Prayer pulls me close and when I'm close… you know what happens there…*

factored in – plus prayer changes you, changes everyone who risks letting go, risks humbling themselves. Prayer pulls me close and when I'm close ... you know what happens there..."

He held the wooden object in His hand out towards me, His face now deliberate – "Here, I want to show you something. I think it will help.

Then, I'm afraid, you have a pretty big choice to make."

Suddenly I sensed the weight of the world was on my shoulders, but I wanted to know all that He was willing to share with me. I reached forward, nervously taking the bat from His hand and immediately the vision began...

I realised quickly that it wasn't actually a bat, it was a baton, like the ones that runners in a relay race use. I saw it at the beginning of creation, then, pass by pass by pass it went forwards and sideways and diagonal and over and under, to every member of the human race, from one to another to another, throughout the earth, since the beginning of time, in specific ways, following specific assignment, at specific hours. The unique and time critical path was coordinated in such a way to ensure the baton arrived at the Plains of Armageddon, at the foot of Mount Megiddo, at an exact point in time for the final battle (**Revelations 16:16**); the battle between good and evil, between God and satan; the battle that sealed Eternity. It was clear to me in the vision that this critical path had been pre-determined from beginning to end – He was the first and He would be the last.

It dawned on me as I watched, that asking God to supernaturally intervene and change, speed up and adapt the path ordained for me (or indeed for someone else) would by default create a corporate shift on every pass thereafter – Thus, making it highly unlikely that the baton would arrive at the intended destination at the designated time. One shift could change everything. Risking eternity for all of mankind.

"Well?" He said enquiringly, jolting me out of the vision – "I can do it. My Father will give me all that I ask of Him on your behalf?

How I love you darling girl and how I hate to see you in such pain. But I have to ask you to consider this carefully. I have to ask you if it's worth it to you. You need only say the word?"

I was horrified.

"No!" I squealed without an ounce of hesitation. As much I I loved my boy, as much as I was hurting, my current needs were trivial when balanced against the future of humankind.

"No, No" I called again with greater urgency, "all of this, my needs, my momentary life; it's all so inconsequential in the bigger picture."

Just imagining it horrified me, being responsible for such a thing was more than I could bear. It suddenly put everything into perspective. He reached across and wrapped His arms around me tightly, pulling me close, tears beginning to flow from His eyes.

I couldn't carry that burden either, that's why I went to the cross.

"Good girl," He whispered. "I couldn't carry that burden either, that's why I went to the cross."

†

Rasha'

(stands motionless in the dark of the night, watching, watching...)

Y'shua

(head down, looks to watchers either side of Him)

Pay no attention to him, he's of no consequence. He just can't help himself.

(placing His mouth against her ear He exhales deeply, then lays His palms gently over each ear, holding them still until He is sure).

Ora

(stirs and sleepily turns onto her side, pulling the sheet up over her shoulder)

Y'shua

She wakes. It's done. (gives a satisfied nod to watchers and then they're gone)

Rasha'

What is He up to now (venom drips from the corners of his pursed lips, despising the things that were hidden from him)? No matter, she will no doubt give me the intricate details in that book of hers and then expand further with all her typical passion and drama when she speaks to those darling babes of hers. What a joke...

In a dream, in a vision of the night,
when deep sleep falleth upon men,
in slumberings upon the bed;
Then he openeth the ears of men,
and sealeth their instruction

Job 33:15-16 KJV

8

The Great Awakening

Those who sought the deepest parts of her soul, had to be brave enough to leave the safety of the shallow waters.

C.S.

The **3ʳᵈ REVELATION** came that evening, but this time in a dream. A much more personal dream that blew my mind.

THE SECRET PLACE

The Dream

Scene 1 – I was inside a car at the bottom of a long street full of old houses, close to a dead-end. The house alongside me was a typical Victorian terrace house, with a small two-meter area of garden at the front, tucked behind a low red brick wall and metal gate that opened out directly onto the pavement. I was in the driver's seat, turning the car around in the narrow street, attempting to park it close to the curb, directly in front of the house facing the direction of the main road that ran across the top of the street. I was not controlling the car well and nearly hit the front wall, but thankfully didn't, so I was happy with myself that I'd done a good job – However, when I looked down out of the driver's window to the curb, the whole side of the car was smashed up, with the driver's side wing literally hanging off. I was confused because I hadn't felt myself hit anything?

Scene 2 – Went inside the house which was so much bigger inside than it looked from the outside. My Mum was in a large open room shaking out freshly ironed sheets, preparing to make up a number of beds. I sensed lots of people were going to come and stay. I went into my room which was much smaller and there was a set of bunk beds there. Lying across the floor were 3 sleeping bags and across the bottom bunk were two more sleeping bags laying diagonally across the mattress. When I went to complain that there were loads of other people sharing my room, they asked how many and at that point I saw another 2 sleeping bags diagonally across the top bunk too; making 7 in total.

Scene 3 – I then saw myself getting back in the car on the street, but in the passenger side. For some reason, the car was now facing the opposite way than I'd left it, with the nose pointing towards the dead end. A girl (I didn't see a face or know who this was) asked if she could drive and got in. Because of the way the car was parked, it had to be reversed all the way up what was now clearly a very long narrow street, towards a busy main road full of traffic. Directly behind our car, almost bumper to bumper, was another car and as the girl began to drive she couldn't work the pedals and lost control, her foot stuck to the accelerator, so we were reversing erratically towards the very dangerous road, at high speed, with the people in the car behind us desperately trying to reverse out of the way.

I became hysterical, panicking that we were going to die or kill the other people and I had no control to stop it happening. As the cars flew out across the busy main road and came to a halt, the people behind were screaming at us saying they were going to call police and report us. I spotted a policeman and calmly got out of the car and went over to him to explain what happened and he was completely chilled and indifferent to what had just taken place.

Scene 4 – I was then back in the house in my room, but now instead of the bunkbeds there were 2 single beds along two adjacent walls. I pulled back the sheets on both beds and both the top and bottom sheets

202

were covered in blood. I called out to someone to say "look, somebody slept in my bed last night and bled all over sheets, then didn't change them; it's disgusting."

Scene 5 – Suddenly my two girls came running into the room and hugged me. They had turned up to surprise me. They looked about five and seven, their hair was cut in short bobs as they'd had it when they were younger and they were really happy and carefree.

Scene 6 – I walked out of the backdoor of the house, directly into a large shoreline scene, where a crowd of people were gathering excitedly at what looked like the edge of a large lake, waiting to welcome the two approaching fishing boats that had nets brimming with fish. As I walked down to the water's edge to join them, crossing a pebbled, gravel area to the strip of sand, I looked down to my feet and saw a half-buried sea horse with its head sticking out of the sand. Thinking it was dead I bent down to touch it; but it was just resting and as I touched it, it got up and went back into the water. I remember thinking that it was much bigger than I'd expected it to be.

Scene 7 – I turned around and ran back towards the house to shout the girls to come and watch the boats bringing in all the fish.

As I opened my eyes, I heard these words; *I am the fisher of men*

Then, in a nano-second, God interpreted every single scene.

Reeling first from shock and then from total AWE; realising this was like nothing I'd experienced before and fearful that I might forget some of the detail; I jumped out of bed, grabbed my journal and a pen and began to scribe. Apart from the vision a few months earlier, these experiences were all very new to me, yet, the way the dream had been constructed and then so specifically deciphered, there was absolutely no doubt in my mind that this was no regular 'too much cheese before bed' dream.

The Interpretation

Scene 1 – I'm in driving seat; thinking I'm in control, trying to do things carefully my way and even though I can't see it, there's a real risk of damage.

Scene 2 – In total, there were seven sleeping bags – my assumption had to be that these represented us; the magnificent seven and whatever this house was, there was space reserved for all of us? 3 years later God would bless me ridiculously with something that fulfilled a lifelong dream and I have come to see now that part of that is wrapped up in this prophetic revelation.

In biblical dream dictionaries, sleeping bags represent travel and not having a permanent home; quite ironic really. And clean fresh sheets represent virtuous living; something I'm happy to accept; however, I've always preferred to establish meaning directly from my Father.

Scene 3 – I'm not in the driving seat; yet despite the panic and fear and feeling completely out of control, even though it looks chaotic and terrifying there's not a bit of damage and I am acquitted of any responsibility or judgement.

Scene 4 – The blood of Jesus has gone before me.

Scene 5 – The girls *will* eventually be as they were before, carefree and happy.

Scene 6 – In the natural, the scene at the back of the house really bore no resemblance to the house itself, but spiritually, it was all connected. There was an atmosphere of great expectation and joy all around, based on what the boats approaching the shoreline were bringing.

And victory...

Shorelines and beaches typically represent where God meets with man and this was my second beach vision; however, as I woke, the one thing I didn't have a really clear understanding of was the meaning of the seahorse so I began to research it and what I discovered was fascinating.

> *,...let the fish of the sea declare to you...that the hand of*
>
> *the LORD has done this...*
>
> *with Him are wisdom and might.* **Job 12:8-9, 13**

Scientists believe the oceans contain about 20,000 species of fish and up to 1.98 million species of animals and plants, such as worms and jellyfish. Whilst we know that all of them evidence creation, evolutionists love to try and disprove that via science and fossils. Trouble is, the fascinating little seahorse is a real thorn in their sides. By the nature of its creation, there is no physical way (nor for that matter, evidence) that it could have survived an evolution process – Today, yesterday and tomorrow, the seahorse <u>remains unchanged</u>.

And this is the reason:

The seahorse swims upright. Even when it sleeps it floats vertically. Within its design is an elaborate balancing mechanism, where an air bubble in the swim bladder that maintains this uprightness, is controlled by a highly sensitive cells at the top of the swim bladder. If the air bubble moves to the wrong place, this cell detects the movement immediately and several complex responses are triggered, causing the seahorse to right itself. The seahorse begins to move until the bubble tells it that it is again upright. Like a well-designed submarine that manipulates gas in order to submerge and resurface while remaining parallel to the water, the seahorse can alternate the amount of gas in its bladder to do the same. Its survival is dependent on a perfectly designed bladder, with the right capacity to hold the exact volume of air and without this a seahorse would simply sink to the ocean floor and die. As a result, there was never any scope for an evolutionary process.

<u>The seahorse had to be designed perfectly the first time.</u>

What a powerful witness for the Creator.

And here are some more amazing facts

Just as every human being is unique and can be identified by our indi-vidual fingerprints, so each seahorse has a <u>unique coronet on its head — never duplicated</u>.

Due to the seahorse's unique head design, it can bend its head up and down, but not from side to side, so its eyes have been designed to move independently. One eye can look left while the other looks right; or when swimming near the surface, one eye can look up into the sky, while the other looks down into the ocean; <u>it has the ability to see all things at the same time</u>.

Its gentle nature and unique design and displacement make it one of the most powerful and dangerous hunters of the sea, as it can get close to its prey almost undetected.

A protective *bony* armour covers the body of seahorses. The female is completely enclosed in this protective armour, while the male is sim-ilarly enclosed except for the lower abdomen, where the opening of his *brood pouch* is located. This armour is so strong that it is virtually impossible to break, even after death.

Seahorses typically live and stay close to the shoreline (*where God meets man*), with a three-year lifespan.

They are monogamous and mate for life. When they begin their rela-tionship, they meet daily for several days and dance together in the water, often for up to 8 hours, tails curled around one another and the same strand of sea grass (*I'm reminded of* **Ecclesiastes 4:12**)

When they let go of the strand of sea grass they swirl upward, their faces touching, as the male forces water through his "brood pouch" at the front of his tail until the pouch cavity is forced open to reveal that it is empty—an invitation to the female to <u>trust him with her eggs</u>.

The female seahorse visits the male during the weeks of "pregnancy" and they have a daily six-minute dance, "holding tails" and changing colours to relays their emotions and intentions towards each other; cementing their bond.

The male seahorse is one of the only animal species on Earth that bears the unborn. The mother deposits many many eggs into the father's *brood pouch* where they are fertilised and immediately embedded into the wall of his pouch and <u>enshrouded with prepared tissue</u>. He then <u>carries the unborn until they are ready to be released</u> into the world.

The father *crazily* produces prolactin, a hormone that female mammals, including us humans, use to produce milk, to instead produce <u>oxygen for the eggs to develop and be nourished in just the right environment</u>.

When the time comes to give birth, fully formed tiny seahorses, each one a mini replica of the Father/Mother, are <u>pushed out by the Father</u>, using forceful muscular contractions to deliver them. Not all survive, the rate can be low — but higher percentage than most fish — due to the <u>careful incubation time with the father</u>.

The new borns are nurtured and protected by their father until they are ready to live on their own.

Scene 6 cont. – As I learned more about the gentle but powerful seahorse, I realised God was showing me Himself. He was meeting me there at the shoreline (my feet in the sand – a sign of im*measurability, His* immeasurability) and reminding me of His total omnipotence and Father heart – that it is *He* who creates, it is *He* who births; *He* who nurtures and grows and prepares and keeps from harm's way; *He* who releases – determining the *day*, the *hour*, the *manner*...

> That it is *He* who **CREATES**, it is *He* who **BIRTHS**; *He* who **NURTURES** and **GROWS** and **PREPARES** and **KEEPS** from harm's way; *He* who **RELEASES** – determining the **DAY**, the **HOUR**, the **MANNER**...

And *He* who still had the power to bring back to life that which ap*peared dead.*

I made a mental note of His gentle reminder of my previous promise of abandonment. That I was not to pick back up the things I had already given to Him. My thoughts travelled back to the valley floor and box I'd so eagerly filled and handed over to Him. I smiled. It was not easy to let go. It was not easy to resist meddling.

Still, it was clear I had witnessed a glorious future moment – the fulfilment of a promise. A 'see I told you' manifestation.

My spirit soared.

I lingered on the beautiful image of the courting seahorses; the way they danced together and hungered to spend time together each day. In many ways, God must surely long to have a relationship with us like this, but also, I couldn't help but see this perfect picture of husband and wife, loving each other much, sharing the load, encouraging, nurturing, building a family – all the while, their tails intertwined together, then intertwined around Him...

A cord of three strands....... Not easily broken. **(Ecclesiastes 4:12)**

There was so much depth and richness to this penultimate scene - I believe over the years I will see a mighty fulfilment of all the different elements, not least, those parts I'm quite certain are still to be revealed?

Common Christian assumptions around the meaning of *God-breathed* dreams and visions would say that the gravel I walked across may well represent that which has been stolen from me. Sea and a gathering crowd, potentially represent many people groups and nations. Boats and cars I'm told often represent a vehicle for our future ministry. All of that has a feel of logic, but was not revealed to me personally. In time my story will testify to the validity of this and to the complete meaning of the incredible message my Father blessed me with, just as the sun was dawning, on that pretty Autumn Alabama morning?

I have come to realise that He often shows us just enough for the next part of our journey. Peeling back the layers, drawing back the veil, as we grow in maturity and look intentionally through the lens of increased wisdom, insight, understanding and experience.

Scene 7 – There was no doubt surrounding this last picture, for He spoke it to me Himself

"I am the fisher of men."

Not me, *Cath*, but Him, Christ Jesus – He was edging ever closer to the shore and bringing with Him a catch so large the nets were bursting open.

> I have come to realise that He often shows us just enough for the next part of **our journey**. Peeling back the layers, drawing back the veil, as we grow in maturity and look intentionally through the lens of increased wisdom, insight, understanding and experience.

I had been praying for some time that God would restore our marriage by Christmas, and now that I was just two weeks away from going home, I was starting to get anxious.

What if he didn't?

I had been in a bubble here. Buffered from reality. It wasn't *real life* - It wasn't my real life at any rate. This had been my *meantime* and it suddenly struck me that if my miracle didn't come soon, I would have to start making grown up decisions about a potentially prolonged meantime.

I had already spoken to a number of people about writing to my boy. To reaching out in love and reminding him what was being thrown away. I had been desperate not to meddle in what God might be doing in the background, but still it felt like the right thing to do and the wise counsel I took completely agreed.

It was almost the end of October and I had nowhere to call home. Without a miracle I had no idea what I was going back to. And Christmas..... I could barely allow that thought to enter my mind.

After much prayer and fasting God had given me this scripture;

I will restore my people to their land
and have mercy on every family;
Jerusalem will be rebuilt, and its palace restored.
The people who live there will sing praise;
they will shout for joy.
By my blessing they will increase in numbers;
my blessing will bring them honour.
I will restore the nation's ancient power
and establish it firmly again;
I will punish all who oppress them.
Their ruler will come from their own nation,
their prince from their own people.
He will approach me when I invite him,
for who would dare come uninvited?
They will be my people, and I will be their God.
I, the LORD, have spoken.

Jeremiah 30:18-22 GNT

It gave me the courage I needed and finally I sat down nervously to write.

The Letter

It was already getting late when I opened up my laptop. I find that I'm able to think more clearly, undisturbed, when I know the rest of the world are sleeping. There is somehow a reassuring peace about it. I didn't know what I was going to write, I would let Him lead me, but I had already settled in my heart that I would allow myself to be vulnerable. The stakes were high, I was risking rejection all over again, but this was important, this was a significant moment – so much balanced on the choice, the decision that was about to be made. There was no place for pride or self-preservation.

I prayed **Psalm 80** and **Isaiah 55:10-12** over it and began to type; *heart-to-heart*, not *head-to-head*. It would not be easy.

It was long after midnight when I finally pressed send; my fingers dancing around the button anxiously, my heart pounding; praying as I did that if it hadn't been His will for this to go, that it wouldn't interfere with whatever He was already doing. I had no idea what my boy felt or thought. I didn't know if his heart was even still available to me, but I knew this was my marriage and I was going to fight for it the only way I knew how –with words – words of truth, words of love, words of life, words of hope, words of forgiveness, words of promise, words that build up. I have never been confrontational, but the gift of words, which have been there from the start, have often been my weapon of choice. As **Proverbs 18:21 says** Life and *Death are in the power of the tongue.* (*the words we say*).

I wanted to speak life back into my family and if an arrow was fired back, so be it – I had tried. Despite the late night, the next day I was on fire. I began to declare victory over the situation and was quite convinced that in a few days I'd hear a knock at the door, believing he would rush to jump on a plane and come surprise me – such was my faith. God had planted a seed of promise in me and I was impregnated with hope and possibility. With adrenaline pumping through my body, I began to sort through all my things, getting it ready to pack to take home. I'd acquired a good bit on 'stuff' over the past three months and had bought Christmas presents to take back with me so some highly creative packing was going to be needed. By late afternoon, feeling pleased with progress, I wandered over to my sister's house and we grabbed coffee.

"I sent it", I said, looking up at her with a mixed half-hopeful smile and a who knows? shoulder shrug.

She walked over and hugged me tight. And we prayed.

And then I waited and waited, as the days passed without a word. And in the deafening silence, so too my courage faded and retreated, while the predictable fiery darts of the enemy came fast and furious. I promised God that I would trust Him, whatever the outcome.

> I promised God that I would **trust Him**, whatever the outcome. And when the word did finally come, it would take all that I had to see that promise through.

And when the word did finally come, it would take all that I had to see that promise through.

My boy *was* out, it was over and he wouldn't be changing his mind...

RAISING UP FOUNDATIONS OF OLD

Ora

I'm so confused Father. I wish I understood myself; wish I understood if my determination to hold on, to believe this is what you want from me *is* actually what you *really* want. Or if I'm meant to simply let go completely. I promised I'd stand in the gap and I've prayed right I think ... do I keep praying? I thought you said to pray without ceasing; but if I do and yet am to move on, how do I manage my heart? And what *if* I just stop now, will all those prayers be wasted, will my promises come to nothing because I stopped. Will satan win because Cath let go?

Father I'm drowning in so much confusion. (anguished face, pleads for enlightenment)

Y'shua

Baby girl, your faith is so bold. I truly delight in you, but you don't have to carry this heavy load on your own sweet shoulders. Here, look (holds out gold bowl) they're all in here, every single prayer. When it's time they'll tumble to earth like precious rain on barren land. All will make sense. But let me be as original with others as I am with you. Let me carry that creative responsibility. (smiles lovingly). You have nothing to prove to me, *ever*.

How about we move forward together, small steps for now, but forward. Do you think you can do that? (leans over and gently slips off the robe from around her shoulders).

Ora

I'll try.

Y'shua

That's all I need from you, that you only try.

(reaching forward) I'm going to need this for just a little while if that's OK?
(steals the white velvet robe of grace to His chest) – (she stumbles slightly)
Keep your eyes on me. I need to unfasten your foot and it might be a little
tender, especially without this, but if you keep your eyes on me I'll make it
as painless as I can. Once it's off, walking will feel much easier.

Afflicted city, storm-battered, unpitied: I'm about
to rebuild you with stones of turquoise. Lay your
foundations with sapphires, construct your towers with
rubies, Your gates with jewels, and all your walls with
precious stones. All your children will have God for their
teacher what a mentor for your children. You'll be built
solid, grounded in righteousness, far from any trouble—
nothing to fear.

Isaiah 54:11-14 MSG

9

Write to Remember

Hear me right, she wasn't mad; her heart just needed to be free.

There was something of the *tameless* and *uncontained* about her, and we need that sometimes, don't we?

As if, by bearing witness to the passion and savageness of *her* heart,

we might somehow find a tiny wildfire ignites in *our own*.

As if, in running our fingers along the trail of *scorch marks* left behind her,

We might one day ingest some of that wild ferocious love.

No, she wasn't mad. Her heart was simply ready to burn for everything she loved.

C.S.

I was looking pretty good when I got back home; I had lost a good bit of weight whilst I'd been in the States and was tanned. Add a bit of lippy to that and you'd have thought I could take on the world. Though things hadn't turned out the way I'd hoped, at least now I knew where things stood and in typical Cath gusto, I got back up and started to get on with the practicalities of life.

The first challenge I faced was where to live. For the sake of my sanity, I needed somewhere of my own; but without a job, I wasn't in a position to buy anything; quite a strange concept for me. Plus, as so much of my future was unknown, I actually wasn't yet ready to make decisions on where to formally plant myself. So, I looked around for somewhere to rent and within days came across a fabulous apartment, super contemporary and sitting in a small courtyard in a perfect location. For a brief moment I berated myself that *Mums don't live in apartments*, but of course this was just another arrow the great deceiver chose to hurl at me.

If nothing else, he was consistent.

All my belongings were in storage, so I hired a large van, loaded it up, climbed up behind the wheel with my *just watch me then* hat on and between us, TFBB and I moved me in to my new cool pad. For the next year at least, this would be *home*. That first night, exhausted, with aching muscles and sore hands, but with a ginormous sense of achievement, she and I threw a mattress down onto the floor, dragged a few sheets, a couple of pillows and some thick socks (it was almost December) out of the packing cases and giggled like a couple of schoolgirls at the craziness of life. Thank goodness for resilience and an unwavering sense of adventure.

One of the first things I treated myself to was an all singing, all dancing coffee machine. It was a statement piece and my gift to myself. If I'd been a guy I would have probably splashed out on a sports car, but somewhere deep inside there was a secret barista bursting to get out and how I loved making *posh* coffee for visitors, with cute cocoa hearts sprinkled on top.

As I decorated the apartment, I began to feel the old Cath re-emerge. More and more, If I shut my eyes and moved out of my head to my heart, I was starting to feel her again, that girl, that *me* girl. And here, I was creating a space for people to come and meet her again in her new world. Don't get me wrong, the pain remained very real, but I knew that I was so much more than the pain and I knew it would not be forever.

There were many firsts approaching; my birthday was only days away, but the one I'd been dreading the most, the one I'd barely allowed myself to contemplate, would be here in just 4 weeks. Christmas. And it couldn't be avoided.

My Christmas dinner table had always been special and beautiful, with lots of noise and laughter around it. My whole life has been about creating lovely and special things and Christmas was no exception. I'd hide clues in the Christmas crackers on the dinner table, with one last surprise present for everyone hidden somewhere around the house, creating a frenzy of raucous activity before the feasting began. The apartment didn't have space for a large table, but the vestibule was quite long, so, determined to make things extra-ordinary, I invested in a long plastic picnic table that ran the length of the space and set it in place. Then, in defiance of the multiple punches satan was lobbing in my direction, I stood back and beheld with pride my creative genius and animatedly, knighted the space *the grand hall*. That year we did Christmas in the *Grand Hall*.

By the time I'd finished it looked exquisite, with lots of tiny candles and fairy lights, pretty napkins and a silver table cloth that draped down to the floor. In the middle I placed a prayer box and after dinner I encouraged everyone to write down their prayers and hopes for the coming year; for themselves and for each other - into the box they went. Of course, there were some wobbles during the day, but we were together, me, my girls, my Mum and the boys and in and through it all, I chose to remember and celebrate all the little victories, the creativity and *grandness* of my very own royal banquet.

New Year came and went – It was a tough one.

But after that the year turned out to be rather significant.

- ‣ In January TFBB's boy asked for her hand in marriage – of course I was delighted to say YES.
- ‣ In February I made the decision to take some time away from *proper* work to begin writing my book

- In March a number of revelations forced me to take a decision I couldn't have ever imagined

- In April I finally put pen to paper (so to speak) and wrote the prologue for my book

- In May I filed for divorce

- In October I bought a house

- In early November my marriage legally came to an end.

- The next day my baby girl became the most beautiful of brides and a wife.

- The following week I said goodbye to the apartment that had kept me over the last year and moved into my very own little house.

- In December I created a picture-perfect Christmas (in a Momma home, not an apartment) - It didn't have a Great Hall, but it had *Cath* and *Momma* written all over it and *love lived there.*

All the while, throughout the course of the year, month after month (night after night) God was shaping me and revealing things to me in dreams and visions and all manner of supernatural encounters.

And I was gorging myself spiritually; gleaning wisdom from a select group of safe hands, reading books and listening to podcasts that spoke life and truth and courage into me. My discernment and awe were growing at break-neck speed and I was becoming hungry. Not for the *ra ra* of the trendy *superchurch* and their creative presentations, but for the realness, the pureness and the simplicity of the Gospel. I wanted to understand more about the person of Jesus and I wanted to know who I really was in *His* eyes, who *He* had intended *me* to be; created *me* to be; who I still could be, despite my backstory (or even *because* of my backstory). What Cath was really gifted at; that unique combination that no one else possessed and most importantly, what the heck I should be doing with it all.

The only place we can find that truth is from the designer Himself.

Behind every great masterpiece ever painted, there is always a story if you look close enough. The great renaissance masters, who painted some of the most valuable paintings in the world, didn't scribble a frame of reference in the bottom corner of each canvas – instead, they anticipated each beholder, in awe and reverence for the artist's great skill, would humbly stand and gaze intentionally. Linger. Ponder. Bring context. Consider. Overlay what we know about the artist, what we know about the subject matter. Discern. Let ourselves feel it deep within, being drawn in by subtle nuggets of information 'hiding' in *plain sight* amid the obvious if we'd only take the time to look that little bit closer: The expressions, the choice and mix of colours, the backdrop, the adornments. Drawing out not just the tangible, but also the intangible. The unspoken story behind this priceless treasure.

We have to discover for ourselves what the one who created the painting is trying to speak to us through his/her skilful work. Then, knowing that, we have to decide how we feel about the piece in light of this new revelation.

As we lean in and fix our gaze, we finally see it. *YES*. In a moment of exhilaration and manifestation, what's been in front of us all along has revealed itself. A reward for our patience. Standing in the art gallery's grand salon, surrounded by other glorious masterpieces, we suddenly feel a strange kind of intimacy with this particular one as the artist lifts the scales from our eyes to reveal his intentions - His heart, his thoughts; all the tiny fragments of himself so delicately and intricately blended in to every stroke. This isn't just a painting; this rare and exquisite treasure is an extension of the one who created it so long ago. It's a piece of his story, a moment in time and with each passing year it is becoming more precious and rare.

A few weeks ago my big girl casually threw out this random question. It was more rhetorical, but it was a whopper.

"I wonder", she said, "how many people actually run the race set before them."

So we must let go of every wound that has pierced us

and the sin we so easily fall into.
Then we will be able to run life's marathon race with
passion and determination,
for the path has been already marked out before us.

Hebrews 12:1 TPT

We have become his poetry; a re-created people that will
fulfill the destiny he has given each of us,
for we are joined to Jesus, the Anointed One.
Even before we were born,
God planned in advance our destiny
and the good works we would do to fulfill it.

Ephesians 2:10 TPT

My frame was not hidden from you when
I was made in the secret place,
when I was woven together in the depths of the earth.
Your eyes saw my unformed body;
all the days ordained for me were written in your book
before one of them came to be.

Psalm 139:15-16 TPT

In my head I went back to little Cath and imagined all the amazing things God had prepared in advance for her to do, or to go, or to be. And I wondered how much I'd missed. How much of the race set before me had I simply sat out, consciously ducked out of or just missed? It was a sobering thought...

There had been no talk of divorce and my faith was stronger than ever. Id gathered together all my journals and spent weeks creating a basic outline for my book, deciding that if I could manage financially, I'd take a year out of work and start the painstaking journey of bringing my unfinished story to life.In some ways it seemed irresponsible, but I knew God was in it and that being the case, He would provide all that I needed. I had so much I wanted to share and encourage people with; so much that God had been showing me; yet, at this stage I remained convinced that ultimately, it would be a book about supernatural love. Still, starting a book shaped towards an ending that didn't exist was tricky to say the least. Even for a maverick like me.

And as I typed the first few words, I knew without a shadow of a doubt that somewhere, in His secret place, my Father was busy working out the finer detail of the last chapter, so all I needed to do was head in that direction.

During those early months, many nights became long and sleep starved. In fact, there were nights I simply led horizontal, eyes open until the light began to appear again from above the curtain pole.

But during the daytime I would dig deep, trying to craft some earthly words worthy of what God was so deeply etching on my heart. Worthy of what was, so graciously and tenderly, being revealed to me; worthy of what my Father had so clearly instructed me to do; yet transparent and kind and rooted in love.

It was **Holy work!**

It was holy work.

And it was intricate work.

When I first decided to write the book, I'd wanted to be certain that it was the right thing to do. I had asked three or four trusted friends to pray about it for me and to share what they believed the Lord was saying to them. All came back with a resounding 'yes'. One friend said she saw the word **HOPE** over me; that hope is something God uses me to give and will ultimately use me to bring to other women. Another friend gave me **Acts 1:8**, she that I *'would be His witness* (through my book) *to the ends of the earth'*; that my book would get to places I could never reach.

This friend also gave me another word, which you'll see, as my story unfolds, turned out to be extremely profound. It was a word God was getting ready to reveal to me Himself, but at the time, no one had previously spoken it out;

"There is such a spiritual light in you, on you and around you", she said, "that draws people to you."

It felt weighty. Having lots of people drawn to *me* felt anything but comfortable, still there was a kind of knowing in some of what she said and I sensed God might use this in time. The light was nothing to do with me and everything to do with Him. My open book style simply allowed Him to shine and I wholeheartedly intended for His resplendence to radiate from every page of my book.

And so, with no knowledge of what writing a book meant and no real certainty of how the story would unfold, with this encouragement, each morning *I cast my bread (my words) upon the water* (**Ecclesiastes 11:1**) believing in crazy *Cath faith* that; whilst it remained with God to fulfil the promise, and though it may take some time; what I was sowing in faith in these barren days, I would surely reap in joy as the seeds sunk deep into the fertile mud of Heaven.

I went in search of little Cath, who had taught me long ago that inside us (she & I) were words that people paid attention to. Showed up to listen to. Words were my sword; they were woven into my fabric and they were about to become my *Divine Roar*. And in the only way I knew how, I yanked opened my bruised and battered and still expectant heart and bled onto the pages of my story, our story, *His* story.

Our purpose is always designed to solve a God-sized problem on earth. God pulls people into His kingdom for particular tasks. And He is very specific about His choosing and selection process and the way He distributes gifts. In **1 Samuel** we see God make it very plain just how *hands-on and specific He is* when He sends Samuel to anoint a young shepherd boy as future king.

> Our **purpose** is always designed to solve a God-sized problem on earth. God pulls people into His kingdom for particular tasks.

Because I've chosen for myself one of his sons as king

1Samuel 16:1 ISV

I will raise up for myself a faithful priest, who will do according to what is in my heart and mind.

1 Samuel 2:35 NIV

This also shows us that He operates and makes decisions and plans from His heart as well as His mind.

God has a **Divine Plan** and this plan is always **Purpose Driven**. Remember satan's *counterintelligence* activities? That word *counter* means opposing, in opposition, adverse. What should we suppose it's in opposition to I wonder???

> In our ordinary moments God is making the finishing touches to **His secret weapon – YOU!**

Our great adversary struts around, busying himself with counterintelligence day and night, *because*, our Great Deliverer, our Mighty Creator, our Wonderful Redeemer has been in the business of **Divine Intelligence** since time began. Everything is directed at Eternity and truly remarkable things are done through seemingly unremarkable people like me and like you (and like young David), because He has provided

US for HIMSELF, **Divinely Designed**, to do a particular task or tasks that only we can do. The fit is that unique. And if we would answer the call, His hand will come upon us; His chosen. And though at times it may seem like we are being forgotten or overlooked, God is always making preparations in the background. In our ordinary moments God is making the finishing touches to His secret weapon – YOU.

David was bringing lunch to his brothers when he was called up. In the midst of battle-ready, heavily armored and experienced (yet floundering) soldiers, David; dressed to hang out with sheep, carrying only the simple tools of a shepherd and no obvious preparation or skill to speak of; boldly stepped up with a slingshot to slay a giant.

His secret, the thing that set him apart, that made his success infallible:

† He knew who his Father was

† He knew who his Father said *he* was

† He showed up as himself

† He knew what needed to be done

† He waited on his Father to bring his target out into the open

† He used a weapon he was already an expert with

† He trusted God with the outcome

As a result, his *Father's hand* came upon him and success was **Divinely Orchestrated**.

I was starting to see that God had a message which He planned to bring through me and words were my slingshot. I had the basic outline of my story, but not the full details of the assignment. However, as I surrendered my words and my time to Him, it became clear that the inner story was still playing out. He was consecrating His message in my life; one holy moment at a time.

And as I wrote by day, at night the wild adventures just kept getting crazier.

It had been a particularly tough day and I had wrestled with sleep, but had finally given in.

THE SECRET PLACE

†

I woke up suddenly. With my eyes still closed and before my mind could start processing, a sense of deep calm came over me.

I could see my body floating and all around me were what looked like a band of glowing angels.

One had a *spanner* or *wrench* in its hand, close to my neck, perched just under my chin. It sounds brutal, but I couldn't feel anything and the angel was using the wrench to lift my head upwards to look at God.

As they did that, I could physically feel my shoulders and neck being stretched, almost like it feels when you're having a back, neck and shoulder massage. It seemed as if I was being physically relaxed while the angel raised my eyes to heaven. I had such peace and was reminded of the **Psalm 121** vision where God had been calling me up the mountain.

†

A few nights later I had another incredibly vivid dream.

THE SECRET PLACE

†

I was aware of drowning in and being tossed around in the most torrential storm and being completely terrified.

Then I found myself half way up a ladder.

Suddenly, Jesus stepped out of heaven, He placed one of His

feet on the top rung of the ladder and lent down out of the cloud and took hold of my hand and pulled me up into Heaven. At the time I believed He was simply pulling me out of the current storm.

†

I shared with a friend the following day.

"That's **Psalm 18**" she declared, '*I will pull you up and make you great*', and I'm seeing the word FRUITFUL over you."

> *⁶from your temple-throne you heard my troubled cry.*
> *⁹He stretched heaven's curtain open*
> *and came to my defense.*
> *¹¹the dense rain clouds were his garments.*
> *¹²Suddenly the brilliance of his presence broke through*
> *with lightning bolts and with*
> *a mighty storm from heaven*
> *¹⁶He then reached down from heaven,*
> *all the way from the sky to the sea.*
> *He reached down into my darkness to rescue me.*
> *He took me out of my calamity and chaos*
> *and drew me to himself,*
> *³³Through you I ascend to the highest peaks of your glory*
> *to stand in the heavenly places (throne room),*
> *strong and secure in you.*
> *³⁴You've trained me with the weapons of warfare-*
> *worship; now I'll descend into battle with power, to*

chase and conquer my foes. *35by stooping down in*

gentleness, you strengthened me and made me great.

36I'm standing complete, ready to fight some more.

39pYou've placed your armor upon me.

Psalm 18 TPT

The volume of dreams and visions I was experiencing were hard to compute. I was straggling two very different paths, each going in different directions; one path that was known, that pulled me backwards into the shadows of a life left behind, but for which I had committed steadfast faith; the other, unknown with limited direction, yet promising all the things my heart yearned for. And the gap between the two was getting more difficult to straggle by the day. I knew at some point I would need to lift one of my feet up, otherwise I'd fall into the endless breach below, but I didn't know how to. It was as if the fulfilment of Gods promises, fulfilment of the giant-sized prayers I'd been praying, depended on *me* holding my position.

As if God might go, *what a shame, here's another one who couldn't go the distance. Oh well, let's chuck all those prayers away. Pity, I only needed a couple more off her and I would have done what she asked.*

And the good girl in me could not, would not, let that happen. I didn't want to be like Abraham, who after waiting years in faith for God to fulfil a crazy promise of a son in his old age, got fed up and decided to take things into his own hands. No not Cath, her faith was unshakable.

When I'd been in the States, I had been listening to an audio version of John's Gospel and had been burdened by something Jesus had said to His father in the garden, just before He was crucified. It sprang right out to me like an arrow in the heart;

Father, not one of those you have given me has been lost.

John 18:9 TPT

John 17:6-8 TPT makes it so simple and so beautiful:

> *Father, I have manifested who you really are*
> *and I have revealed you to the men and women*
> *that you gave to me.*
> *They were yours, and you gave them to me,*
> *and they have fastened your Word firmly to their hearts.*
> *7And now at last they know that everything*
> *I have is a gift from you,*
> *And the very words you gave to me to speak*
> *I have passed on to them.*
> *They have received your words and carry them*
> *in their hearts.*

Shame told me that I *had* lost someone and I felt like a failure. I'd have to stand before my Father one day and say sorry, unless...

COMAND HQ

Clink.

The chain wrapped around her ankle and the padlock clicked into place, as the serpent circled unnoticed on the ground, flicking out its forked tongue, enjoying the smell of the innocent target.

Using both sides of its tongue it easily maneuvered the grubby string, making a knot through the links and tucking the label in so that it was hardly visible. The words **FALSE RESPONSIBILITY** rubbed against the side of her foot leaving an imprint.

It suited her well. *To the death.* He chuckled.

Yes, if he couldn't get her any other way, this would paralyse her nicely.

"SSSSSSSSSSSSilly girl", he sniggered as he slithered away, "such a SSSSSSSSilly, silly girl."

Those words weighed heavy on me and I settled that I would intercede for the rest of my life if I had to, petitioning heaven for the *one* I'd lost.

THE SECRET PLACE

†

"Baby girl this is going to hurt I'm afraid. I'm helping you, even though it won't seem that way at first.

You're going to experience some things that are unfamiliar and uncomfortable, but it's necessary. It's time. Arrows will fly and some will unfortunately hit. Things will get a little messy for a while...

But we've got this, you and I haven't we? We can do this together.

And you have the armour remember, you've been doing just brilliantly with them, I'm so proud of you.

Remember to put on the Breastplate from the box and nothing will stick. Keep your Shield up and ever fiery arrow will be put out. The Belt will help you see what's really going on and your Sword will give you the right words to say. Stand in the Sandals and you will walk through this next part of the journey with a peace that can't be explained and everyone will wonder how you're doing it. I do need to take your cloak for a while as it will get in the way – but you'll have the Helmet, so nothing can touch you."

†

And so, I wrote and prayed and grew and dreamed (and cried) and proclaimed and read and listened and talked. In my heart was an unshakeable excitement and anticipation of the glory God would get when the miracle I was believing for came to pass. I had such a certainty, such a picture in my head about what that would look like, the wonder and astonishment on people's faces. It was going to be a 'WOW' moment for sure. My book would be such an amazing testimony of hope and faith and love and the incredible power of God.

I'd been trying to find some information for my book for a few days but was struggling to lay my hands on the notepaper I'd scribbled it down on. I was pretty sure I had a document saved on an old iPad somewhere with the information on, so I rummaged to the back of the drawer where I'd pushed the iPad when I'd emptied last few packing boxes several months earlier. I hadn't opened it for over a year so it would need charging but I was hopeful I'd find what I needed in there, so I plugged it in to charge overnight.

Moment of Impact

THE SECRET PLACE

†

"That's my girl", a tender voice uttered deep inside me as He exhaled a knowing sigh.

†

The next morning when I eventually opened it up, I discovered much more than I was looking for.

Truth came hammering on my door, forcing it open, as the hordes of hell pushed their way into my little apartment with quivers full to the brim of fiery darts.

Benefit of doubt is an act of Trust, underpinned by Grace and Love. Up to this point, the latter two had been my superpower. They had come easy to

Somehow, I *always* see the **wounding** (the cause), as clear and as quickly as I see the ***mess*** seeping out of the wound (the impact). And this, inescapably, gives birth to compassion.

231

me, much to people's astonishment (and frustrations at times I think, LOL). Occasionally (and justifiably I feel) some anger and judgement would show up, but it didn't stay long. It hadn't been so much a conscious choice for me, more, just the way I'm wired. Somehow, I *always* see the wounding (the cause), as clear and as quickly as I see the mess seeping out of the wound (the impact). And this, inescapably, gives birth to compassion.

In an assessment I had done many years ago, as part of a professional personality profiling exercise, it had been noted:

> *You notice new as well as unusual configurations in facts, evidence, or data. Others, however, can see only separate, unrelated bits of information. You are fascinated by problems that puzzle, confound, or frustrate most people. Instinctively, you comprehend what has gone wrong. It's very likely that you customarily pinpoint the core problems and identify the best solutions.*

In a corporate environment, this can be highly frustrating, because even when you know, that you know, that you know, there's a whole load of red tape between you and delivering the solution needed. You firstly need to take others on a journey of discovery, to help them see what you see and then you have to bring a compelling case for change.

With people, it becomes even harder because we're dealing with human hearts and feelings and beliefs. On top of the usual hurdles, there's often a bunch of generational, psychological (spiritual), emotional and egotistical/prideful nuances to navigate too. Not mentioning our severe resistance to personal examination and change. It's hard work and often uncomfortable.

When you're on the receiving end of someone's wound; when all that hurt, all that expectation, all that loss, all that abuse, all those lies, all that neglect........whatever it may be, is pouring out of them in your direction, it's easy to form hasty opinions and judgements about who they are. But we should never forget that always, despite what we see or experience, underneath it all is a much loved son or daughter, with wounds and bruises and scars and baggage just like me and you. And we can be pretty sure that satan has been meddling in their lives, the same way he's been meddling in ours.

So, we can choose to to shout angrily *look what you did to me*. Choose to believe they're not worth it. Choose to believe they can never change.

Or

We can choose to look a little deeper, choose to witness their wounds with compassion and grace. Choose to become a bridge between what hurt them and the LOVE† that can heal them.

Hear me right, each of us is accountable for our own actions. The choices we make as adults will have consequences - positive consequences or negative consequences. Consequences that bring life or consequences that bring death. Having compassion and showing grace is an act of love, but know this, *that* love still requires wisdom and clear boundaries.

For me, there are rare moments like this, full of raw emotion, where compassion was ripped up from its roots. It was as if God had instantly lifted grace off me and shown me truth, the ugly truth. He'd narrowed my field of vision. And as successive conversations ensued and self-preservation raised its haughty spirit, an unfamiliar feeling of contempt bubbled up, causing a paradigm shift in position. I knew instinctively that the direction of my story was about to change and that some key characters would probably not make it through to the next chapter. I was beginning to understand that they would write their own story and *He would write mine*.

> They would write their own story and *He* **would write mine**.

God was showing me things in real time and I was having a job keeping up with Him.

Despite everything I had been standing in, I knew without a shadow of a doubt that this was God at work, and I knew he was repositioning me.

Reluctantly, the torrid process of divorce began. I didn't understand how this could be happening for a second time. My life had become a paradox that I could no longer rationalise with the girl I knew myself to be. But there was one thing I did know with all certainty - this process was not breaking my marriage covenant; that business had already been taken care of – I was merely releasing myself legally, to step into the next part of my journey. It had to be one of the most difficult things I've ever walked through. I neither believed in it, nor wanted it, but I no longer had a choice and over the following months, I hung on to the hem of his garment every single day; along with the biggest box of *Kleenex* you ever saw.

It forced up so many questions:

- † Where does the grace and mercy end?
- † The bible says forgive seventy-seven times or more. (**Matthew 18;22 - Luke 17:4**)
- † At what point does my responsibility for standing in the gap and interceding expire?
- † Can interceding become an act of defiance rather than faith? (that was a hard one for me)
- † How do I reconcile The Father heart of God vs The Holy Anger of God?

Day after day I wrestled and tortured myself with these questions. In-fact, some days I still do. But only because I want to get it right. I want to give my very best. My big girl once said to me that I bully myself – OUCH. Told you she was a wise one ☺

There are things of God as I've already said that are a mystery and what I have learned over the past few years is that there are no black and white answers to mysteries, you simply have to stay close enough to Him to be led and affirmed (or corrected) in the moment. There isn't any other way, or if there is, I haven't found it yet. I do my very best to follow my Fathers lead and when I slip, He picks me back up and sets me straight.

I wandered into the bedroom, tired but resilient. The process of unbinding *one-whole* back into *two-wholes* doesn't add up – do the maths. It's unjust, unmerited damaging to many and it hurts like heck, but somehow, I managed to find a renewed sense of direction and hope. With a little intervention, I'd finally managed to get both feet on the same path and though the directions were still pretty sketchy, I found peace of mind.

I'd spent the week creating lovely big hot glue gun blisters on the tips of my fingers, whilst the sides were a criss-cross of wire lacerations from the bouquets, button holes and venue decorations I'd been busy making. TFBB was getting married in just over a month. I'd even made my own hat. My big girl had married almost two years earlier and now I wasn't sure I was quite ready to let go of my Bubba too. She'd found a good one, just like her big sis, and I was so happy for them. God had been crazy faithful, still my heart wanted her to be mine just a little while longer.

I'd packed away early; it was Friday and I worked hard all week and as it was such a lovely afternoon I thought once I'd cleaned myself up, I'd take a nice walk outside.

I wandered into the bedroom to shower.

THE SECRET PLACE

†

Draped across the bottom of my bed was the familiar white velvet cloak. I looked around to see if He was still here. I was certain He was, but I sensed He was leaving me to work through this one alone. I walked over and reverently ran the back of my hand over the wonderfully soft fabric, letting out a breath. I hadn't felt right without it and I had some big things coming up that would have been impossible to manage in my own strength. I pulled it to myself and nuzzled my face into it comfortingly, inhaling its pureness.

This time I knew how it would feel and with no hesitation draped the beautiful garment around my shoulders, feeling the same shift in my spirit as it cast its grace and peace and love into every fibre of my being.

"Thank you", I whispered, grateful He had kept His word. And just out of sight, He smiled silently.

The huge box that had been sitting alongside it on the bed had not gone unnoticed. How could it, its gold shining paper and purple satin ribbons reflecting the brilliance of the early Autumn sun blazing through the bedroom window, casting flashes of light against the bedroom wall and ceiling. It had been a hot summer and I had missed having a garden; but writing a book, preparing wedding decor and ....had kept me busy.

I reached out and slid the unusually large box nearer to the edge of the bed. Dangling from the ribbon was a label and a key. The label read: **ACCESS ALL AREAS**

I had been listening to some amazing podcasts and one particular one had got me excited. It was about praying from your seat of power. It talked about us being seated in heavenly places, with Jesus and His Father. One with His Spirit, we have the power of Heaven at our disposal. When we pray, we shouldn't be looking up pleading, but standing in the throne room, in the presence of the Almighty Judge, displaying all the authority and power that brings. I was kind of itching to go.

I untied the ribbon and peeled back the paper, prising the top flaps of the box apart. Inside were 3 separate items, each with its own label.

1. A Trowl - **INTECESSORs BUILD THE WALLS OF PROTECTION**
2. A Pocket Telescope – **WATCHMEN STAY AWAKE & WARN**

3. A Peruke (Barristers Wig) – TRUTHBEARERS PLEAD THEIR CASE

In the bottom of the box was a separate piece of paper that read:

You must fight for justice to prevail for them. I have given you access to the Judgement Room and now I am making your authority plain. Keep watch daughter; you have always seen, but now you must use that to build the walls that protect and strengthen others, even when they don't know they need protection. And you must warn them. Work discretely and diligently - though others may not see, I see and I will reward you. Justice and Mercy are mine to give but your secret pleading has weight in my courts. You must persist in reminding me of this, you must never stop. You have position and power. Use it wisely. Use it lovingly. But use it, do not waste it Mighty One.

I have posted watchmen on your walls, Jerusalem;
they will never be silent day or night. You who call on
the LORD, give yourselves no rest, and give him no rest till
he establishes Jerusalem and makes her
the praise of the earth.

Isaiah 62:6-7 NIV

Your prophets, Israel, are like jackals among ruins. You
have not gone up to the breaches in the wall to repair it
for the people of Israel so that it will stand firm in the
battle on the day of the LORD.

Ezekiel 13:4-5 NIV

I looked for someone among them who would build up
the wall and stand before me in the gap on behalf of the

†

By the time I went to bed that night I was stirred up in full chain breaking warrior mode.

The apartment block I was in had around six modern apartments, but only two were occupied. It was a lovely large building in a pretty courtyard that housed a few shops and a spa and restaurant, but at night it was deserted. I'd gone to bed late as had become my habit, so inside and outside everywhere was silent and in total darkness. I'd just bought a small digital alarm clock so I set that and then I pulled my head right under the quilt and marched intentionally into the throne room. I began to visualize myself sitting next to my Father, looking down over the town, over the house, over the bedroom where the source of my battle slept, declaring very loudly and audibly the breaking of chains and victory. Suddenly I became aware of a bell ringing. *How frustrating!* I pulled my head from under the covers assuming I'd set the alarm clock incorrectly, however, holding it to my ear I realised quickly that that the ringing was actually coming from the small hallway outside my front door, And I was pretty sure what I could hear was the building's fire alarm.

As I jumped out of bed, throwing on my dressing gown, an odd thought dropped into my head. Lingering on it only briefly I opened my front door and stepped into the small hallway where my neighbor stood equally embarrassed in his pyjamas. It was one of those 'I hope this never happens' moments. With the fire alarm hollering loudly we went to the public area only to discover that the main entrance was locked and we were unable to get out. It was a managed building with digitalised access and for some reason the doors had locked shut. There didn't seem to be anyway out and no one was around, but thankfully there was no evidence of a fire.

"I have no idea what could have triggered the alarm" he said, "nothing appears to be amiss?"

That odd thought I'd had earlier crept back. Inside I smiled. I wanted to say *I have a sense it might be my fault.* But I couldn't, he would think I was some kind of crazy person. Instead, I let him do the heroic thing of going in search of the alarm control panel, which turned out to be back down the long hallway to the far end of the building and down the stairwell. Eventually the airways fell silent.

"Still have no idea what triggered it," he said as he reappeared, "the panel was showing that the alarm was tripped either in the attic above your apartment or the area of corridor directly outside your door?"

As far as I was concerned the alarm panel confirmed what my spirit had discerned. My prayers were bugging satan. I pictured, as I battled intently; me under my prayer blanket in Lancashire, my spirit petitioning in Heaven's courts; I pictured the enemy of our souls, of our calling, of our destiny, screeching and wailing in anger "Noooooo STOPP" as he frantically loitered listening-in, knowing he was losing his grip. Thrusting his fist on the alarm button like a spoilt child throwing a tantrum - *cause that's all he had!*

If I hadn't experienced it myself, it would be hard to comprehend, but that night I witnessed firsthand the damage and disruption we do to satan's evil strategies and plans, each time we plead our case and the case of others in the court room of Heaven; where the merciful and just Judge is waiting to bang his hammer down and declare:

NOT GUILTY

FREE

RECORD ERRASED

Rasha'

I believe I have something of yours (smugly wafts the charred remnants of the discarded covenant in the air)

Y'shua

It is written *'A thief has only one thing in mind—he wants to steal, slaughter and destroy. But I have come to give them everything in abundance, more than they ever expect.'*

Rasha'

(dismissively) Do tell Y'shua, who will you pass her assignments to now - which little evolving ray of sunshine should I have my eyes on?

Y'shua

Oh Rasha' (pitifully), don't you see, whilst you've been busy devouring, I've been busy building. Your evil strategies are becoming my Divine Victories. She had to be all that she is, live all that she has, see all that she's seen; to become all that she is becoming. So that, in due time, she will carry TRUTH to the nations. Carry ME to the nations. Her sacrifice is my gift to them. Her life is my revelation.

The Divine Plan, her Divine Purpose; neither are in chaos. I am about to name her, validate her, elevate her, send her. And redeem it all.

And I will speak to her of things as yet untold.

And you should be worried, Rasha', very, very worried.

While you were ministering, I watched Satan topple until he fell suddenly from heaven like lightning to the ground. Now you understand that I have imparted to you my authority to trample over his kingdom. You will trample upon every demon before you and overcome every power Satan possesses. **Luke 10:18-19 TPT**

10

Lifting the Lid

Eventually, we all have to face the fire – even Dragons.

C.S.

One year to the day from moving into my little apartment, I loaded up yet another van and proudly and excitedly moved myself into my very own home. It had been time. The wedding had been beautiful and TFBB had looked exquisite as she'd walked up the aisle towards her equally *dapper* and tearful bridegroom. The church and the venue looked magical and the blisters on my fingers were hardly noticeable; and even with slightly unglamorous *mother of the bride* hands and a few hard moments to navigate I was delighted with how wonderfully everything had gone. It was just as she'd wanted and hoped for.

God had really worked a miracle. I still wasn't working, but by some crazy unheard-of blessing, I was able to secure a mortgage off the back of my past income and imminent job hunt. Originally, I'd planned to find a house that needed fully renovating; after all that's what I'd always done and loved to do; but on the last minute, wisdom and a good dose of common sense, led me to a fabulous place. It was just eight years old and in a perfect location, so with a good bit of man-management and juggling, I was able to complete the purchase a few weeks before the wedding. In that two week period, woven in to all the last minute wedding preparations, the determined warrior in me set-to repainting the whole house and laying new flooring so that the girls and I could roll out temporary mattresses on the floor, pop open something fizzy and spend my baby girls last night as a single woman all together, giggling, reminiscing, hugging, giving praise for every little victory and just loving-on each other in Momma's new home – it had turned out perfectly.

And that wasn't the only miracle God had been organising on my behalf.

As Christmas approached, I'd shared with friends that in the New Year I would need to begin my job search in earnest. As much as I enjoyed writing, I knew I couldn't survive indefinitely without work, so I would park the book for a while and see what was out there. By mid-January, before I'd even started to refresh my CV, I got a call from a good friend to give me a heads up on a role that an old colleague was looking to fill. It was a senior position and he thought I'd be a perfect fit. If I was interested, he'd give the guy a call and put in a good word for me? Never one to pass an opportunity, I enthusiastically and naively said I'd love a chat to find out more. The role was heading up Customer Strategy and Customer Experience for a Commercial Bank. Whilst I'd been consulting directly before going to the States, this was a promotion from my last employed role and the salary was amazing; however, there was one huge elephant in the room....it was in London.

I was in the North West and I'd literally just moved into a new house. The adventurous spirit in me had always enthusiastically pushed on swinging doors to see what was behind them and this was no exception, though I didn't think for a minute I'd get it. On paper I had all the skills and experience they were looking for, but I felt sure it would go to a guy and someone already London based; still I figured having the conversation would get me back into the right head space and force me, if nothing else, to get my CV in order.

It turned out they had been struggling to find someone with just the right blend of specialist skills and broad experience that I had and having read through my CV, so keen were they to talk to me, that just twenty-four hours later, at 8pm in the evening I found myself having an exciting pre-interview chat. Two trips to London, plus two heavy interviews later, they offered me the job. I couldn't believe it. There was a brief moment where I questioned what I'd got myself into and if I was up to it (and if I really wanted it), but mostly I just giggled and got massive joy from how blooming proud the girls were of me. God had opened a door that no one could shut, and I'd hardly had to lift a finger. I hadn't had to spend hours researching job vacancies – this had dropped straight into my lap. I felt like an imposter, but I also felt like someone had pinned a huge *badge of honour* back on me and validated my worth.

Well, I reflected, once the euphoria had subsided, there's just one small issue to resolve now.

And so, *He* did.

I'd decided that I would live in London during the week and commute home at weekends, using the train as a mobile office on Friday afternoons. I looked at the location of the office and corresponding tube stations and established I would ideally need to rent weekday accommodation somewhere along the Central Line – and a Christian landlord would be a bonus. A few days after getting confirmation of my appointment, I was chatting to my sister in the States about it. 20 minutes after I'd said 'bye' and put the phone down an email with photographs landed in my in-box. The pictures were of a cute little bed-sit on the upper floor of a large three story old Victorian terrace house located on the outskirts of London. Underneath the photos she'd typed: Hey, some old friends of ours who we knew twenty years ago have just sent these. It's their neighbour. She's a single Jewish lady who's been looking for the right person to rent one of her rooms to. She's quite particular. The house is in South Woodford and she's only willing to let it weekdays so she can keep weekends to herself. I don't know if that works for you?'

I chuckled – that worked perfectly for me. I looked on the tube map and was not surprised to find that South Woodford was a mere 20 minutes outside London on the....Central Line. The monthly rent was crazy cheap for normal London rates too. It had God written all over it.

Within a few more days He gave me this word and I knew for sure that He was *sending* me and it was right to go.

> *Seek the peace and prosperity of the city*
>
> *to which I have carried you into exile.*
>
> *Pray to the* LORD *for it, because as it prospers,*
>
> *so too will you prosper.*

> **Jeremiah 29:7 NIV**

I also knew this was not going to be a permanent thing. I just knew this was a *meantime* mission and I wasn't meant to decorate it. I would go to London, God would bless me financially, whilst restoring my credibility and self-esteem, I would pray for the house I was to live in, for the local area of South Woodford, for the City of London and for the Company I was working for. And for anyone else He prompted me to. I would work my socks off and when the task was complete, He would bring me back.

So here I was. An unbelievable job in the bag, a London pad lined up, my lovely little Lancashire home looking all *Cath'ed* (as H would say about my interior prowess) and just over two months to kill before the hard work began. The book was packed away for now, so I concluded I'd use the time to get organized at home, figure out what I'd need for the London bed-sit and catch up with friends and family before I left.

I certainly wasn't anticipating any great moves of God in those two months; I was still basking in all that I'd just seen Him do and this was simply about killing time. But God moves when God decides and sometimes His moves are clustered around our refining and shaping and growing seasons.

Oh, how we underestimate him and try to fit Him in our perfect little boxes. The cascade of revelation He was about to pour out over me would completely liberate my understanding of who He created me to be and begin a *near obsessive* pursuit of the real *ME*. It would take me on a journey to the place where the *Good Girl* first showed up with her sense of duty and awkward humility. And it would shine a flashlight into the dark and confusing world of *unauthorized insight*, exposing the realities of Spiritualism and satan's meddling that would turn out to be a profound lightbulb moment for my backstory and a critical part of my testimony.

'I've decided to set up a ladies bible study starting next Monday,' H said nervously as we sipped the take-out coffees she'd just called round with. 'I'm not sure how many people will sign up for it, but I've been reading a great book called *Really Bad Girls of the Bible* and I think it will make a great eight-week group study, what do you think?'. This was one of her real gifting's. Although she never saw it in herself the way others did, she had this amazing way of gathering women together for *straight talkin, no messin, life bringin* biblical truth. I knew our church gals would be tussling to join.

"I think it's a fab idea," I replied. "Put me on the top of the list. I'll just have time to do all eight weeks before I leave for the retreat." I had a five-day wellbeing retreat in Majorca Spain booked the week before I started in London. It had been something I'd spotted about a year ago and had finally plucked up the courage to book (typically) right before I knew about the job, but in the end, all the dates had lined up perfectly.

So she quietly publicised it and *now*, Monday night had arrived and as predicted, H's house was crammed.

And boy were we were ready - with our righteous scales of justice we could not wait to dissect and weigh our first Bible Bad Girl and proclaim how bad she really was.

And in this first week the jury was unanimous - this old gal was *very very* bad indeed.

REVEALED AND REDEEMED – The Witch of Endor

Babylonia, you fought against me,

and you have been caught in the trap

I set for you, even though you did not know it.

Jeremiah 50:24 GNT

We must not slay the dragon in the dark. We need to see clearly what we're dealing with and just as David waited until God brought Goliath out into an open space where he was fully exposed before going in for the kill, we too must wait for God to bring the father of all lies, his evil demons and their murderous strategies out from their hidden pits, to a place where they can be seen clearly, before we take our position on the front-line of the battle field.

> We must not slay **the dragon** in the dark.

So. Remember the irrelevant tape I dropped in a box of old photographs along with a mountain of confusion and unanswered questions around twenty years earlier? The words of a spiritualist that I'd never planned to hear. The delicious, enticing words that tiptoed up behand me and caught me off-guard with their accuracy and familiarity. Peddling hope-filled promises that tenderly massaged my battered and lonely heart. Well, tonight I was about to get those esoteric questions answered. It would come in two waves of powerful revelation, and as we piled into H's living room, pouring ourselves a coffee and getting comfy, the swell of wave one was rapidly gathering its roar.

Tonight, and over the next few days God was about to drag satan out from his dark lair by the scruff of his neck, into the revelatory light of truth. Growling, hissing and convulsing, he would be laid bare as the prowling wolf and wizard that he was; *is, always has been, always will be...* until he's taken care of for good. This awkward topic that had quietly and secretly troubled and perplexed me for so many years was about to be decoded. And as I, with the help of H, picked my way through the detail, breaking apart and dismembering everything I had personally witnessed all those years before, challenging and weighing each and every fact against a new found knowledge and against scripture, I was sensing that what was being entrusted to me was about way more than satisfying my own vain curiosity.

I had just been handed the *Dummies Guide to Spiritualism.*

The ultimate slaying of this aspect of satan's personal strategy against me would not take place in the immediate days of deconstruction and rebuilding ahead; *that* victory would come a few years down the line following wave two of the revelation; but here and now, as we studied the *old woman of Endor*, God was about to show me one of satan's significant operational strategies for stealing destinies and spoon-feeding us falsehood.

God has made it plain long ago that witchcraft is *detestable* to Him.

And do not let your people practice fortune-telling, or use sorcery, or interpret omens, or engage in witchcraft, or cast spells, or function as mediums or psychics, or call forth the spirits of the dead. Anyone who does these things is detestable to the LORD. It is because the other nations have done these detestable things that the LORD your God will drive them out ahead of you. But you must be blameless before the LORD your God. The nations you are about to displace consult sorcerers and fortune-tellers, but the LORD your God forbids you to do such things.

Deuteronomy 18:10-14 NLT

Do not turn to mediums or seek out spiritists (those who

consult the spirits of the dead),

for you will be defiled by them. I am the LORD your God.

Leviticus 19:31 NIV

Saul and the Medium at Endor

This part of the chapter really isn't about Saul and this medium '*per-say*', it's about what God revealed to me through their story, but it will probably help if I share a little of the background for context?

In Saul's and David's days witchcraft was as prevalent as it is today. As God's anointed, King Saul had made witchcraft and all its associated practices illegal. However, over time, Saul's divine relationship with God had been undone and severed due to Saul's intentional disobedience and as a result, his anointing had been removed - His days were numbered.

Here, we find Saul in a place of terror, about to enter an uncertain battle without his wingman, the Prophet Samuel, who he'd typically turned to for advice, but who had now died *and* minus the ear, wisdom and protection of God, who he'd alienated.

And just look what happens in the space of one verse below when that vulnerability and uncertainty is exposed.

³Now Samuel was dead, and all Israel had mourned for

him and buried him in his own town of Ramah. **Saul**

had expelled the mediums and spiritists from the

land.

⁴The Philistines assembled and came and set up camp

249

at Shunem, while Saul gathered all Israel and set up
camp at Gilboa. 5*When Saul saw the Philistine army, he*
was ***afraid; terror filled his heart****.* 6*He inquired of*
the Lord, but the Lord did not answer him by dreams or
Urim or prophets. 7***Saul then said to his attendants,***
"Find me a woman who is a medium, so I may go
and inquire of her."
"There is one in Endor," they said.
8*So Saul* ***disguised himself****, putting on other clothes,*
and at night he and two men went to the woman.
"Consult a spirit for me," he said, "and bring up for me
the one I name."

1 Samuel 28 NIV

In his fear and panic Saul went looking for answers and a quick fix in a place he knew he shouldn't. Just as we often are, in difficult seasons of our lives, he became a sitting duck for satan. Dropped by his own side and hungry for some useful intelligence, temptation came *a knocking* at Saul's door. It tied a leash around his neck and led him into a humongous error of judgement, where he stepped over his own professed *forbidden* boundaries. Such was his hunger for assurance and direction, that against everything he knew to be true and right, he ventured out in disguise into the dark night, to visit a woman in Endor who claimed to consult with the dead - hoping to speak to Samuel the Prophet and get the answers he longed for.

> Temptation came *a knocking* at Saul's door. It tied a leash around his neck and led him into a **humongous error of judgement**, where he stepped over his own professed *forbidden* boundaries.

It's worth mentioning here that there's nothing in the Word of God (Old or New Testament) that suggests we can speak to our dead relatives or friends – just saying...

If you read the whole story, you'll discover that, the medium, much to her own surprise *ironically*, did see an apparition who spoke with a strong message for Saul. There is much debate as to who this apparition was and with much of the detail left out, we can merely guess? The general view seems to be that God himself showed up – but we simply don't know for sure.

One thing we can be fairly sure of is that the old woman wasn't making up what she saw; nor was it likely to be satan in disguise on this occasion as he does not know the future and as it turned out, the hopeless message Saul received was indeed fulfilled the very next day, when Saul and his sons were killed in battle by their own swords.

It's hard to pinpoint the exact moment the scales fell from my eyes, but as the evening went on and as I drove home that night, then later, as I lay in bed remembering and piecing together the events in my past, reflecting on all we had read and talked about that evening, a clear picture of the unnerving simplicity of satan's strategy and tactics in the area of spiritualism, fortune telling (or whatever you choose to call it), began to manifest.

Moment of Impact

'Hey it's me. Are you free later today? I could really do to call round for a natter. There's something from last night I really need to share with you and talk through.' I pressed send on the text and later that evening I was back in H's house walking her through parts of my backstory that we'd never really spoken about before, whilst testing and evaluating together all that I was sensing against God's word.

Back in the day, as a brand-new Christian I don't think I really gave consideration to the fact that mediums really *can* call up spirits. Mentally, I'd just assigned it a label that read **NONSENCE.** Then, when I'd heard first-hand unquestionable facts about my life flowing out of the mouth of a stranger, I simply replaced the label with **UNEXPLAINABLE/ UNRESOLVED**, like some crime series on TV. And for some unfathomable reason to me now, this usually zealous private detective left her unsolved mystery collecting dust in a cardboard box full of other random keepsakes.

As my own spiritual maturity and relationship with the Holy Spirit grew, somehow, I had never thought to revisit the case with wiser and fresher eyes. Not until, *that is*, the Witch of Endor picked me up and thrust me full throttle in that direction, where she finally cleared up a few outstanding questions.

Whilst many spiritualists and mediums are frauds, some are undeniably receiving information from an invisible source.

The bible is absolutely clear that all involvement with spiritualism and the occult is a sin. There is no sin in Him and therefore any unauthorised insight through these channels can only be coming from enemy territory. The words of an authentic spiritualist are coming from the mouth of hell, *no matter how lovely and full of promise they appear or sound.*

Not all who perform spiritualism activities do it with evil intent or knowledge. Many feel they are bringing a service to help people. But God leaves no doubt that all who dabble in this area are aligning themselves and serving satan. It's not only our Father who has a purpose for our lives – satan does to and he can, and regularly does, disguise himself as an angel of light to entrap us. But every word is intended to steal, kill and destroy.

Satan does not know the future (**Isaiah 46:9-10, Ecclesiastes 8:7, James 4:13-14**). He uses an abundance of facts about our past to dazzle and convince us of the authenticity of the speaker.

He uses his hordes of counter intelligence to tantalize our senses and build trust. And then he throws his *Value Hook* to set the scene for an imaginary future that fits our vision of bliss, which he's been busy orchestrating in the background; identifying, matching and manipulating people and situations perfectly, so that when a small element of this picture presents itself, we're so familiar with it that it already feels like part of our life. Subconsciously, we've accepted a lie as truth (even if innocently or naively) and walked into a future that God did not design for us.

Have you ever wondered why the devil always brings up our past? Why his crushing's and manipulation's somehow always press on the tender places of our heart - the things we've lost, what someone did to us, our failures and our old mistakes (past tense)?

It's because that's all he's got.

He only knows the stuff he or his demons have seen with their own eyes.

Remember the fifth shelf back in Command HQ, all those personalised tin boxes holding his you and me strategic profiling: How calculated assumptions are factored into his secret coding?

The dictionary defines assumption as 'a thing that is accepted as true or as certain to happen, without proof'. Satan takes our past and a whole load of assumptions to fool us into thinking he knows the future, when the truth is, all he has is the past. So often, we allow him to ensnare us and go all out to define our future using *out of date* intelligence.

> Satan takes our past and a whole load of assumptions to fool us into thinking he knows the future, when the truth is, all he has is the past. So often we allow him to ensnare us and go all out to define our future using **out of date intelligence**!

But God says our past *does not* define our future and He is the only one who knows.

I am God, and there is no other;

I am God, and there is none like Me.

I make known the end from the beginning, from ancient

times, what is still to come.

Isaiah 46:9-10 NIV

As I processed this new knowledge, I realised that my own life had become the revelation and I was thunderstruck that this smart, wise, discerning, good girl had been a sitting duck.

> I realised that my own life had become the **revelation...**

Many times, we expose ourselves to witchcraft and spiritualism naively, but be in no doubt, when God made it abundantly clear that we are not to entertain any of it, He meant it. Satan and his demons are skilled assassins that operate in the dark and excel in painful places. We are children of the light and that is where we must stay – in the light. Every answer we'll ever need can be found in Him. His Holy Spirit is the only spirit we should ever entertain and He is *with us always.*

> Satan and his demons are **skilled assassins** that operate in the dark and excel in painful places. We are **children of the light** and that is where we must stay – in the light.

The Lord your God is in your midst,

a mighty one who will save;

he will rejoice over you with gladness; he will quiet you

by his love; he will exult over you with loud singing.

Zephaniah 3:17 NIV

Be strong and courageous.

Do not fear or be in dread of them,

for it is the Lord your God who goes with you.

He will not leave you or forsake you.

Deuteronomy 31:6 NIV

Teaching them to observe all that I have commanded you.

And behold, I am with you always, to the end of the age.

Matthew 28:20 NIV

It should be said that I had done the critical and necessary clean-up work with God many years before. This regrettable event was part of my distant past and had been fully redeemed and severed through time with God in prayer and repentance, but only now was He revealing to me the day-to-day realities. The word <u>occult</u> means *hidden*. That tells us a lot. Our focus should always be on Jesus and the things of heaven, but that first week of BBGs had quickly taught me the ignorance and recklessness of leaving **UNEXPLAINABLE/UNRESOLVED** labels on things so dangerous and offensive to our Father.

Y'shua

(chuckling to Himself)

Well, my little wanderer, how are you feeling – now that you know?

Ora

(kinda chuckling too)

Hmmm...Happy. Relieved. Amused. Potent. Known. Giddy.

A little dumb too if I'm honest. If only I'd *got it* sooner, it would have saved me so much self-judgement and confusion and doubt.

Y'shua

(smiles)

Yes it would. But don't be too hard on yourself – you're not alone.

And I've enjoyed showing you and seeing you grow in wonder and realisation.

Increase is coming, so enlarge your tent and add

extensions to your dwelling. Hold nothing back. Make the tent ropes longer and the pegs stronger. You will increase and spread out in every direction. Your sons and daughters will conquer nations and revitalize desolate cities.

Isaiah 54:2-3TPT

11

Jael & Me - Tent Dwelling

Silly girl, the old lady smiled;

Your difference was you're beautiful all along.

ATTICUS

Week 1 had proved to be a huge milestone in my Christian walk and after such breakthrough I was not prepared for week two to be equally life changing.

Justified and Sanctified – Jael

Jael is a Hebrew name, from Yaél meaning 'ibex' or 'chimois' (which are species of wild mountain goats), from the root yaél meaning *to profit, to ascend* (perhaps in reference to the goat's nimble ability to ascend mountains with ease).

The Hebrew words *Ja'el* literally translate to *he shall ascend or go up.*

I'm sure when most of us imagine God aligning us directly with one of the women from scripture, we hope it will be Mary the Mother of Jesus who shows unusual faith and humility, saying 'yes' without hesitation to God's plan for her life, despite the confusion and fear she must have been feeling. Or the stunningly beautiful and brave Esther who showed great wisdom and spiritual discipline, to win the heart of a king and save her people. Or the generous, loyal and loving Ruth, who despite her own heartbreak, displayed great compassion for her mother-in-law, putting all her efforts into dealing practically with life's unexpected circumstances.

And what we would all give to hear our Heavenly Father lean in and whisper to us that we are His perfect example of the Proverbs 31 Woman – Her husband adores and praises her, her kids think she's the best Momma in town, she is an *entrepreneur extraordinaire* that works harder than anyone I know and everything she touches turns to gold; yet, she remains serene, dignified, God fearing and thoughtful of everyone around her in the process. That would certainly be a result wouldn't it.

Week 2 - BBGs and I was about to be introduced to my bible *twinnie* and she most certainly didn't belong with the aforementioned pool of *women to be highly esteemed...* or did she?

We were studying Jael, of whom the great Judge and prophet, Deborah, said *Most blessed of women be Jael, the wife of Heber the Kenite, most blessed of tent-dwelling women.* **Judges 5:24 NIV**

And why did Deborah rain down her praises?

> *Her left hand reached for the tent peg, her right hand for*
>
> *the workman's hammer. She struck Sisera, she crushed*
>
> *his head, she shattered and pierced his temple.....and he*
>
> *fell dead at her feet*
>
> **Judges 5:25-26 NIV**

Hmmmm...

Jael was part of a Nomadic tribe aligned to the Canaanites (Judges 4); enemies of the Israelites; but Jael and her husband had separated themselves from their people and set up their tent a good way from camp. Despite being a descendant of Moses' father-in-Law, Jael's husband had made peace with the Canaanites; still, the survival of these typically nomadic people was dependent on them keeping out of local disputes, which we can only assume is the reason for the separation?

Unless of course, God had somehow orchestrated their geography?

We have no insight on their feelings towards the God of the Israelites (*of Moses*), but it's clear from what we do know that Jael, whether she was aware of it or not, was in some way being led by the Spirit of God. The Canaanites and the Israelites were at war and the Israelites had been floundering. In fear for over twenty years, people had been keeping away from main highways and byways, staying hidden in their homes and tents. The Commander of the Canaanite army, Sisera, was a cruel oppressor with the might of nine hundred chariots fitted with iron at his disposal. On the day of Jael's *bloody moment of glory* her husband was AWOL. In a different location, across the valley, Deborah the Prophetess had decided to take charge, declaring a promise from The Lord that the Israelites would see a great victory that day.

She would take some of the men and lead Sisera's army into an ambush where The Military General, Barak, was commanded to wait with the remaining men to finish off both the Canaanite army and the evil Sisera. He was being handed *Hero* status on a plate. However, Barak, not feeling his usual brave self that day and clearly not fully confident enough in Deborah's prophecy, announced that he would only lead the charge on the enemy if Deborah came too. REALLY BARAK... Well Deborah agreed to this, but...

Beep Beep - News Flash Just In – Update From The Lord

> *Due to an act of cowardly disobedience from General Barak, the ultimate victory will no longer be his, instead... The Lord will sell Sisera into the hands of a woman.* **Judges 4:9 NKJV**

And so it was, the battle, led by Deborah with Barack in tow was indeed won. But the cowardly and worn-out Canaanite leader Sisera had managed to make a sneaky run for it, ending up tired, bruised and thirsty right outside Jael's tent. Jael, being such a *hostess with the mostess* came right on out of her tent to greet him, offering him a little milk and a lie down. I'm guessing she omitted to mention the small matter of a tent peg?

There is so much more I'd love to know about Jael:

▸ What prompted her to come right out of her tent to greet Sisera?

▸ How did she know it was him; we'd have to assume she'd never been in his company and there were no social media posts with his tyrannous mug-shot on?

▸ Why would she want to bring a victory for the Israelites, when her tribe were aligned with the Canaanites?

▸ Was she a prophetess too-she clearly has some kind of strategy, but why?

▸ Was she a leftie (as in left-handed) – unimportant but just some Cath curiosity?

Whatever the answer to those questions are, Deborah the wise, godly and highly respected leader of the day and well established judge, declared Jael to be *Blessed above all nomad women* and following Jael's *slam dunk*, forty years of peace followed for the Israelites.

Once we'd debated and dissected this interesting saga and agreed that Jael was less of a Really Bad Girl, but more of a fearless (or perhaps desperate) heroine, displaying spiritual discernment, courage, wisdom and strategic vision, divinely used by God; we began to talk about what we each needed to 'step outside our own tents' for. What was God calling us to weaponise up for, to step up to, to walk out of our safe place (or tents) to grab hold of. What kingdom things were we being called to do, yet cautiously holding back on?

As the evening had gone on and the conversation became more intense and deep, we'd all somehow shuffled closer, some of us with our shoes kicked off, sitting cross legged on the floor, others with the *poufs* they'd been demurely sitting on around the outside of H's living room at the start of the evening now dragged into the middle of the candle lit room, as we sat huddled together in a circle with our measuring line and scales. H was still sitting in her high back chair like the wise women that she was, holding us all in this holy place, her unneeded notes on her lap, her prudent questions opening up the conversations in a way that drew out truth and light.

As we each threw into the conversations some things that we maybe needed to revisit or step up to, I suddenly blurted out without thinking," I don't believe I need to come out of my tent... because my tent is always on my back – It's like I've become my tent and I just carry it wherever I go."

THE SECRET PLACE

†

As I looked up, in the middle of the floor was a long thin box. It was about one meter long, but only about 4 inches wide and high. It was wrapped in the same gold paper and the familiar purple ribbon adorned one end. I looked around our intimate gathering, realizing no one else could see the giftbox. His presence was undeniable, but this I knew was for me. I straightened out my left leg as far as I could in front of me, straining to hook my heel over the top of the awkwardly shaped parcel to draw it close. With expectancy, I discretely lowered my gaze to the label, my heart pounding with anticipation of what clues might be there.

It read **POWER & PURPOSE.**

By now I had come to recognise that something significant, typically, was unfolding in these holy moments.

I reached down and pulled loose the ribbon and carefully peeled back the gold foil. The box opening ran the full length of the parcel, so with one hand either side I carefully prized open the lid with my thumbs. Inside was an exquisite piece of carved wood. It wasn't smooth or straight, but nobly and undulating. It had a broader part at one end, like a hand carved walkers' staff, but I could tell it had been carved by a craftsman.

I lifted it out and smelled it, then ran my fingers over its surface. Since I had been a little girl spending time with my dad in his workshop, the smell and feel of freshly carved wood had brought life to my soul - it still did. As my hands navigated the knots and features, I felt some unusual markings in the wood. I pulled my fingers back to reveal two small rows of lettering.

CATHERINE - Pure - Righteous - Without blemish - Vindicated

STAFF - Power - Purpose

Immediately, I heard Him respond, "you're a Nomad, I made you that way."

†

Moment of Impact

No·mad (nō′măd′) n. A member of a group of people who have no fixed home and move according to the seasons often moving to and from the same places. An Itinerant, a wanderer.

Itinerant (i-tin-er-ant) n. A person who alternates between working and wandering. A person who travels from place to place, especially for work or duty. In Latin, *iter* means way or journey. That root was the parent of the later Latin verb *itinerari*, meaning *to journey*.

My hand went to my mouth in shock. This moment was beyond significant, God had just identified me by a name that was scarily familiar, but one I'd always used as a jokey self-deprecating term.

In that moment, my Father, the one who created me, who knew my innermost being, who'd knitted me together perfectly and completely for a specific purpose here on earth, smiled, heaved a huge sigh of relief and gave me permission to just be *me*.

Supernaturally, everything about Cath that had *always* been there; things I'd always considered odd about myself because they seemed 'different'; things I'd even chastised myself over and internally labelled Stubborn Independence, were legitimised. My life which, thus far, seemed to be defined by a constant moving from place to place, by upheaval and restlessness and constant change began to make sense. I thrived on *loving-on* people and encouraging and blessing them wherever I happened to be, but often people would want to pull me in to the centre of *their thing;* something I instinctively knew would create constrains and hinder my ability to navigate freely the next instruction to 'GO'. It all made sense; I made sense.

I wasn't odd or messed up or irresponsible and stubborn or never satisfied or an outsider who didn't fit in – those were words belonging to The Father of Lies.

The Father of Truth, The Father of Life, the One who created the blueprint for me, said I was exactly as I was meant to be.

It seemed to me as I dug deeper into Jael's story, that she was positioned in the right place at the right time in a specific season, for a specific task. A nimble mountain climber, a wanderer, a southpaw; a strategic and wise watchman who displayed great bravery and insight (and a few other things we might want to skip over); culturally we may find her actions hard to praise, but she heard that inner voice and acted on it. The prophets praised her, the nation was delivered from war and death and fear by her hand and God exalted her by making sure her actions were recorded for all of eternity; that everyone who read His word would know the name of the woman whose hand had conquered and slayed the mercenary and now cowardly Sisera.

All this time, all along from the beginning, without realising, I had been walking in purpose, desperately clinging on to the inner voice of the One who formed me, who called me by name, who set me apart, who appointed me, who cherished me and thought of me constantly and whose design and creation was *mysteriously complex and marvellously breathtaking.* **Psalm 139:14 TPT**

...as satan, The Father of *Lies,* relentlessly and cunningly bid to bring me down, trip me up, turn me around, question my value and my worth, Drip-feeding doubt – exactly like he had with Eve in the garden.

He's nothing if not consistent and predictable.

COMAND HQ

Did God really say...?

But Our Father's, our Dad's Word is INFALLIBLE and UNCHANGING. It is LIFE FORMING, GLORY BRINGING TRUTH.

Before I formed you in the womb, I knew you...

before you were born I set you apart; I appointed you...

as a prophet to the nations.

Jeremiah 1:5 NIV

I thank you, God, for making me so mysteriously
complex.
Everything you do is marvelously breathtaking.
It simply amazes me to think about it.
How thoroughly you know me, Lord.

You even formed every bone in my body when you
created me in the secret place,
carefully, skillfully shaping me from nothing to
something.
You saw who you created me to be before I became me.
Before I'd ever seen the light of day, the number of days
you planned for me
were already recorded in your book.
Every single moment you are thinking of me.
How precious and wonderful to consider that you
cherish me constantly in your every thought.
O God, your desires toward me are more than the grains
of sand on every shore.
When I awake each morning, you're still with me.

Psalm 139:14-18 TPT

For we are His workmanship [His own master work,
a work of art], created in Christ Jesus [reborn from
above—spiritually transformed, renewed, ready to
be used] for good works, which God prepared [for
us] beforehand [taking paths which He set], so that
we would walk in them [living the good life which He
prearranged and made ready for us].

Ephesians 2:10 AMP

Awareness was coming faster than my mind could comprehend it. I was making connections between things I previously looked at independently and I was wondering why on earth I hadn't seen all this before. The persistence and regularity of His instructions to **GO, PRAY, BUILD/REBUILD, WRITE/RECORD.** The frequency of mountain climbing references. And now this. When I took these new revelations about my identity and folded in my own core temperament, almost like mixing the ingredients of a cake together, it was as if a supernatural explosion was going off deep within me. And I'm certain in Heaven too...

What had felt like the real ME for all these years, *was the real ME* after all.

He had created me to live an *ad hoc* life on purpose (*in purpose*).

What had felt like the real ME for all these years, *was* the real *Me* after all.

When I reached home that night, I opened up my daily devotional and this was the scripture:

> *Then the few remaining in Jacob will be amid many*
> *peoples like dew from the Lord [a source of blessing];*
> *like spring showers upon the grass, which does not hope*
> *for humans or wait for human ones.*

Micah 5:7 CEB

I knew right then that God *sends* me to sprinkle Jesus, like dew on the early morning grass, wherever I found myself. Even as a wasteland wandering nomad; a term that would embitter or terrify many, yet filled me with the comfort of liberty and hope; He had so remarkably multiplied and shaped me whilst flooding His *torn tent* with

All I needed to do was turn up as myself. *Cath* needed to act like *Cath*, dress like *Cath*, carry *Cath* shaped weapons, have a *Cath* shaped heart (shaped by a Christ shaped mind) and be ready to say yes.

the brilliance of His light, hidden deep in its inner room, its *holy of holies* by Him at the design stage. A light carried to sprinkle His glow and refreshing on those my tent encountered as I roamed. Right now, that was about to be London, but the most exciting thing was that there would be other places, other people and all I needed to do was turn up as myself. Cath needed to act like *Cath*, dress like *Cath*, carry *Cath* shaped weapons, have a *Cath* shaped heart (fashioned by a Christ shaped mind) and be ready to say Yes.

What a liberation and relief.

Weeks 3-8 of BBG hadn't disappointed either. Every week God seemed to pour out revelation to one or many of us. One week a friend gave me a vision of seeing me knocking skittles down. She said it was a picture she believed representing me knocking down spiritual barriers in people's lives through prayer. It really had been a profound and inspired couple of months and now I was almost ready to get out my briefcase, my heels and my lippy and hit the big smoke (aka London City)

But first I had one last treat to enjoy. I could almost taste the fresh fruit and feel of the Majorcan sunshine on my face, as I boarded the plane to my first ever health retreat. Five glorious sun-filled days, a tribe of beautiful women, exquisite life-bringing, body healing food and the gleaning of such exceptional wisdom – that its impact would abide, long after the days' incandescent sun and the late discussion-filled, friendship-building balmy evenings' full moon and incalculable stars, had long since set across those captivating Majorcan skies.

A CITY WITHOUT WALLS

Rasha'

(watching uncomfortably from afar, as shards of divine light explode from Him with the luminosity of an erupting supernova in the heavens.)

Y'shua

I haven't seen you here for a while Rasha'; you've clearly been amusing yourself elsewhere? (Her skills in battle had been increasing exponentially, He mused to Himself, knowing she'd put the serpent in his place – she hardly broke a sweat these days.)

Rasha'

Keeping busy Y'shua, keeping busy (his eyes following the nauseating radiance that flowed from Him to her, to them; his body coiling back in repulsion)

Y'shua

(observing) After all this time, that light still perplexes you; still fascinates you – still *out-whit's* you doesn't it Rasha' (breathes out, as each beam of light erupts into a billion billion particles; photons of light and energy flowing from a Father's heart to each of His children. Delivering HOPE. PROMISE. LOVE. JOY. LIFE. A demonstration and reminder to the vile onlooker...)

Go back to where you came from you serpent of death – your darkness can never, and *WILL NEVER*, overcome the light – *NEVER*.

A fountain of life was in him,
for his life is light for all humanity.
And this Light never fails to shine through darkness —
Light that darkness could not overcome.

John 1:5 TPT

12

Getting My *Shine On*

She's completely unexplainable. You think she's the good girl, but she's everything. She's crazy, she's funny, she's honest and you never know what she'll do next.

AUTHOR UNKNOWN

Majorca, Spain - Who told you you can't shine?

Mirror Mirror on the wall...

Funny isn't it how we remember the exact moments when significant people drop into our lives?

And here was another one of those moments.

Remember I mentioned that when I first felt the pull of writing my story, I asked a friend to pray about it with me. She'd come back fairly quickly with a resounding 'yes,' stating that she'd felt God answer that my book *should* be written and would reach the far corners of the earth, to places and people I could never reach personally.

Fantastic I'd thought at the time, *this is it, if God is for me who can be against me - it's sealed, I'm going to be a world-famous author.*

Well, what I didn't share was that a week later I bumped into the same friend and we got chatting about my plans and she told me that she had sensed more; as she'd continued to pray for me she'd seen a picture of an old fashioned stagecoach, the type I guess, that would have been used by my old Highwayman back in the day. She said she'd felt as though God was saying that spiritually I was still growing and was not yet fully ready to tell the whole story; that there was more to the story and that I had more learning to do... *well heck I knew that already* - I didn't even have an ending at this point, *duhhhh.* But that wasn't what she meant. She said she saw me on a journey and just like the old stagecoaches would pull into at every town to restock and shoe the horses, with some people getting off and leaving the party and others joining, she saw my book-writing journey just like that; random scatterings of glorious little chapters evolving en-route to the *ta daaaaa.*

How can anyone straighten out what God has made crooked?

Ecclesiastes 7:13 GNT

A seemingly accurate prophecy as it turned out: One fifteen-chapter draft outline, one prologue, one glorious opening chapter, a couple or monologues and twelve months of life later, so much of my story still unwritten; still untold...

Cue significant person - Who knew God was on Facebook.

So look, I'm pretty skilled in the field of marketing and not easily distracted by fancy ads, particularly the mountains that flash up across my social media pages. But this one was different. There was just something mesmerising about the delicious face staring back at me; promising health, vitality, total relaxation and sunshine, wonderful wonderful sunshine - Everything about that face screamed 'energy', 'well-being', 'life' - and before I'd even processed what I was doing, I'd clicked *save post* and boom, another tiny miracle sneaked in unnoticed, as Orly [a beautiful Hebrew name meaning *surrounded by light*] was eternally woven into the messy, crinkled, adventure-filled, nomadic pages of my story.

Ironically, it would be another year before I saw that post and that sweet face again but by that time, I was ready. Mentally ready, physically ready, heart & soul ready and financially ready and right on cue there she was, like a blessing straight from the storerooms of Heaven.

Orly understood true health, she understood how to sensitively unravel the tangled history maps of the mind, she knew how to truly nourish and love, she knew Jesus and soon she would know me; every single tiny intricate detail of me; way more than she could ever have bargained for.

We each have bits of our stories that are best kept just for us - Gods little building blocks, His little leg-ups to our self. A chance for Him to hold a mirror up to us and say 'just see how exquisite you are, how incredibly wonderful and breathtakingly messy you are'. My time with Orly was just that and honestly, could not have been timed more perfectly, coming straight off the back of God's last big revelation, it became a precious time of awakening, of deeper revelation, of growth and of transformation.

Now, do not, I repeat *DO NOT* be fooled by this beguiling word *transformation* - the process of change. It may roll easily off the tongue, but there is certainly nothing easy about the process. It's tricky and untidy and painful and there are always, always casualties and sometimes those casualties are parts of you that are familiar and feel like home, but which no longer serve you well.

> The process of **change is tricky and untidy and painful** and there are always, always casualties and sometimes those casualties are parts of you that are familiar and feel like home, but which no longer serve you well.

When a caterpillar enters the cocoon, it intentionally offers up the familiar, crawling in and out of the shrubbery on the ground looking like every other caterpillar, for the potential of one day emerging majestically with strong new multi-coloured wings that might carry it way above the ground to

> Before the butterfly can make its bid for freedom it has to **dispose of all the parts of its old self** that its new wings will be **unable to carry**. Strong as they are going to be, they will **serve a much greater purpose** than dragging around old skin.

a beautiful new world and a brand-new viewpoint. As its miraculous transformation begins, deep inside the cocoon a gooey sticky matter is forming. No longer exists a furry, wiggly caterpillar; yet, the wonder that is to become our glorious butterfly is still growing its wings. If we tested the DNA of this gooey sticky mess, we would discover our precious butterfly is already making its mark on the world, but to the untrained eye all we would see is a caterpillar leftovers. You see, before the butterfly can make its bid for freedom it has to dispose of all the parts of its old self that its new wings will be unable to carry. Strong as they are going to be, they will serve a much greater purpose than dragging around old skin.

And just like the butterfly, as Orly and I peeled back, layer after layer, I quickly learned that there were some parts of Cath that needed to be left behind if she was going to reach her full, divinely designed purpose and potential.

And the first thing that had to go was the *good girl*.

I don't quite know how she spotted it, but as we talked about my childhood and my younger school years, Orly blurted out boldly, "Who told you you can't shine?"

Moment of Impact

For a moment I fell silent, meditating on her question and on the story I'd just shared with her, slowly seeing what she had seen straight away and smiling impishly as I wondered what I was going to do with this little rascal of revelation. I'm not sure if it's the same now, but when I was at school the good girls with nice clear voices always got narrating parts in the school play. And good girls who had half a decent singing voice were also put in the choir. So, as a *not so tall* 'good girl', most times you'd find me hidden behind a large wooden lectern with the microphone dragged down in the direction of my mouth or in the middle of a *not so angelic sounding* primary school choir. One particular year the teachers were

Who told you you can't shine?

auditioning in the classroom for the nativity play and invited pupils who were interested to step forward and give their best Angel Gabriel performance. Silence. Complete Silence. No-one moved an inch. More silence. The discomfort and false responsibility started to bubble up in my chest, I felt an intense awkwardness and embarrassment for the poor teacher and I knew I had to do something quickly to rescue her.

With no practice or prepared script I took one huge lunge forward. Adorned in my knee length white socks, little grey skirt and navy-blue jumper, I impulsively flung both arms high into to the air and taking a deep breath, released the best angelic voice I could muster and declared, "Behold, I bring you glad tidings of great joy."

"That was wonderful, Catherine," the teacher beamed and just like that I saved face for my teacher and became Angel Gabriel. I was so happy and proud and excited. I hadn't planned for this but I was going to relish it.

My big girl was born for the stage. Her whole life she's performed in one way or another and she has used that stage for so much good, as God has opened the craziest doors and platforms for her. Even so, as she bounded through her younger and teenage years, doing and savouring all that she was clearly made to do, embracing enthusiastically every new random opportunity that came her way, we would often simultaneously cheer her on whilst rolling our eyes and grinning, as if to say 'what is she like.' As if this ability to seize her platform with boldness and vivaciousness was somehow a shortcoming - in that good old British way of 'being seen and not heard.' I had been raised on it, I had lived and breathed it and I wore it proudly like a halo on my head. The lie had embedded itself so firmly in my moral code that false humility was holding me in bondage, contending with the bright star in little Cath that was created to shine. And Orly was on to it.

> The **lie** had embedded itself so firmly in my moral code that **false humility** was holding me in **bondage**, contending with the bright star in little Cath that was created to shine.

The only reason my moment of glory had come up with Orly in the first place, was that she'd asked me to write a long list all of my childhood memories, anything at all that dropped into my head. I believe this is quite a standard practice that psychologists use to help expose unconstructive things from our past. The concept is, that we typically remember key moments that impact our beliefs and values, the things we believe to be true and importantly, carry into adulthood (good or bad) and by unravelling them and seeing them for what they are, we are then able to also unravel any associated mistruths or unhelpful beliefs, behaviors, habits, hang-ups etc.

Now remember I was on a health retreat and we were actually doing this exercise from the context of food and wellbeing, but we'd somehow (thankfully) gone off down a very interesting little track.

And sadly, my nativity story doesn't end with my glorious casting. It turned out that my primary school tribe were just as reluctant to volunteer for choir and reading, so I found myself being championed for both, traded between teachers, with my starring role snatched away and handed over to someone else (who, by the way, in my book, had not earned it); my own sparkly star pushed back into storage, the good girl placed back on duty, doing all the right and proper things as she'd been taught.

Everybody's little angel apart from The Virgin Mary's.

And there it was again, Orly's obstinate question – I could hear from her tender but firm tone that she was fighting my corner - she'd gotten to know me pretty well over the week and had seen something I'd been suppressing for a very long time.... .

"Who said you can't shine, Cath?" She wasn't going to let this go.

"I don't know," I replied honestly, my head down, my eyes surveying the ground.

And I didn't.

I thought of all the moments I'd been out with my girls, them wanting to take lots of group photos of us together in one busy place after another, me getting increasingly flustered in case we were making a scene or drawing attention to ourselves in public. How that good, compliant girl had robbed the world of the full extent of the effervescent Cath that was mostly reserved for a close group of loved ones, or for extra special impromptu occasions, when her star spontaneously popped out and she danced on the table. Or for work events where she could more easily manage her dazzle in heels, lippy and a good suit. Oh, she could shine then. Because that wasn't about *her, her behaviour or her character; it was about her capability.*

I made Orly a promise, that I would commit to paper my journey back to *naughtiness* and *mischievousness* and *breaking the rules* and *courage* and *boldness.* The craziness was, the fierce part of Cath, the core, the part that had been pushing and screaming and dreaming and scheming forever it seemed, was not a good girl at all. She was a gypsy; a bare footed, wild hearted, boundary pushing, restless, romantic, wandering Nomad, full of adventure and a need to be free to make her own mark on this world. But for the most part, the really really good girl had stolen so much of my truth.

The craziness was, the fierce part of Cath, the core, the part that had been pushing and screaming and dreaming and scheming forever it seemed, was not a good girl at all. She was a gypsy; a bare footed, wild hearted, boundary pushing, restless, romantic, wandering **Nomad**, full of adventure and a need to be free to make her own mark on this world! But for the most part, the really really good girl had stolen so much of my truth.

And oh, how people loved and depended on that good girl.

And oh, how *she* loved to please.

Trouble was, piece by piece, day by day, the good girl was sucking the life (and the heart) out of me - I was exhausted and it was time to take back control.

But how?

"Here's what I want you to do" Orly said; "make a list of all the things you wouldn't have done if you hadn't been such a good girl..." I knew what her game was of course. Once I'd got the list, she was going to present me with a *and what now?* But the truth was I wanted this for myself, I was ready and so my list turned out to be *huuuuge.*

Now I'm a prolific list maker, in fact I'm never without one, ever, so writing the list was a piece of cake. However, crossing off...., becoming a bad girl (or a liberated girl for want of a more acceptable phrase) quickly... that was certainly a whole different game.

Yet, something deep inside had shifted. I wanted to shine. I wanted to feel like it was actually *OK to shine. No...more than that...,* I was ready to fully accept that My Father, my Dad, had actually created me to shine; had placed His light deep within the bones and flesh and airways and veins and senses and organs and hands and feet; so that as I carried and released it, others would see Him. And for every moment I kept that light hidden, I kept Him hidden. And that meant I wasn't being who he had created me to be, nor doing what He had called me to do. I was a fraud, a counterfeit version of Cath.

But not anymore, I was tired of living only half alive.

As huge as my list was and as hard as it was going to be to shift some of these prehistoric facades, I was feeling miffed now too and I had some pretty impressive cheerleaders on the sidelines willing me on to victory, so I took a deep breath, did some serious reflecting and began to devise my *good girl* exit strategy.

My List

[a work in progress]

- I'd have been less accommodating of everyone else's needs at the cost of my own.
- I'd worry less about what people thought.
- I would have been more vocal about my own desires.
- I'd have realised sooner that I'm not responsible for fixing the world in my own strength.
- I'd have stopped justifying other's wrong-doings and called out wrong as '*wrong*'.
- I'd have use less words and listened more.
- I'd have realised I didn't have to always justify myself.
- I'd have stopped trying to plug every gap.
- I'd have made less commitments – '*No*' is an OK word.
- I'd have tackled conflict more directly.
- I'd have learned to value silence in conversations.
- I'd have learned to dance on the table and sparkle and shine without inhibition or angst.
- I'd breathe in and out more.
- I'd have learned how to protect myself better from negativity.
- I'd have lived less rushed.
- I'd have talked more slowly.
- I'd have written less lists.
- I'd have stopped overthinking and over analysing.
- Tattoos... an interesting one all in its own.

Gosh I really do have issues.

And practically:

- I wouldn't have allowed my history teacher to convince my parents I should go into banking at age sixteen.
- I'd have chosen a career that fed my soul.
- I would never have touched sugar (that's a whole other story, for next time perhaps?)
- And I would have learned my craft.
- I'd have done much more world-wandering.
- And settled a little further from the nest.
- I'd have fallen in love with a beautiful heart who would have treasured my creativity, my spirit, my quirkiness and my nomadic disposition and who would have loved me forever.
- I would have studied psychology and interior design and architecture and theology.
- I would have bought a little house by the sea in a sunny climate and written stories in the morning and lay in the sun creating the next chapter in the afternoons, then eaten glorious food and sipped chilled rose in the evenings.

Is it a life lost... *heck no...*

If God really has made this path crooked and if He really has created me perfectly and with purpose; and if no one can open a door that God has closed, nor close a door that He has opened; then perhaps it is all just as it's meant to be - right on time, right people, right place, right path.

> I am in the process of **transformation**; no longer the Cath I once was, the one the world tried to hijack; but still not the Cath I am becoming.

And as I hear the final call from the stagecoach driver announcing the imminent departure, I lay down my pen once more and get myself ready to move forward into the next chapter of this great adventure we call life.

Because, I am in the process of transformation; no longer the Cath I once was, the one the world tried to hijack; but still not the Cath I am becoming.

And I found myself wondering about Y'shua's promise, to *build on the old foundations.* – And I wondered...could these be *my* old foundations, *Cath's* foundations, the ones He laid in place before He knit the Carpenters Daughter together and called her by name. Could it be possible that despite all the messy chapters, all the craziness and the mistakes, the victories and the silliness, the shakings and the shattering; was it truly feasible that her foundations hadn't moved an inch – they hadn't crumbled or fractured or even subsided any – in fact as the earth around them shook and displaced, a reinforcement had been taking place, embedding them so firmly that they were now considered *Kingdom Building* worthy?

Despite all the messy chapters, all the craziness and the mistakes, the victories and the silliness, the shakings and the shattering; my **foundations** hadn't moved an inch – they hadn't crumbled or fractured or even subsided any – in fact as the earth around them shook and displaced, a reinforcement had been taking place, embedding them so firmly that they were now considered *Kingdom Building* **worthy**?

THE SECRET PLACE

†

They endured as He had known they would on the day He set them in place. Foundations on which He would build His City, generation after generation after generation. A city without walls, where His Glory would descend, a city that he would defend with the fire of heaven. She would be the apple of His eye and He would raise His own hand against any that dared to plunder her.

†

Hmmm I contemplated curiously, aware that if this developing realization was true, it was going to require a willingness on my part to fully let go of all that I had hoped in. If these ancient foundations of mine were truly what He planned to rebuild on in the days still to come, rather than the ones I had been imagining, then every expectation I had for my life would need to be laid down in faith.

> If these ancient foundations of mine were truly what He planned to rebuild on in the days still to come, rather than the ones I had been imagining, then every expectation I had for my life would need to be **laid down in faith**.

THE SECRET PLACE

†

And not for the first time, in His secret place, a proud and joy-filled Father who had been setting her up for greatness from the start, smiled and murmured lovingly,
"that's my girl."

†

Zurgena, Andalucia Spain 1569 and 2019

Rasha'

The world is so large Y'shua. So much of it more pleasant and less pungent than *this* dry and barren... *and* blood-stained valley. I have never quite understood why the echo of your voice continues to reverberate in the wind o'er a small, seemingly insignificant place such as this? I choke every time I pass over this contaminated piece of land ~ I can still smell the wretched stench from the blood that dripped onto the ground from his broken, worn-out body, as he knelt there defiantly holding on to some futile faith that his words might reach you and you might just show up and save this valley from my hands.

I kept a close eye on him that afternoon; this soldier far from home, almost overcome from the heat, fighting a hopeless battle against a foe who had already subdued the land (smirks smugly). They had thought they could hold the settlement...

(nods down the valley and across the rambla, towards the now pretty white-washed ancient village of Zurgena, then just a basic fortress)

...but it was no use, their enemy was too strong, too determined, too close ~ so they retreated along the Ruta Verte towards the ravine yonder (flicks his wizened chin upwards, roaring with laughter).

Though time was against them, he held back as they passed this way; I could see something in his eyes, like he had unfinished business here (moderating tone). No doubt hoping the others wouldn't spot him, he stole away unnoticed, slithering into that ditch there (points ahead), before scrambling up here, beholding the whole valley like he owned it. I pitied him, as he dropped alone on this very spot; where *she* now pours out her oil whilst the other one speaks with her to evict me (turns and stares in loathing to where the two sat minutes earlier, feet in the water, speaking words of agreement); his spear thrust into the ground as if somehow that gave him dominion – praying to his Christ for territory, claiming it for Y'shua's glory (fake curtsey of acknowledgment and snigger).

Foolishly clinging on to false hope that you might come through. And when the ground didn't shake, nor the mountains tumble, the wounded soul slipped back, unmissed, to march alongside his defeated *soldados*, imagining, I expect, some sweet miracle to have taken place (pfff). And now you have *her* here, floating on the water over his spilt blood – it's all so very peculiar Y'shua (yawns indifferently).

Y'shua

What troubles you most Rasha' – the fact that his prayers held power, or the impenetrable wall that remains around this place, still, after so many years? It must surely grieve you to see how the valley became fertile again, its trees bowed and stooped under the weight of ripened fruit.

To see my people take back their homes and villages and land and streams, singing their praises to me as they gathered in the harvests? His blood and holy anger poured out for me, right here, as mine had poured out for him. He brought this land before my alter, just as she now does. *You* see a land that is dry and barren, Rasha'

I see a land that is as fertile as Eden, overflowing with living water.

The LORD will always guide you; He will satisfy you

in a sun-scorched land and strengthen your frame. You will be like a well-watered garden, like a spring whose waters never fail.

Isaiah 58:11 NIV

13

A Life Less Ordinary

There she was, all dressed up in adventure; straddling the edge of
a star.

JONNY OX

London City

I made two declarations as I left for London, I would not wear flat
shoes to get to the office and I would not carry a back pack. Both, I
considered to be un-classy and un-ladylike, plus at 5ft 2 ½ inch, good
4" heels were not only a work staple for me, but a non-negotiable.

By the end of the first week, I was doing both.

The fifteen minute walk from my digs to the tube every morning and
evening demanded smarter footwear and increasing workloads, plus
excessively overloaded tube carriages (where resting a heavy briefcase and oversized handbag on the floor wasn't an option), pushed
me reluctantly into the backpack brigade. I also had to have a rapid
wardrobe rethink. I arrived in late spring in the middle of a heatwave,
discovering that a heatwave in the south could not be compared to
what we in the north considered a heatwave.

The extreme heat of the tube, which my landlady kindly explained heated up on the first part of my over-ground journey and then transformed into an oven as the now heated metal carriage moved into the insulated tunnels of the London Underground, became the enemy of my hair, my makeup and just about every part of my body and sanity. With every minute that passed, once that train entered the tunnel, we were being cooked alive. Perspiration dripped down my forehead, the foundation and mascara I'd skilfully applied only thirty minutes earlier dissolving into oily rivers of mud on my face, the weight and bulk of my trendy but way too full backpack adding an unhelpful layer of padding that made me question whether I'd actually applied deodorant that morning, as more and more expectant people compressed their sticky bodies into the already overcrowded carriage.

Think *Bridget Jones*. In the tangle of people, my 5ft 2½ inch melting frame; graciously moving wherever I could to make room for other equally deserving passengers; switched into survival mode, scanning any potential gaps where my arm might squeeze through to grab hold of some available fixed object before the train doors closed and the carriage lurched forward. I had already seen people fall into embarrassing postures during these critical moments and with the absence of my faithful heels I was no longer able to reach up to the overhead metal rails to steady myself, meaning the middle space of the carriage was to be avoided at all costs.

Losing my composure in front of the many arresting 6ft something city chaps, dressed in Tom Ford and radiating a mix of fresh perspiration, charm, nonchalance and their signature La Labo fragrance, their Bottega Veneta tucked perfectly under one arm as they scanned the Times en-route to Chancery Lane or St Pauls, was about the most humiliating thing I could imagine. If I could make it to a corner of the carriage close to the doors and stake my claim rigidly, avoiding all eye contact and remaining unruffled by huffs and tutts, I knew I was safe, at least for this journey.

It was a baptism of fire, literally.

But despite the chaos and heat and twice daily challenge to find my corner and resist serious physical crushing, I loved it. The work was intense and fast passed, but it was what I was good at and I loved feeling like I was bringing something to the table again and the people were fabulous. Walking into the office from the tube, amongst the hustle and bustle of the city, with its noise and smells and diversity, I couldn't believe how God had blessed me and elevated me. As I paused by the exit of the tube station each morning to quickly slip out of my flats and into my trusted and dependable heels, I felt alive for the first time in so very long. Is it wrong to say I was proud of myself? Well, I was. I'd been through the worst thing, yet I had stood and I had conquered. I hadn't just survived, I had flourished.

Had I imagined that in my fifties I'd be leading this kind of frenetic life; heck no, it's the sort of thing I dreamed of in my late teens and twenties, but nothing about my life had been what I'd imagined and I was going to embrace this moment for all that it was and for all the grace and blessing that God had poured into it and for all the guts and tenacity and resilience I had shown to get here. So yes, you better believe I was proud of myself and I was going to give it all I had.

I got in a great routine, flying like a lunatic along Southampton Row to make the Friday afternoon train out of Euston, finishing off the week's work and emails on the 3-hour journey back home. Then hopping on the return train each Monday, back to the City. It was tiring, but it was worth it and always, I knew, that this was a meantime place.

I missed the girls terribly, but God was so busy doing great things in their lives too and we facetimed regularly. TFBB had been promoted and was finally doing her dream job; Executive Assistant to the CEO of her company and they loved her. Why wouldn't they, she had her Momma's people and leadership skills and she *organised the socks* off them. She had dreamed of this since she was a little girl, scrambling to grab the letters from the post man, and here she was all grown up and killing it like a pro. My big girl and her boy were part of a Christian band that were going from strength to strength.

The band's mission was to lead young people to Jesus. They spent a lot of time in high schools all across the UK, dealing with knife crime and self-harm, but mostly sharing the Gospel and they were seeing phenomenal results. The rest of the time they were travelling the world performing to growing audiences and as they'd dipped their toe into main stream music, in an attempt to get in front of young people who would not ordinarily be exposed to the Gospel or know they had a real hope and a future, incredible opportunities had been opening up.

I read an article once, in which a mother had said something about raising her girls to think they breathe fire. I didn't fully resonate with the entire article, but boy do I love the sentiment of the statement she was making. My girls breathe the fire of Heaven. They know it and they live it and God has ridiculously blessed and anointed it.

The band had just been asked to support a top R&B artist on their European tour the following year, something unheard of for Christian musicians. Not only that, but in an unexpected show of heavenly favour, TFBB's boy, who was also a gifted singer and musician working in a different field, was invited to replace a member of the band who was leaving. God was certainly stretching out the ropes of our tent in every direction, as my precious seed began to conquer nations and revitalize desolate cities.

And spiritually, God continued to grow me at pace.

My upper room as I came to call it – my little 3rd floor bedsit where I lived a strange sort of isolated existence four nights a week, became my inner chamber. There was a skylight directly over my bed and on clear nights I could lie and watch the stars. At the level I was working, nearly all my work colleagues escaped the city most nights. Few people remained in town, so there wasn't the busy social life you might imagine. Plus, I

Because I'd done the ground work with God, I was able to confidently unleash His power with all the sass of a **royal daughter** strutting her stuff, knowing she was completely backed up by the might of a king and His armies. And that ignited boldness. It became a joyous daily routine.

worked long hours and often till late, sometimes going out and grabbing food from the many amazing eateries and bringing it back into the office. Then I'd make the 20–30-minute journey home when the tube was quieter.

From the tube, I'd have a fifteen minute walk back to my house, where I'd usually have a brief catch up with my landlady in the hallway or kitchen on how each of our days had gone – she'd tell me off for working to late and I'd giggle, then I'd climb the two steep sets of stairs up to my *quiet place*. The route back to the house involved walking through an unusually long tunnel, which crossed underneath the main London circular road and a motorway. It was the only real scary part of my journey, especially if I was late.

The walls were decorated with brightly coloured tiles and there was some low lighting, yet, for a country girl, this was the type of tunnel you'd see in movies, where dark deeds took place. Where some unsuspecting person made it halfway through, as evildoers up to no good and accompanied by a dramatic overture, blocked the exits, entrapping their victim. I was never really worried in the mornings, as it was light with lots more people around on their way to the tube, but at night it was pretty daunting.

At first, in the evenings as I approach the steps that led down towards the entrance I'd begin to pray and cover myself. As time passed, I began to cover the tunnel and everyone that might walk through it in the future. I would claim it as a safe place for people to walk through, binding up any evil intent. I had a realization that as I did this I was walking in purpose. It was so energizing. Because I'd done the ground work with God, understanding who I was *really* and the unique ways He used me; I was able to confidently unleash His power with all the sass of a royal daughter strutting her stuff, knowing she was completely backed up by the might of a king and His armies. And that ignited boldness. It became a joyous daily routine – I'd see the steps and out would come my sword, as me and my Dad slayed every dragon in that tunnel.

And after we'd fought the good fight, I'd make my way back home, unlock someone else's front door, shout 'Hi' and make my way up the stairs, dropping my bag on the flood, kicking off my shoes and flicking on the kettle, before flopping on the bed and exhaling the day.

On one such night I had a Vision.

THE SECRET PLACE

†

I was in my bedsit, but I was aware that this room was actually part of the inner palace of the invisible Kingdom of Heaven here on earth. Inside the Kingdom's walls. In the middle of the room was a set of ladders that went up through an opening in heaven, into the throne room, where I saw a cupboard full of wrapped parcels which I knew were all the gifts of heaven that are available to us and as I watched I could see myself going up and down the ladder, walking over to the cupboard and taking from it the gifts I needed for whoever I happened to be praying for. Popping them under my arm, I'd totter back down the ladder to deliver them. I'd pick up a gift-wrapped *healing*, or a gift-wrapped *peace* etc. and off I'd go.

I had this absolute clarity that I was *of* the kingdom, but that every day I went out through the fortified doors into the daily 'earth' world, returning back each night to the inner sanctum. I was always royal and here, in this inner place, I had privileged access to all areas; *but* I wasn't designed to live inside these walls exclusively. I had to step outside every day - still maintaining my *royalness*, yet being part of the world I was born to live in.

†

The frequent appearance of ladders in my dreams and visions hadn't escaped my attention and I knew they were scripturally and spiritually significant for many different reasons.

It was a year of immeasurable favour. As well as all the spiritual and emotional prospering, financially the storehouses of heaven seemed to endlessly pour out over me. He was taking such good care of me and it felt so undeserved. And as an unexpected event triggered the beginning of the end to this season in London, God was about delight me by fulfilling a lifelong dream.

My Mum who was now in her 80s got sick and it was uncertain how it would materialise. Up to this point she had been very active and well and so my commuting nomadic lifestyle had worked well. In London I spoke to her every morning and evening, then at weekends I would visit and sort out anything she needed. Both my big sis and little sis lived out in the States and so I was the only one who was local. Mum was fiercely independent, meaning it wasn't particularly a hands-on kind of looking after, but since my dad had died almost thirty years earlier, I'd taken care of all her practical utility/administrative/paper-work type things.

I'd been doing these things at weekends for the last year, but now, the uncertainty about her health brought a new tension and conflict in me. London felt like it was too far away should she need me urgently and such was the level of my role, that I didn't feel comfortable professionally operating under such uncertainty and conflicting needs and responsi-bilities. Not bringing my all and my best had never been an option for me. I'm an *all or nothing* kind of gal. I did consider working remotely from the North West for the bulk of the week, but the job I did required leading and attending meeting across multiple London sites and deep down I realised that just wouldn't work. So, with some reluctance, but also with a certain knowing that it was perhaps time, I handed in my notice. Just like my little apartment, it would be almost one year to the day by the time I said my final goodbyes, three months later.

As the countdown began, a fresh idea invaded into my thoughts. My whole life I had dreamt of having a place in the sun and with all the tribulation and struggles and exploits of the previous few years I longed to create a little sanctuary somewhere hot, where we could go as a family, hang out and eat good food and just have fun together.

I had some money that had just been made available to me, plus I had saved money from working. With my gang mostly working in the charity space, having a family holiday home would remove the worry of paying for expensive holidays, especially when grandchildren came along. I could see us all sitting around a pool together, with a glass of rose' or a cute fruit cocktail. Someone floating lazily around the water on an inflatable sun lounger, reading a great book. There'd be a little tiki hut and a few palm trees decorating the backdrop, providing shade in the height of the afternoon sun. And laughter, lots and lots of laughter, late into the evening.

I also imagined a place I could renovate and put my own stamp on, making it super special, almost like a Beach Club/Spa vibe that would bless friends and family. I knew God had given me a gift of being able to create inspiring spaces and environments and I dreamt of creating a tropical paradise where people could kick off their shoes, throw down their bags, pull out their sunnies and straw hat and just be.

But where to start?

I was on the train heading back into London one Monday night in February and I decided out of the blue I'd email **A Place in The Sun** TV show with a comprehensive list of what I was looking for. I googled the email address and although I knew they got 1000's of applications, there was no harm in giving it a go. I knew my big girl would be up for going on the show with me if we happened to get picked, so I attached a handful of photos to my email and pressed send.

Moment of Impact

And then I carried on with the rest of my journey. The next morning at 9.30am I was sitting at my desk when my mobile rang; 'Hello,' the voice on the other end of the phone went, 'this is one of the producers from A Place in The Sun, do you have a moment to chat about your email?' My heart pounded, how could this even be possible, it was barely 12 hours since I'd sent the email. I hadn't even used their official application form; I'd just rambled on *Cath style* and sent some old photos? This isn't how these things work. Not only that, having established what we were looking for and where, they told me that they had a film crew going out to Spain in three weeks' time and "would we like to screen-test tomorrow afternoon in our studios just outside London to see if we might be a good fit?"

My big girl would have to be present and if we passed that screen-test and the producers liked the look of us they would then need to send the film crew to my house in Lancashire that Sunday to do a further *at home* shooting and then, if that was approved, we would be on a plane two weeks later to look for our dream house and film our episode of A Place in The Sun. I was stunned. My tummy was doing summersaults and a giddiness was welling up inside of me, as I reminded myself that all of this could fall flat if my big girl wasn't able to make the screen-test the following day. Let me just show you how our amazing God works for good. My big girl was working in a school with the band just on the outskirts of London that week. She was actually meant to be running a youth evening for some of the girls at the same time, but moving that around would be pretty simple, so she could hop on a train in time, do the screen-test with me, we could then enjoy a lovely meal together before both jumping back on our respective trains to *business as usual*. Isn't He just spectacular and clever.

So that's what we did. And for whatever reason, they loved us. And after following us back north that weekend and filming the second part of our screen-test in my little Lancashire home, they still seemed to love us. And so, a mere three weeks from impulsively sending a random email, overflowing with VERY specific requirements, to a TV production company *just to see*, we found ourselves on a flight to Almeria, Spain like two animated school girls, wondering what the week ahead would hold.

I knew exactly what I wanted. I wanted something that was quite modern in structure, a square building with a contemporary feel. I wanted a detached house with its own pool and I wanted all white. I would turn it into a Balinese paradise, bringing an Ibizan chill-out vibe to the décor. Close to the sea is always nice, but I didn't want anything in a touristy, built-up area. Someone I worked with had recommended Almeria to me for its natural coastlines and desert-like climate, so I was satisfied we were looking in the right location. In the beginning I'd been pretty clear that I didn't want a major renovation project - I would be out in Spain working alone and I wouldn't have access to tradesmen, but I was keen to put my own stamp on it.

We had the most amazing week. The film crew and presenter were amazing and the whole process was such great fun. And none of it felt awkward. And best of all, we found our place. It was as if it had been lifted straight off the pages of my email. It was inland, in a small Spanish village, with a 360-degree mountain view. It was a large detached house on a fabulous plot with a fantastic pool. It had two huge palm trees standing proud and a massive roof terrace where you could watch the sun rise and later, watch it set.

At the front of the house stood two lemon trees dripping with fruit and between them was a delicious heavily laden orange tree. As the world's most expert orange peeler (a skill I have so far not yet mentioned, nor bragged about, but one for which all who know me will vouch); that sealed the deal. The orange tree I took as God's nod, to say 'this is the one Catkins.' And even better, it was way below my budget.

What this house was not, was white, nor was it in need of *just* TLC. The owner had hardly used it since it had been built 10 years earlier. Almeria is Europe's only desert, in fact many of the old Cowboy and Indian movies of the 1940/50s were filmed there and unmaintained houses, closed up for extended periods did not cope well with the blistering heat and humidity, the heavy winds and pounding rainfall that came infrequently, but ferociously.

Everything about the inside was dated and unloved. The kitchen needed updating, the bathrooms definitely needed replacing, as did the floors and everywhere was in need of a general refresh and love. Outside the house was a nice shade of yellowy/mustard and drooping from the two large palm trees were several seasons of melancholy shrivelled brown leaves that had long since perished. Many of the plants were over grown and the pool was not quite the same shade of turquoise from those 1980 Wham videos. However, there was so much potential.

The shape of the building was square and contemporary just as I'd imagined and so much bigger than I'd dared to dream. The space inside was light and bright and completely open plan. The kitchen area was huge too and my mind was already in overdrive thinking of all the things I could do with it. The earlier reluctance to take on a big renovation project quickly became a distant memory - I knew this was the one and I knew bringing this house back to life and blessing the sock of my family and friends would bring me joy beyond measure. And later, as we sat having lunch with the film crew, me mesmerising them all with my world-class orange peeling talents (using the exquisitely sweet and juicy orange that one of them had plucked for me as we'd left the property), I let them know that we'd just found my dream place in the sun – of that I was absolutely certain.

I was also certain that this miracle in the midst of uncertainty, this answer to nearly fifty years of wild imaginings and hope, was yet more evidence of the goodness of my Dad – my Father - not that I needed evidence; but can't deny, *renovation Spain* was fast becoming my *favouritest* adventure *EVER* ☺

And in true *Cath* style (when you know, you know), before the week was out, I'd negotiated and bought **el asilo** as I went on to call it; *shelter, refuge, sanctuary, haven.*

As I completed my last few months in London, I *to'd* and *fro'd* between my Spanish solicitor and surveyor, as all the legal work was undertaken and *I,* filled my head (and reams of notebooks) with plans and designs for the summer. It was going to be the most amazing summer ever and I could not comprehend how blessed I'd been. I printed the words to *Club Tropicana* and framed them, the anthem had always been a part of our family vacations and now we were going to have our own Club Trop paradise. But this house was going to be so much more than a personal holiday home, I wasn't completely certain yet, but I knew God would use me to bless others through this place. In some ways I should have been worried that I was walking away from a good

This house was going to be so much more than a personal holiday home, I wasn't completely certain yet, but I knew God would use me to **bless others through this place.**

salary to zero, but I wasn't – God had always taken care of me and I knew His hand was on this as it had been with everything else. I should have also been worried that I was singlehandedly taking on a major renovation project in a foreign country where I didn't know anyone and the only word I could speak was 'Hola', but I wasn't. In fact, by the time my days in London drew to an end I had already amassed a vast array of tools, furniture, half a DIY store, cutlery, crockery, curtains and bedding, juicers... really just about everything I could possibly need for a fully functioning luxury retreat in the sun, including a bulk supply of flip flops and pool towels for all the guests I imagined hosting there.

My vision was that people would travel light, that everything they might need for a relaxing and restoring break would be found in *Casa Cath* and that 'everything' was currently bubble wrapped, boxed and precariously stacked in my garage awaiting collection by a great little local Spanish removal firm I'd discovered. I'd cleverly coordinated delivery on the other side with the week I would be over signing contracts and picking up keys, and waiting for that week to arrive was agonizing.

Almeria, Spain

But finally, here it was. As I sat with my Mum outside on the pavement of a small Spanish café, the early morning Spanish sunshine casting its light across our faces, I stared down at the contract lying in the middle of the rusting table; two *café con leche* either side, the keys to el asilo resting on top; I looked at my Mum in wonder and grinned "eeeek, I did it Mum, I own a house in Spain, no going back now." Not that I wanted to, but this was BIG. I took a quick picture of the table - I had been dreaming of this moment for what seemed like forever and I wanted to capture its gloriousness.

"Shall we go?" I said, finishing up the last dregs of the coffee, pushing out the small metal chair from underneath me and scooping up the precious documents and keys.

Pushing the fob into the ignition of the hire car whilst tuning in the radio to Spectrum FM, I tapped the address into Google Maps, handed the phone to my Mum and began my summer of adventure.

The first week was all about clearing out, ripping out and *sussing* out. I was flying back home in a week with Mum then I would come back on my own to begin the real work. H had planned to come over quite soon for a sneaky peek which I was super excited about. We would have a girlie few days and I would show her round the area; some light relief from all the work; but also, she was going to help me prayer walk and dedicate the land and the house - the thought of having my first guest was thrilling, though I'd warned her there would be dust. I'd planned to pull out the kitchen and all the flooring and I was counting on finding good people to help with the bigger jobs. The whole house needed painting inside and out to get that sparkling white vibe that I wanted, but the dirty work had to be done first.

That proved to be a much bigger job than I'd anticipated. Strangely, it seems it's quite normal to simply lock up and walk away from a house when you sell in Spain, taking only that which is precious. As I turned the key in the door of my Spanish dream home, I was catapulted into Miss Haversham's house in Charles Dicken's Great Expectations. The cupboards and fridge were all full of food and drink and pots and pans, the wardrobes and drawers in all of the bedrooms were full of clothing and toys and DVDs. The beds were still made and everything had a layer of dust and grease – I was dumbfounded.

I arranged them lovingly until I could once again **see in faith**, that which did not in any way shape or form exist in the present - it gave me back my sense of **purpose**. It reminded me of my goal and it gave me a tiny peek of **what *would* be**. Here in the middle of all the mess and rubbish I got a glimpse of the future I was creating and I was reminded how extraordinary it was going to be.

That week Mum and I all but killed ourselves bagging everything up, lugging it down to the municipal garbage containers, then scrubbing till our fingers bled. There were moments, I have to admit, where the dream became a little tarnished and a few tears threatened to push through my exhausted eyelids. I was passionate and a hard worker and very used to building dirt, but this was not building dirt, this was the leftovers of a family's entire Spanish life and we had the job of disposing of it, before we could even begin to do any of the other things I'd planned so meticulously for that week. On day four, in a defiant show of *I will not be beaten*, I ripped open one of the packing boxes that had now been delivered from the UK, delving into the treasure trove of cute ornaments and retrieving victoriously a few rare and beautiful finds. Clearing a space on the now sparkling kitchen worktop and hob I arranged them lovingly until I could once again see in faith, that which did not in any way shape or form exist in the present.

This was far from practical, but it was a very *Cath* thing to do and it gave me back my sense of purpose. It reminded me of my goal and it gave me a tiny peek of what *would* be. Here in the middle of all the mess and rubbish I got a glimpse of the future I was creating and I was reminded how *extra-ordinary* it was going to be.

By the last day, worn out, cracked hands, aching backs - but blooming proud of all we'd achieved, Mum and I sat in the dark with our feet in the pool, the lights below the water's surface turning the ripples into a kaleidoscope of turquoise, white and baby blue, the tall palm tree fluttering in the gentle, but warm evening breeze – It was hard to comprehend that all this

Sitting here in my dirty clothes, under the starry Andalusian night sky, my feet floating in the tepid water of my own pool, I could not fathom the **indescribable blessing and inexpressible Grace of God**.

was mine. I knew it was, I'd signed the paperwork and taken possession of the keys, but sitting here in my dirty clothes under the starry Andalusian night sky, my feet floating in the tepid water of my own pool, I could not fathom the indescribable blessing and inexpressible Grace of God.

"It's beautiful, isn't it?" Mum reflected as she sat in the dark in her nightdress. I'd had to persuade her to come down and sit with me. She didn't swim, but she loved to put her feet into the water from a safe place.

I inhaled deeply, "It is - Aren't we lucky?" The words floated out, resting on my breath as I exhaled sensuously, echoing her sentiment and soaking it all up. It *was* indeed beautiful; the night, the house, the teamwork, the enchantment of the floodlit water cooling our hot and dirty feet, the sound of hundreds of male crickets rubbing their wings together hoping to win the girl - the *once in a lifetime* moment; it was all so incredibly beautiful.

"I dare you." she chuckled looking in my direction mischievously, "I dare you to jump in." Perhaps it was the exhaustion or simply the magic of the moment, but in I went without hesitation, fully clothed I swam up and down my own pool like an excited teenager high on life.

That summer I worked my socks off. God really did bless me with some amazing neighbours, practical and knowledgeable help and great ongoing contacts. I found a huge store which sold just about everything and virtually set up camp inside. I got to know the area well as I drove around the small villages and down to the coast and joy flooded my soul. Day by day, project by project, I was breathing life back into the villa and it was becoming all that I had imagined and more. And always, as I worked day and night, to complete what seemed a near impossible task in the timeframes I'd given myself, my eyes were fixed on a specific date. It had to be spectacular for them.

It simply had to be...

Yes, originally this had been *my* dream. Since I was a little girl day-dreaming on a swing at the bottom of my garden I had pictured this and in His goodness my lovely precious Father had made it happen; yet now, most of all, I discovered I wanted it for them. I was merely a custodian, I understood that and I would try to pay it forward as I was prompted. But for now, right here in the summer of adventure, as I worked like a crazy women to trasform a tired and unloved house into a tranquil oasis of peace and restoration, into a happy family *home;* in my heart I wanted it for THEM. I wanted *them* to be proud, to be wowed, I wanted them to be blessed, I wanted them to also be blown away by how their Father had showered them, showered us, with such unmeritted favour.

I left the large gate open for them as I'd prepared a platter of olives and salamis and cheese. It was late, so they wouldn't get the full wow of this place until morning, but still I was giddy with excitement for their arrival.

And as I heard the sound of their hire car pull on to the gravel, my joy was complete.

My girls, my boys, were home.

Y'shua

I see your conflicts precious one. And I see how tired you are behind that big smile. You don't have to keep so busy. And you don't have to carry the weight of others on your shoulders. Come and lay it all down and be with me in the place I have provided for us and rest a while.

How I delight in you Hephzibah, my beloved bride, who's heart is like a resplendent jewel, radiating in all its brilliance. Yet, still so carefully protective of the piercings that linger there. I see how you catch your breath in private, when something jolts it unexpectedly – I am there with you Beloved. Hear my promise, Beulah, no one will ever again call you forsaken or deserted, because they will see how I delight in you and how I care for you and your home and your girls. They will see that I have taken possession of you and your family as my own and I will give you a new name that you have never had before.

People will seek you out, for what is buried in your heart. I too will bring you before great men.

And I will pour my spirit upon your seed and my blessing on your offspring. I will multiply your seed for my Kingdom's purpose and they shall have nothing to fear from their enemies. They will be strong and mighty and through them nations will be blessed - because you have listened to me and you have known me well and because you have brought them before me and battled for all of them who will be your generations to come...

Rasha'

Not so quick Y'shua...see how her heavy head droops on the side of her bed. I have her shackled. Blind to the fact that the weight she naively and virtuously bares for them belongs to you. It's crippling her, yet she persists. How do you propose to unfetter such a noble yoke ? (roars with laughter).

Ora

(raises head smiling victoriously) **AMEN.**

Rise up in splendour and be radiant, for your light has dawned, and Yahweh's glory now streams from you. Look carefully. Darkness blankets the earth, and thick gloom covers the nations, but Yahweh arises upon you and the brightness of his glory appears over you.

Nations will be attracted to your radiant light and kings to the sunrise-glory of your new day.

Isaiah 60:1-3TPT

14

Hephzibah

A familiar light spread out from her and the whole world seemed to
open up and change into a rainbow of beautiful bright hues. After
the darkness of winter, it suddenly felt good to be alive.
The day seemed warm and inviting, as if anything was possible.
Hope danced on her windowsill,
as promise teased open the curtains; reminding her that there were
no longer any limits.
Everywhere she looked goodness and loveliness reverberated
from the faces of passers by and just like that,
she realised she no longer felt alone or afraid,

C.S.

As autumn arrived, I started to feel the draw of writing again. Though
logically it made more sense to start looking for work, now that the first
phase of the villa renovation was complete, I couldn't get this niggle out
of my head that it was time to pick my pen back up. I'd planned a short
five-day trip back to Spain with H to close up the house for winter and
we'd agreed we would spend some time whilst we were there praying
into the following year and where God was directing each of us. We
were both serving at a church conference the last week of October and
would fly out the day after it ended.

For early November, the weather was beautiful – there were some wild
windy days but that was just Almeria and in the shade the sun was
still super-hot. We had a blessed time just relaxing and chatting about

the outrageousness and wonder of the last year, in awe of our good fortune, to be there in our very own villa in the sun and we celebrated together how far we'd come over the past few years. As much as she'd walked shoulder to shoulder with me through the dry and desolate places I'd had to travel, she too had been dealing with some things of her own and through the gift of our friendship and sisterhood, God had brought us both a really long way.

I was still unsure how God planned to fully redeem my story and who that would involve; if indeed it would involve anyone other than me & my Father? I could not deny that the landscape was unrecognisable (in a good way) from where I'd stood only three years earlier, yet there remained some unanswered prayers that, for whatever reason, I was still not able to lay down. I wasn't sure whether this was stubbornness or even arrogance on my part, or whether it was, as I'd believed all along, the intercessory anointing that God had placed inside of me? Whilst I consider myself to be more of a watchman, I also know there is a fierce and bold intercessor lurking, which rises up whenever I sense injustice.

Intercessors are bridge builders; they become the bridge between where a person is and where God is calling them to be. They stand in the breach, believing in others when often they're not able to believe in themselves, when those around them have given up or walked away, when things have been a certain way for so long it's simply accepted that change could never happen. Intercessors believe in the unimaginable, the impossible – indeed, that's what we count on. We don't limit God by what we see, by past experiences, by human understanding and formulas; we allow God to be as creative with others as He's been with us. Sometimes it feels (as it did then for me) as if you're carrying their burdens/ their sins/their wounding's on your own back; with some kind of holy anger you run ahead, clearing the ground, declaring war on it, speaking to the root of it, obstinately refusing to put it down until it manifests into that which your heart imagines - even though your eyes do not see. And over time that can be exhausting.

I questioned God often, desperately wanting to get this right – I knew I had been standing in faith; it really was what I believed I should be doing, but I was tired and, in all honesty, ready to put some stuff down. Deep inside, however, I continued to carry this fear of disappointing God. That good girl wasn't letting go easily...

As H and I talked about my book and how it had been shaping up and what I should do next I had a bit of a lightbulb moment. Directly before going to London, I had been running a small life group for some of our older teenage girls. I'd been really keen to help them establish properly who God created them to be; helping them to see who He *didn't* create them to be, peeling back the layers of lies and expectation, the smoke and mirrors and the daily comparisons that seemed to engulf this vulnerable generation - exposing and celebrating all that was unique and exquisite about each and every one of them. Giving them permission to verbalise what made them come alive, what they dreamed about when they led alone in bed, in the quiet of the night, what day to day things conflicted deep inside with who they felt they were, and we had fun calling out all the things we just didn't feel we were great at or simply didn't enjoy, giving ourselves permission to let them go and to stop pretending or agonising over them. It had been such a precious and revelatory time and I remember feeling frustrated and sad that so many people either, never get to do this work of discovery, or leave it so late that most of their life feels burdensome and unfulfilled as they masquerade their way through their own story.

I began to see a parallel between this work and the ways that my own story and book had been unfolding. As much as I had been convinced when I committed the first words to paper that this was going to be a supernatural love story (which it was/is on so many levels), as I lived out the journey in real time, piece by piece God had been revealing *me*. Not me as part of something else, but me as ME. As I've already said, I have always been pretty comfortable in my own skin and with who I am, enthusiastically embracing those personality assessments that dissect you and nuzzle into the murky detail, consistently desiring to build on and improve who I am and get to know myself even better. Yet God had been doing a much deeper work and reveal in me of late than I ever could have done on my own, even in a thousand lifetimes. He had walked me through a process that had left me convinced I finally knew who I was created to be. Like really. And such was the clarity, that I was now brave and bold enough to call it out.

"You're so good at this stuff Cath," H said as we lay and prayed on two sun loungers that we'd dragged up onto, what I'd termed *my reading terrace*. Stepping straight out of the back door, sheltered from any wind and under the shade of the majestic palm tree that stood tall for the whole village to admire, from day one this space had the presence of God all over it. I'd furnished it with a big comfy sofa, a faded linen covered rocking chair, a small coffee table and a small wooden book trolley and I imagined (hoped) every visitor to the villa would be drawn to its allure, just as I had been, *always was*, to soak in its peace, its restorative qualities and perhaps I hoped, meet with Him?

"You've made me believe things about myself, I never would have ordinarily," she said, "you've made me believe anything is possible, because *you* believe anything is possible – and I've seen it happen. I think your book could really help so many others."

I'd been struggling where to take the book. I was getting all these feelings to pick it back up, but I still didn't have an ending and let's face it, it's pretty hard to gather pace in a story when you've no idea about the direction of travel. Deep down I knew this book was important. In fact, the week before we came away someone from church had come to me and said 'There is something in you that God wants to get out for the benefit of others.' And I felt it too, I just wasn't sure what all that was going to look like. Each January our church undertook a twenty-one-day prayer and fast period and every year it seemed like God showed up and revealed something profound to me, so I'd already made my mind up that I would see what happened during that time and from there, decide on writing V real work. And if my book came out on top, then I was trusting that I'd also get a sense of where I needed to go with it?

On the last day as we were packing up, I was in the kitchen and God spoke to me. He said "Prepare for the King." – I was taken aback and shared with H. Immediately I was transported to Esther and how she spent twelve months preparing herself to be presented to King Ahasuerus and so I took it to mean that God was saying prepare for something to come my way in twelve months' time. But it turned out that I wouldn't have that long to wait.

Back home, with the house in Spain all safely packed away for the winter months, I began to prepare for Christmas. My first gift arrived early. My big girl had called to say she'd be dropping in for a quick visit – she was over my way doing something and would pop in to say 'Hi' before heading home. "I've got you a little gift," she smiled as she pulled herself up on one of the kitchen bar stools. I was touched. "That's so lovely of you," I smiled, taking the pretty bag from her and placing it on the table. She smiled back giving nothing away, as I carefully pulled open the ribbon that was holding the handles on the bag together, cautiously removing the crumpled tissue paper on top. As I reached in and began to lift out the gift inside the realisation of what I was holding caught me off-guard. I gasped for breath, turning to look at her in disbelief. There, between my thumb and my two forefingers was the sweetest and softest white and grey baby grow.

My baby was having a baby. Inside of her a seed was growing that had once been inside of me. The miracle of life is so mind-blowing. Usually so intuitive, I had not seen this one coming and within seconds the tears were flowing as I laid hands on her tummy and then tightly around her, covering and speaking life into this precious growing baby, seeking new Momma and Daddy gifts and graces for her and her boy. And more than anything else, thanking God for His crazy favour, yet again, to our little family unit.

It was a strange moment for me, that brought a barrage of mixed emotions. Of course, I was beyond ecstatic, but with my own life so upside down, there was this niggle that said, *how can you become a Nannie when you've not even got your own life figured out yet? (and when there's no Grandad...)*

Hmmm are you recognising that old boring predictable voice?

I knew that was nonsense of course and I quashed it quickly, but what I wasn't as certain of as we stood in a holy embrace, tears of joy and amazement running down both our faces onto each other's shoulders, was how this was going to change the dynamics of a three-way relationship on which the bedrock of my life for so long had stood – it had always been the three of us #original3; Momma Cath and her two girls. That supernatural bond was almost tangible and even as they married, there remained an undeniable knowing. It never interfered with anything, it never demanded anything from one another, it was just there when needed, but now there would be another layer and I wasn't sure if I was ready just yet to say goodbye to *us?*

"God's given me a word over my baby Mum," she whispered smiling, stroking her hand gently across her tiny bump, as I finally let her go.

"Victorious... He said he or she will be Victorious, Momma."

Her seed, my seed would be victorious. How wonderful that He was confirming to her, all that He has promised to me so many times.

Her seed, my seed would be **victorious**. How wonderful that He was confirming to her, all that He has promised to me so many times.

Jerusalem will be rebuilt, and its palace restored.

The people who live there will sing praise;

they will shout for joy.

By my blessing they will increase in numbers; my

blessing will bring them honour.

I will restore the nation's ancient power and establish it

firmly again.

Jeremiah 30:18-20 GNT

...I will pour my spirit upon your seed, and my blessing

upon your offspring.

Isaiah 44:3 NKJV

It was a wonderful moment, and I couldn't wait to see her bloom over the following seven months.

Though.... none of us could have ever imagined how those seven months would unfold.

The following week our church had its last ladies gathering of the year. As I'd arrived in the meeting, I'd felt a heaviness in the room and all through the service I'd felt as though I was holding up a heavy covering of something invisible. At the end of the meeting one of the ladies who I knew well and trusted came to me and said that throughout the meeting she'd been standing at the back and had seen a bright beam of light coming down over me during the service, as I'd worshiped. I didn't know what to do with that information, but I thanked her and left.

Christmas came and went and fairly certain that I was going to start writing again in the New Year, I'd purchased a highly recommended book on Discernment by Jane Hamon to study during our 3-week fast period and I was feeling expectant.

Within a day of the first week, things began to happen.

The first thing was a direct approach by a Professional Recruitment Agency asking if I'd be willing to meet with the Chair of a large Christian well known charity with a view to sitting on their board. They were looking for someone with a strong banking background who was a committed Christian and having reviewed my profile on LinkedIn, felt I'd be a great fit. Initially I was incredibly flattered and a little shocked that I would be counted worthy of such a significant role. I knew I could bring something to the table, despite feeling just as equally inadequate; though my curiosity (and yes, I must admit a tiny bit of ego too) remained rather excited throughout several subsequent exploratory conversations.

The role, whilst not a full-time, was London based and would require a good amount of commitment and input from me and in the end, as much as I liked the concept, I could not shake this feeling that right now God was calling me to finish my book. I knew full well that this could be an amazing opportunity from God, but I was also acutely aware that it could also be a rigged diversion/distraction; a carrot dangled by the opposing side, trying to draw me away onto a different path? Distinguishing (discerning) between the two is not always easy. Quite ironic that the book I was studying covered that very subject matter.

Knowing myself as I did, however, I was sure of one thing - the two simply couldn't and wouldn't coexist harmoniously; remember, I'm that *all in* girl – when those fireworks start, they fill every part of the gray and white matter of my brain. The book was going to require all of me - all of my thoughts, all of my heart, all of my energy, all of my blood, sweat and tears. And so would this position. I prayed and then I thanked them for the huge honour of being invited and shared that I believed God had different plans for me, at least for the next twelve months and I wished them well.

I had booked to fly out to Spain the 2nd week of February. I'd offered the house out to a couple of different people in March and I wanted to open it up properly, so that it was all lovely and ready for them. I was taking my Mum with me for a little break and I had decided I would begin to write as soon as I got back in early March. The baby was due at the end of April, which hopefully would afford me time to get a good chunk done amid helping my big girl with anything she needed, as she prepared for the arrival of the treasure that would be her precious bubba. She planned to work right up to the birth which bothered me, but financially she had decided it was worth the struggle, to give her more time at home with the baby afterwards.

I knew how hard those final months are and hated to think of her struggling on the morning commute into the city, jostling with the hot and crammed met, walking the long streets of the Northern Quarter to the office. But she was determined – and I had to let her make her own tough, yet wise decisions - even though I still wanted to carry every burden for her. She soon would understand the weight of a Momma's love.

She soon would understand the weight of a **Momma's love!**

By the end of the first week of prayer and fasting, the <u>Discernment</u> book I was reading had me captivated. Revelation was pouring off every page and I was soaking it up. I've already alluded to the fact that some of the big prayers I had been bringing before my Father for several years had started to feel outdated and heavy, still I had held my position, like a soldier refusing to leave his post. Fearful that the fault would be mine if the battle was eventually lost, I had wrestled between the good girl, the enemy and God for too long over the tricky questions.

As my future began to hold a certain charm again, stirring me once more to lift my head and feel the wonder of the sunlight on my face, to grow majestically towards the light; much the same way a sunflower awakens, standing upright to raise its head in unison with the rising morning sun, then holding its position as it gently follows the arc of the sun across the afternoon sky, its bloom somehow knowing without ever being told that as long as it faces the sun, as long as it continues to grow towards the light, then its energy, its vibrant yellow hue and its lofty grandeur will remain unrivalled; I knew it was time I found my peace and the truth;

Can I or can't I stop now please?

Am I going to disappoint God if I let this one go?

Will blood be on my hands if I give up too soon?

If I stop now are the agonizing hours, tears and copious prayers just wasted?

Am I still genuinely holding on in faith, or has it become a habit?

What does God want from me?

And there it was in black and white – the answer I'd been searching for – across the pages of the book now tightly gripped in my hands; the words you've already heard me use, but which I first saw on the pages of this life changing book; **FALSE RESPONSIBILITY**

Moment of Impact

For a good girl, the most liberating thing she could possibly read is that what she's been holding onto, the thing that had to some degree been keeping her in bondage, was completely wrong thinking. A misguided view on my job description V God's job description.

THE SECRET PLACE

†

"See."

He held out one of the large golden bowls in front of her. The pleasant aroma that wafted from it was intoxicating. As she arched a little closer, encouraged by His invitation, she began to hear faint

314

sounds that resembled earthly pleadings and appeals, as names and words and dates appeared to swirl effortlessly in the spicy mist that rose to fill the royal chamber. She couldn't be sure, but she thought for a brief moment that she heard an echo of her own voice amongst them?

She straightened back up, watching as He plunged His head into the mist, breathing it in for what seemed like an age to her - lost in His own divine joy.

Lowering the bowl finally, He smiled across at her; "The prayers of my saints. Not a single one lost or wasted. Each one handled with the love and faith of the heart that brought it here."

He leant down to his right and handed back the bowl.

"See," He repeated, indicating first to the twelve sitting to His right and then to the other twelve on His left. In union, the twenty-four elders held out their bowls as the room was overpowered with the same sweet ancient perfume. A great peace and knowing settled on her.

"At the right time, as these bowls fill and overflow, how I delight to pour the *very best* of heaven's answers over my children."

†

And when he had taken it, the four living creatures and

the twenty-four elders

fell down before the Lamb. Each one had a harp and

they were holding

golden bowls full of incense, which are the prayers of

God's people.

Revelation 5:8 NIV

Prayer activates heaven and faith wrestles with God on behalf of others and ourselves, but God carries the burden of responsibility for how and when the solutions are released on earth. *WE* do our bit and *HE* does all the rest, promising that every prayer is treasured, kept and answered with heaven's best, right on time.

> **Prayer activates heaven** and **faith wrestles** with God on behalf of others and ourselves, but **God carries the burden of responsibility** for how and when the solutions are released on earth.

So, there it was, my *honourable discharge* - I could pray if I felt called to, but likewise I could lay certain things down if I felt the need; either way my faith filled wrestling's with God were firmly established in the *prayers to be answered* golden bowls, that the twenty-four elders of heaven continually brought before The Lord.

For faith to breathe/ exists there has to be some element of mystery. As much as God makes some things really clear to us in scripture, there are other things we don't get to see or understand. And in that unknown space, we must not make assumptions about God to plug the gap, we must take up our shield of faith and walk blindly but confidently across the bridge of mystery, until we reach the other

> For faith to breathe/exists there has to be some element of **mystery**. As much as God makes some things really clear to us in scripture, there are other things we don't get to see or understand. And in that unknown space, we must not make assumptions about God to plug the gap, we must take up our shield of faith and walk blindly but confidently across **the bridge of mystery**, until we reach the other side, where we get to look back and see what God was up to all along.

side, where we get to look back and see what God was up to all along. We can hope of course and continue to cry out to Him, but practically our job is simply to bring it before Him in the Throne Room and trust *Him* to provide the perfect solution. All the while, allowing *ourselves* to be transformed in the process.

Do not conform yourselves to the standards of this
world, but let God transform you inwardly by a
complete change of your mind. Then you will be able to
know the will of God
--what is good and is pleasing to him and is perfect.

Romans 12:2

Look at those two words conform and transform. The enemy in the world tries to *con* us, to 'con'form us, to trick us in to thinking and acting like him. But in yielding to God's way, in walking faithfully in the mysteries of the things we just can't understand, He 'trans'forms us. The origin of the prefix 'trans' means 'across', 'beyond', 'through'; so as our Father 'trans'forms us, He is 'trans'cending' all that we're going through and have been through, changing us and growing us into something else – a new character, a new nature, a new spiritual condition - that ultimately takes us further, raises us higher, removes every ceiling/limit, surpasses in quality and eclipses and outperforms everything our mere human minds can conceive.

> The enemy in the world tries to **con** us, to *con*form us, trick us in to thinking and acting like him. But in yielding to God's way, in walking faithfully in the mysteries of the things we just can't understand, He **trans** forms us. Transcending all that we're going through and have been through.

I knew I had been travelling this journey with Him for some time now and I sensed a pivotal season was fast approaching? I had been going through a time of significant spiritual growth, where I was being randomly invited to join groups at church, based on giftings people seemed to be assuming I had. I'm not a label girl, I've always just responded to God's leading, so when someone asked me 'are you an Intercessor?' I just replied with 'I don't really know?' Of course, once I'd done a bunch of research, it became clear to me that I probably was operating in an

Intercessory annointing, but also (and more dominantly), a Watchman gifting.

The frequency of dreams and visions I was receiving was multiplying too and people at church would randomly bring me words that they felt God was speaking to me. A few people began to call me a Profit, which shook me a little and made me quite uncomfortable and I'd brush it off; but in all of this, what was clear was that God was beginning to do a new thing in me and around me and the divide between my past and my future was widening by the day. The air smelled fresher, the past, a little less raw.

Thinking back, the girls and I had been through so much together, that, on occasion, I'd wondered whether there had been some sort of curse over us. That sounds rather dramatic I realise, but life had been one heck of a ride, which as I've said before, simply didn't seem to line up with who I believed I was or how I conducted my life. With what I'd come to learn about the access satan gains via mediums, to some degree, I'd had to accept this as a real possibility - if only for a season? And perhaps not a curse as such, but through his trickery I could not deny that I had naively given him a certain amount of access to meddle. And that was on top of his standard level of interference.

The crazy wonder of all of that, though, was the fact that we had remained.... I guess I can't say untouched....'*kept*' is probably a better word. *He* had kept us magnificently and He had made it clear to me two years earlier that *He himself* had given us 'safe passage' and brought us up *His* holy mountain, to this high place, where He had lovingly pruned us and watered us and fed us and showered us with grace and favour. Restoring and then completely redeeming any lingering damaged. He had poured His treasure into us, so that we in turn could pour it out into others. The dark and damp of the valley floor seemed a million miles away.

And yet, even now, there remained just this small *tag*. It's hard to explain what it felt like, it was almost like a fine thread in an elegant garment that inconveniently catches on something sharp and pulls unexpectedly. It doesn't change the fall of the garment or even the way it looks to others, but you know it's there and as much as you try to smooth it out and blend it back in, each time you put on the garment there's a small pucker around the tag that gives it away. Well, there was a small *pucker* in me and with every step forward I took, I would frustratingly feel a small tug that had me believing I would never feel completely healed and released from all that was behind me.

I talked to H about it a lot. I genuinely wanted absolute freedom from it; to feel unrestricted in my right of passage into the future and into my true destiny – I wanted this tiresome and gruelling doubt and constant tug-of-war gone completely; no more imposters playing with my head and my heart, intersecting my progress at every opportunity; no more intermittent double mindedness.

Let's go back to the things I shared about healing not being linear. Well, healing from the trauma of divorce and loss and rejection is not only incomputable, it's also one heck of a battle, both physically, emotionally and spiritually.

The opposite of linear is deviating. The dictionary describes this word as *to turn aside, to depart from a route or course of action. To digress from a thought or reasoning.*

The thesaurus offers the following comparable words:

- **Devious** (*departing from the proper way or most direct way. shifty, crooked*)

- **Serpentine** (*snakelike, shrews, subtle, artful, crafty, cunning, sinuous*)

- **Interpose** (*to put a barrier, remark or question in the midst of a conversation or thought-to bring influence or an action on behalf of one party*)

- **Interfere** (*to come into opposition, to meddle, to strike against*).

There was no denying how far I'd come, no denying at all and it's hugely important to call that out and to celebrate it; however, bringing some objectivity and realness to the party and a businesslike assessment of what's going on in almost every journey of healing and growth (particularly when the purposes of heaven are involved); we need to go right back to the beginning and reacquaint ourselves with what (or who) we are dealing.

If you could humour me briefly, I'd like to dress our *charming* satan, our **Master Marketer**, in a slick, expensive *Armani* suit and sit him where he likes to be, at the head of a prestigious board room table and explain the dynamics of strategic marketing from a corporate perspective.

The role, and ultimate skill, of the strategic marketer is (or at least should be) one of the most material/influential roles in any board room.

MARKET DOMINATION (growth) as appose to **STRATEGIC WEAR-OUT** *(irrelevance)* completely hinges on how effectively the strategic marketer:

▸ Understands the overall **CORPORATE OBJECTIVES**

▸ Identifies and segments their TARGET MARKET (*potential new clients*)

▸ Gathers **EXHAUSTIVE INSIGHT** on those clients to get underneath who they really are, what makes them tick and the inner value system that drives them

▸ Funnels down into this new treasure trove of insight, to pinpoint the **KILLER USP** (*unique selling point*); or the **VALUE HOOK** that will draws the clients to you rather than your competitors

▸ Consistently tracks **COMPETITOR ACTIVITY** to make sure they always remain one step ahead

▸ Develops a **COMPELLING PROPOSITION** (*offering*),

built around the value hook

▸ Then, at the right time and with all their available resources in place, mobilises an **AGRESSIVE CAMPAIGN** to finally win them over.

Taking your time to do this well and thoroughly will typically drive a high rate of success.

Get complacent, fail to keep abreast of the changing landscape, or underestimate your competition; and whilst you might make some short-term gains, ultimately you risk strategic wear-out and critically, market irrelevance.

Of course, satan knows his competition well; heck, he used to work for them, so he already has insider info. Not too happy about being fired, he's now out to build his own empire, bigger, greater, more impressive than his old boss; with a strategy focused on plundering their people - you and I are his target market. Visualise an ambitious young exec - doesn't sleep much, phone on 24/7, continually monitoring the market to gather every snippet of information; schmoozing useful key players; muscling in on conversations, snooping through old records, hungry for that *big picture view*.

That little black box on the fifth shelf, the one with our name on the lid, is the key reason he continues to strut around over confidently, because, despite our changing landscape and our brave and victorious progress, he thinks getting a high ROI (*return on investment*) from his next targeted campaign towards '*us*', will still be a piece of cake.

COMMAND HQ

There it is he sniggers, as he cruelly takes hold of the small thread again. He watched her smooth it out last time, hoping no one had noticed her flaw. He had to admit, Y'shua had been doing an impressive job with her. He had been certain the tasks he set his minions would have crushed her spirit by now. No matter, he had enough material to keep tugging until she gave up. And what a blinder she'd played for him, storing his wizardry in her own house. He let out a chilling holler. Darn it, he snarled, he would get her eventually, after all the work he'd put in, however long it took.

Out of the box he lifted **REMEMBER, UPHOLD, RESILIANCE, ENDURE, FORTITUDE, TOLERANCE, CONSESSION, GRIT, GOOD GIRL**

He was pleased with his choice – he knew she would consider these to be strengths; it was why he enjoyed this game so much, why his double-dealing always worked so well.

One by one he threaded them onto the strand and then, with one huge and by now irritated yank, he went to work.

So skilful is he at knowing how and when to tug that thread, that if we're not tuned in, he will hold us in a place where confusion and just enough uncertainty and longing will drag us back, slow us down, tire us out, disturb old wounds, immortalise the familiar in our memory-bank and our hearts, suppress hope and in time, paralyse us. I can't stress enough how incredibly important it is for us to understand this and to exercise and stretch our *discernment muscle as we begin to walk in purpose.*

> *But solid food is for the mature, whose spiritual*
> *senses perceive heavenly matters. And they have*
> *been adequately trained by what they've experienced*
> *to emerge with understanding (discernment) of the*
> *difference between what is truly excellent and what is*
> *evil and harmful.*
>
> **Hebrews 5:14 TPT**

322

As I prepared for bed on that Friday evening, the end of my first full week of prayer, I had no inkling of how God was about to spectacularly expose and loosen my own hidden thread. That's how He works, how faith works – we never know when and how He will move on our behalf - we just know He will.

That's how He works, how faith works – we never know when and how **He will move on our behalf** - we just know He will.

I'd decided to read in bed that night, which was unusual for me, but I was enjoying the book and thought it would be cosier snuggled up inside my big duvet. I'd put some nice oils in the bedroom diffuser earlier in the evening, filling the room with the aroma of bergamot, ylang ylang, lavender and vetiver, whilst I took a long soak in the bath surrounded by candles and soft music. Feeling very relaxed and sleepy I wandered barefoot across my velvety bedroom carpet, flicking on the reading lamp as I climbed up and nestled under the quilt, pushing two oversized pillows behind my back. I wondered how many pages I'd actually manage before my eyelids surrendered, unaware that the second wave of revelation, from that now dreary, obsolete, but unyielding episode with the spiritualist all those years ago, had been gathering pace throughout the day. And as I leant over to the bedside table to pick up my book, opening it where I had left off the night before, chapter five released its thundery and momentous roar, breaking wide open for one final and dramatic time, the dark and hidden pit of the enemy. Inescapably, just like Goliath, God had brought him out into the open, his limitations laid bare; and the day for me to take up my slingshot, move towards the now exposed target, stand shoulder to shoulder with David and slay the dragon, had dawned.

In chapter five of Jane Hamon's Discernment – The Essential Guide to Hearing the Voice of God (2019, p. 95-95), Jane describes a highly successful businessman in her church who found that, after becoming a Christian, all his business enterprises began to fail. Perplexed, Jane and her husband prayed with him and in a dream, God showed her husband a pictured of playing cards. Without going into all the detail, it turned out that as a young man this businessman had happened across a fortune teller at a funfair. It was light-hearted encounter but the fortune teller had taken a dollar bill from him, spoken some kind of spell over it, folded it up and told him that as long as he carried the dollar bill in his wallet, he would have good

Finally, just like Goliath, God had brought him **out into the open**, his limitations laid bare; and the day for me to take up my slingshot, move towards the now **exposed target**, stand shoulder to shoulder with David and **slay the dragon**, had dawned.

fortune. Without much thought or seriousness, he'd kept that folded dollar bill buried in his wallet all these years and forgotten all about it. After he'd become a Christian, it had never entered his head, yet without realising, he'd been walking around day after day carrying *mystic promises* and this was seriously hindering his walk.

Moment of Impact

As I read those words a bolt of lightning struck me – somewhere in my loft, tucked away in a cardboard box of keepsakes, I remembered the recorded transcript of mystic promises. Seductions from the depth of hell were sitting on an old tape-recording gathering dust in my loft. I had been carting them around, move after move, house after house, year after year, without any thought or awareness and I was suddenly well and truly spooked. Even for a *royal warrior princess,* who by now was getting pretty apt at wielding her sword around, this was unnerving. All I could think about in that moment was 'satan is in my loft...' He wasn't of course, never the less, I was spooked. It was late and very dark and very quiet and even though I wanted every trace of him gone pronto, I established extremely quickly that 'NO WAY' was I taking myself up into the loft tonight to deal with it. So, I put down my book, switched off my lamp and led back in deep reflection, praying and repenting, resolute that I would find it and destroy it first thing in the morning, making sure that the broken pieces ended up in the waste, as far away as possible from my house. And I meant it - Early the next morning, I yanked down my loft ladder and armed with a torch I climbed into the cold dark attic space like a woman on a mission; if it was there, I'd find it. I was cleaning up my house and I was getting that pesky devil out of my loft.

Now if you don't know me, reading all this might make you think I'm a little bit crazy, but you have to remember, the very unique and unfolding journey I'd been travelling with God on this. I believe He was growing my vision and understanding by showing me some home-truths. That, in keeping the tape originally, I'd clearly given it some coun-

> Knowing what I now did, and in the connecting of all the dots, I **could no longer label it innocent**; in fact, not sorting it out quickly would have been down right dumb.

terfeit weight or value. Unwittingly perhaps, but we can all fall prey to these types of traps and knowing what I now did, and in the connecting of all the dots, I could no longer label it innocent; in fact, not sorting it out quickly would have been down right dumb. God speaks and teaches each of us differently and this was the final piece of the whole medium/ spiritualist puzzle for me. It was giving me the complete picture, so I never had to say again 'I don't quite get it?'. And in the process, the whole sorry saga was finally and unreservedly being redeemed and released.

"Please let me find it Lord", I prayed, as every lid of every box came off. I rummaged through old photographs and medals and baby keepsakes and school tea towels with tiny painted handprints all over them, almost forgetting at times that I was up there on serious business, but it was becoming increasingly clear as I worked my way through each box that what I was looking for wasn't there.

What if I couldn't find it? I agonised, as I called out for some fatherly intervention; *I'm doing all the right things here Lord, surely you could give me a small break...* The words tumbled out pleadingly through chattering teeth, as the adrenaline that initially fuelled my eager expedition had all but retreated, leaving me suddenly aware of the freezing and cramped space around me that I was now fully persuaded to vacate. Discouragement began to raise its jeering head, stirring up an uneasiness. An uneasiness that only creeps in when we forget that, when we're about our Father's business and walking in purpose, victory is guaranteed. And just like that, I remembered the other box, the one stored in my Mums loft. I'd stuck it up there a few years earlier and had been meaning to collect it for ages – *maybe the tape was in there?* I had promised to take her out for coffee that afternoon, so I would discretely check then.

As I pushed all the ransacked boxes back into some resemblance of order, I spotted an old plastic wallet lying on the floor that I'd had for years. I'd kept a number of personal letters from my dad in it, plus some special cards and keepsakes, it had to be at least thirty years old? Switching off the torch I soppily reached over and grabbed the wallet, before scurrying down the stepladders, back into the warmth and pleasant space below.

Moment of Impact

I never tired of reading my dad's old letters to me, they never got old and reading them periodically made me feel close to him again.

But God sure does work in mysterious ways.

Having closed up the loft access and put away the ladders I placed the plastic wallet on my bed, unzipping it and pulling out its contents. The pale blue airmail envelopes addressed to me – Dafnis Street, Paleon Psyhikon, Athens, Greece - were so familiar and I ran my fingers across the name and address on the front, remembering fondly the carefree girl I had been back then. My Dad wasn't a big letter writer, which is why the letters he sent me when I was away from homein Greece that summer of discovery, so very long ago, were more precious than gold to me. He told me things in those letters – things he felt, things he saw in me, things he dreamed for me - that we'd never really talked about face to face and wouldn't do again. I lifted one up and pressed it into my cheek; I wasn't holding his letter close; I was holding him close. My biggest advocate, the one who always believed in me, who taught me I could do anything, be anything. How I wished I could hear his words of love and encouragement now.

Lost in thought momentarily, a couple of unfamiliar things that had fallen out of the folder caught my eye. Lying underneath a large faded birthday card with *Daughter* written across the front was what appeared to be a concertina'd ream of *old-school* fax paper.

First, I picked up the card and read the words from my Mum;

> *You were always such a sweet little girl, my little helper, and your questions helped me find new beauty in the world· I learned a lot from watching you· And even though I love the woman you've become; confident, talented, self-assured; sometimes I miss the little girl you once were·*

My Mum had never been one who easily expressed her feelings and I knew that who I was and had always been was quite different to who she was and at times, the freedom and unstructured way I'd lived most of my life had typically filled her with real angst - and whilst the words on the card were written by someone else, her choosing them seemed rather significant to me and it struck me how much those words focused on little Cath...

And then I reached down for the folded paper. I had promised God that when I found the tape, I would destroy it without playing it or re-checking what was on it – I would give it no regard and dispose of it as quickly as possible. So, when I opened the paper and saw what was on it, I couldn't help but wonder if satan was playing his old games with me? For, handwritten across the long script was what appeared to be notes from the session I was so sincerely trying to extinguish once and for all. I was stunned. I had no recollection, whatsoever, of ever writing anything down. Yet here, tucked away inside a small plastic wallet that I'd brought from my loft for sentimental reasons only, was an additional link to the event I was desperately trying to release to history, something I hadn't known even existed. But as my eyes traced the scribble in front of me, something in my spirit shifted and I quickly sensed that this was in fact God at work and not the trickster I'd first considered.

My lovely Father was taking care of business and of me, by making certain that nothing got left behind – I would never have hunted for something that I simply had no recollection of. But there was more. He was about to show me more, something that would consolidate an area of my unique design and purpose that he'd been drip-feeding me over the course of this *journey of discovery* and though I had no intention of reading the whole transcript, the few lines that God had used to identify for me what I was holding, were illuminating a critical word of knowledge that I was being invited to recognise, accept and own.

> *Your Dad says that when you were a little girl, there was a light in you that drew everyone to you. When you walked in a room, you lit it up. There was this aura of joy and happiness all around you.*

There was that reference to *light* again?

Somewhere, in the design phase of Cath and then in the knitting together in the depth and darkness of Mum's womb, He had woven His light into me, *on* purpose and *with* purpose, in such a way that it was visible to others. Perhaps it was more about designing the openness and curious parts of my character, that would allow *Him* to *filter through* as He set me upon my inimitable path? I won't truly know the manufacturing intricacies for sure this side of Heaven, but what I do know and now must acknowledge is that it had been there at the beginning and according to some, remained today. I've shared this important thought with people who I've worked with to help navigate this breath-taking journey towards the discovery of true purpose – We have to be courageous and open, setting aside our learned modesty and self-effacement, if we sign up to go on this voyage of discovery with Jesus.

Let me say that again...

We have to be courageous and open and set aside our learned modesty and self-effacement, if we sign up to go on this voyage of discovery with Jesus.

We have to **be courageous** and open, setting aside our **learned modesty** and self-effacement, if we sign up to go on this voyage of discovery with Jesus.

And I say this because as someone who has spent a lifetime being bound by a false sense of humility, declaring that there is a light in me that people can see would make the old Cath feel wretched; desperate to add a whole load of 'well what I mean is.... Of course, it's nothing about me...Of course I don't think I am.

And I *don't* think I'm anything, other than an evolving version of a perfect design, created with some very specific eternal tasks in mind. I'm messy, I'm flawed, I'm human, but knowing there really is and will only ever be one version of me, able to do heaven's work on earth in my own incomparable way, then surely, I owe it to myself, to those whose paths I'm sent to cross and to the one who designed me for the job; whose mark I carry and whose reputation balances on the quality, suitability and success of 'me'; to figure out my unrivalled weapons, gifts and attributes. Otherwise, I'll show up ill-considered and ill-prepared, instead of bringing my divine power. I'll show up as someone else instead of the crazy, wonderful, potential-filled me. And seriously, what's the point of that?

> I owe it to myself, to those whose path I'm sent to cross and to the one who designed me for the job; whose mark I carry and whose reputation balances on the quality, suitability and success of *me*; to figure out my **unrivalled weapons, gifts and attributes.**

Every single one of His designs is good and perfect and tested and purposed, before it's ever placed in its Momma's womb, so you need to be ready and brave enough, as you peel back those layers, to celebrate and call out the gold you're about to find, because you will find gold ....and diamonds and rubies and sapphires, in places you never imagined. This isn't about telling everyone how amazing you are, it's about identifying it and acknowledging it with your Dad and with yourself. And maybe a small group of trustworthy people, with whom you can work through what it all means and figure out what you're going to do with it.

One of the things I had to work through and ultimately park, as I pondered and reflected on this new revelation, was why; if this observation about a light in me as a little girl was spoken out through what I now understood to be a hellish channel, meaning, it must have been something that had drawn attention behind the veil; why would God let that happen? Surely, that would make me a sitting-duck, at an age where I wouldn't have the awareness, maturity or skills to protect myself? I know it sounds a funny question to deliberate, but I kept thinking about Job and how God gave satan access to him, all the while confident that Job would stay the course... and I wondered. Had that light been real and had it been there when little Cath daydreamed on her swing, barefoot in the grass, building sandcastles in the sky? Was the Holy Spirit truly with me back then, before I even knew Him or had invited him in? So many unorthodox questions were exploding uncontrollably in my wonder-filled and hungry brain.

And what did that mean in the overall plan and purpose for my life? I had so many questions, but I also had a whole load of fresh insight, which, piece by piece, were beginning to join the dots on a, thus far, incoherent understanding - divinely unveiling *me*.

I quickly tore the transcript apart and pushed the shreds into my pocket, as I grabbed my keys with the other hand and headed in the direction of my Mums.

> I had so many questions, but I also had a whole load of fresh insight, which, piece by piece, were beginning to join the dots on a, thus far, incoherent understanding - **divinely unveiling *me*.**

"I need to just get something out of your loft before we leave, Mum." I said nonchalantly as I walked through her back door and she never questioned me. It didn't take long to locate the tape and with one victorious punch in the air and a whopping sigh of relief, I pushed it into my pocket, on top of the torn shreds of paper and almost melodically chanted "come on Mum let's go and get that coffee."

Fifteen minutes later, in an out-of-town shopping complex, whilst my Mum happily browsed unaware, I slipped away to a public waste bin where I tugged, stretched and unravelled the 20-year-old tape that had sat curled around the vintage spools for far too long, until a messy mound of curly brown plastic sat in the palm of my hand. Closing my fist around it and with one last tug, both ends snapped and with a feeling of finality and relief, the irretrievable tape recording, its clear casing and all its schemes and conspiracies coasted into the trash, along with the torn-up *account* in my pocket.

As I glanced around, to regular people enjoying a regular Saturday out shopping and drinking coffee   , I couldn't help but chuckle inside, imagining what they would think of this crazy girl and her crazy exploits.

But this final act had been my graduation ceremony, the last part of my schooling. The closing of a *best forgotten* (or perhaps not) chapter and what an education it had been. I was quite sure that God would not waste it; if I was ever brave enough to document and recount my emergent journey, then maybe there would be purpose in it after all? It had been a wild ride and I was never more thankful that I'd got to journey it with Jesus as my teacher and my upholder.

I was reminded as I worked in my garage that weekend, beginning the renovation process of a dusty old and battered rocking chair that I'd sourced for my big girl to nurse and sing over and declare over and wonder over her precious first born, that we must be prepared to go through all the arduous and painstaking (and somewhat boring in my view) stripping back and sanding down of the old paint, the rooting out and replacement of any rusty screws or sub-standard framework, the careful unpicking and replacing of worn and dated fabric and inner padding; before we get to enjoy the creative delights of restoration. Not unlike that old three-wheeler bike in my dad's garage. Just like him, I loved to make beautiful things and I couldn't wait to present my girl with the finished product, which would be placed proudly in the place she'd prepared for it.

As much as all the stripping back and preparation secretly frustrated me and seemingly stole my time, I knew that nothing but the best would do for my grandchild and its Momma - this repurposed chair had to be just right. And as we choose to bravely repurpose our own life, back to its original and wonderful design, there is a Father, lovingly and patiently, stripping back, rooting out and unpicking - believing that nothing but the best will ever do for you.

And so, with all the personal uprooting and unpicking firmly behind me, my mind could focus on packing my bags for Spain. It was the last week of January and I couldn't wait to get out to the house in just over a weeks' time, to open it back up for the year. This would be my first full year of being able to enjoy it as a family, but also bless others.

> And as we choose to bravely **repurpose** our own life, back to its **original** and wonderful **design**, there is a Father, lovingly and patiently, stripping back, rooting out and unpicking - believing that nothing but the best will ever do for you.

There was so much going on at home in the UK around our exit from Europe, and around the world there was lots of crazy stuff happening, especially in China, where some random virus seemed to be spreading at pace. I was longing for some rest and relaxation and a break from all the chaos. My big girl was blooming now and at six months, had a mere twelve weeks to go, so I was excited for the big countdown and baby shower celebrations on my return.

Ora

I don't understand Father, how can this be? (looking at the large door before her)

Y'shua

Not by your might, but by mine, sweet girl.

Ora

But I can't go through there; I can't do what's needed. I'm not up to that.

Y'shua

Just trust me and enjoy the adventure. You and I together can do anything; never forget that; but what's through that doorway may not be all that you assume.

You may find there are other doors for you to try. But first, you'll need to let this door swing shut.

Scary hey?

Ora

Yes very scary

Y'shua

I'm right here (slips His arm lovingly around her shoulders)

Always have been – Always will be.

Nothing can separate us.

'For I,' says the L*ORD*, *'will be a wall of fire all around her,*

and I will be the glory in her midst.'

Zechariah 2:5 NKJV

15

The Great Shaking

She has been feeling it for a while - that sense of awaking. There is a gentle rage simmering inside her, and it is getting stronger by the day. She will hold it close to her - she will nurture it and let it grow. She won't let anyone take it away from her. It is her rocket fuel and finally, she is going places. She can feel it down to her very core - this is her time. She will not only climb mountains - she will move them too.

LANG LEAV / THE UNIVERSE OF US

Funny (not so funny) how the words *rest* and *relaxation* somehow never seem to go in the same sentence as *Cath*. Just as I was thinking life was easing up a little, in true Cath style, yet another mind-blowing moment was hovering on the horizon.

Just two days before I was due to fly out to Spain, I received a call from a firm of *headhunters* in London. They wanted to talk to me about a role they were managing. It was a Christian Bank and they were hunting for a new CEO.

And when I was told the name of the bank, the words that I'd heard just three months earlier lunged straight back into my head - *Prepare for the King.*

Not only that, a friend had also given me a word a few weeks before

A man's gift makes room for him,

And brings him before great men.

Proverbs 18:16 NKJV

He'd said that he sensed the Lord saying that because of the treasure within my heart, I would be invited to the King's table.

And now this – I was stunned. Not just because of these different words, but because inviting me to apply for the CEO of a Bank was just about the most crazy bonkers thing I'd ever heard.

I'd held some relatively senior roles in big banks but there were many degrees of separation between those roles and the CEO. I realised that this was a very small niche bank, and I couldn't deny that the idea of developing and leading a christian bank didn't intrigue me and get my strategic and spiritual juices flowing; however, I was certain they had got the wrong person and would quickly realise this soon after a conversation. Just the regulatory environment wrapped around financial institutions in the UK and the associated personal responsibilities assigned to the boards and CEOs were something about which I had zero experience, nor did it interest me.

I'm a visionary, a storyteller, a big picture girl, not an accountant or a risk and compliance analyst. But what did interest me a little was how exciting it would be to be part of a financial organisation that was led by godly people, operated by godly people, serving godly causes; where team prayer was top of the daily *to do* list and where business decisions were not just focused on growing the balance sheet, but also on growing the kingdom – it was certainly an exciting proposition. Still, as much as I was, once again, flattered and even more amused than I'd been a few weeks prior, and as much as I knew *all things are possible with God.* (**Luke 1:37/Matt 19:26/Job 42:2/Jer 32:17/ Gen 18:14/Psalm 62:11**) I was also a realist... (kind of)

They wanted to have an initial conversation the following week, when

I would already be in Spain. I explained the situation, indicating that I'd be happy to chat from there and they wanted to do that, so they emailed me the full recruitment pack, which I printed and placed in my case along with my CV. I would be professional and do the prep thoroughly ahead of the call, but of course, I was sure that would be the end of the process. As much as the concept excited me and terrified me in equal measure, this really wasn't the direction I felt my life was moving in. I would never say 'no' to God and if a door opened that could be Him, then I'd walk through it until it closed, but deep down I'd said goodbye to the manic exec London/commute lifestyle, plus with everything in me, I believed that the book I knew I'd been called to write was significant too.

There was so much inside of me that needed to be heard, in a way that only I could voice – only I had walked my path, only I had experienced God the way I had, only I could bring my truth and an eyewitness report of all that had been revealed to me. Taking a job such as this would only push-back further the recording and telling of my story. *Many others could lead the bank and do it so much better than me.* I concluded that once the initial conversation was done, they would quickly realise I wasn't the right person for the job. I'd have shown obedience, but with a huge sigh of relief and gratitude, I'd be able to get on with the task at hand.

Only it didn't happen quite like that...

At the end of that first call I was asked "So what do you think, are you interested?" To which I replied, "I guess my response has to be, what do you think – based on all the other candidates, does it feel like I have the skills and experience you're looking for?"

"Well," the reply came, "you're certainly a very interesting candidate for us."

WOW - I hadn't seen that one coming.

By the time the call wound up, I'd agreed to meet in London on my return, for a face-to-face meeting. That meeting went really well and I was told that, in all, there were fifteen candidates who would be presented to the bank's board for selection the following day. From those fifteen, four candidates would be taken through to the next round.

The call came late the next day and it shook me to my core. They had selected the top four candidates and I was one of them. Three were men, all of whom had CEO experience, then there was me, the wild card. It was my broad experience right across the banking sector and my strategic expertise that was of real interest to them. My heart sank. Hear me out, I was so humbled and proud to be included with these amazing people, but in my heart of hearts I just didn't want this right now. As huge as the prestige (and salary) were, there was also a weighty job to be done and though it sounded phenomenal, something inside of me could not shift the thought that this *is not for me*.

But the good girl always had an answer. *If God wants me to do it, I will and He will be my teacher and my counsellor and my navigator, but oh Father I'm really not sure about this?*

As the main interview was approaching, the whole world turned on its head. The virus that had been plaguing China had invaded and ravaged Italy and now it seemed to be tiptoeing across almost every country on the globe. And the UK was no exception. People were starting to panic. I was sure it wouldn't take long for things to be sorted, but for a few weeks everyone was asked to travel a little less and work from home temporarily.

And then the whole country went into total *lockdown*.

This meant the panel element of the interview, four days later, had to be managed over zoom. It would not be quite the same as meeting people in person, nevertheless, I put in the hours, did my research and preparation, developed a *first 100 days* plan that presented a number of strategic thoughts and options – all the while feeling absolutely certain, deep in my belly that this was not the direction I should be going. All the while, retaining absolute trust in a father who knew me better than I knew myself and who had already prepared my path.

And then the day arrived.

I sat in my office on zoom, making small talk, whilst studying the panel of highly experienced, highly esteemed, highly prominent, highly influential men who were smiling back at me and I wondered how on earth I had found myself in this position. Truly, there was only ever one conceivable explanation. It could not be explained by logic, capability, hard work or anything in between – I was out of place through favour. God had brought me before great men, me, little Cath, crazy Cath, impulsive Cath, tell it like it is Cath, barrier bashing Cath, dream big dreams Cath; I was sitting in the presence of true greatness and I was considered worthy of their time and regard. As long as I live I'll treasure that moment and be glad I didn't say 'no' and miss out on that reminder, that anything is possible with God. It will remain one of the great wonders of my life.

In the end I didn't get the job, it went to a perfect candidate and I'd never been so relived. When the call came through, I almost cried with joy and I realised as soon as I put the phone down, that in that moment, God had just drawn a thick line under my career in banking. Time and time again He had brought me back to it, but I knew there and then, that it had finally come to an end. I didn't know what the future would look like for me professionally, ministerially or financially, but I was sure of one thing, the rest of the year would be given over to writing my book and after that...... well God would let me know, when I needed to know.

Just enough bread for today, as my big girl often reminded me.

And remember that missing spleen, the one I'd exchanged for that very same extra-ordinary girl, well, with a world falling into chaos, the gap it left was about to supercharge my writing journey.

WALKING ANCIENT PATHS

Rasha'

Behold, oh King, from your high and mighty places – I bring destruction and death like never before.

See how it spreads, like toxin, contaminating the entire earth.

Y'shua

(laughs loudly) Do you feel it yet, you ground-dweller, can you feel the shaking from your lowly hiding place?

Can you hear the birthing pangs of my children?

The seasons are shifting, the tide is turning, the armies are assembling, the voices are rising. The highway of holiness is being revealed and along it, a new generation are preparing to write history.

(holds up the standard, then thrusts it deep into the ground, as the earth begins to shake violently)

Look at the nations and observe — be utterly astounded.

For I am doing a work in your days that you would

never believe even if someone told you.

Habakkuk 1:5 BSB

16

Beneath the Broom Tree

An elephant carries her unborn for 22 months;
longer than any other mammal;
but when it's finally born, the earth feels its weight.

UNKNOWN

Resting my head against the murky windowpane of the tram, gazing on the late-night city centre comings and goings; tired but happy after a wonderfully fun and girly night with H & my two girls in a Manchester football stadium, dancing and singing and reminiscing with just under fifty-five-thousand other Spice Girl fans; God tapped me on my shoulder and said, "That's enough for now, no more projects." As a leant there, my mind drifting back to the period just before *life as I'd known it* changed forever; when I'd been recovering from designing, dressing and managing my big girl's wedding and finishing up what had been a heavy but highly successful business consultancy contract for a bank in Manchester; I began to count up all of the significant changes and things I'd embraced and undertaken with my predictable enthusiasm. A devastating separation, packing away and dividing up my world, the wider family wounding that had left its mark differently on each one of us, then of course, the divorce itself.

Moving to TFBB's and onwards to my Mums – before flying out to the

States, where I'd thrown myself into the strategic restructure of three large charities (which just happened to border three different continents.) And in the midst of that, landing myself in a John Grisham style murder/mystery. After all that, three months later I found myself, once more, back at my Mums, from where I moved to my lovely apartment, that gave me a year of stability. Finally, I put down some roots; buying and moving into my own little sanctuary.

In that same period, I'd had a couple of big job interviews, which in the end I'd decided not to take. Then came London... and Spain.....
All in all, in the course of just under four years, I'd moved home eight times, I'd bought and singlehandedly renovated two houses (one in a different country), I'd spent a year commuting between the North West and London, project managed a second wedding for TFBB, made a TV programme, held down a very stressful job in the City, created a detailed business proposition for a wedding business (which I ultimately decided not to do). I'd got the bare bones and initial chapters of my first book down on paper and I'd boldly (and courageously in my humble opinion) stepped up to the challenge of the CEO role.

It really was quite shocking to put it in that kind of context. 'No wonder there was a constant sense of weariness inside of me,' I mused. Part of me secretly liked that bit of Cath, the bit that was unstoppable and resilient. 'It's just who I am, isn't it?' I wanted to bounce back to Him cheekily, hoping He'd chuckle and tell me how brilliant I was. But, instead, as my stare remained transfixed on the flashing lights of the city streets beyond the streaky windows, He gave me that real Dad look, that one which says without words, 'come on now baby girl, I think we both know it's time to take a breath?' To slow down. To restock and recharge. It's time for time-out. No more big adventures or changes or creative ideas for a while.

No more hiding.

He was telling me that I needed to just *BE*.

I knew He was right, but just thinking about it made me want to crumble into a ball on the floor and cry. Right there on the floor of the Met, surrounded by incognisant revellers singing along to 'Spice up your life'. The intensity of the dread I was suddenly feeling caught me off-guard. The prospect of actually stopping and creating space in my head that would allow all that stuff access, seemed nothing less than undeserved punishment. And it struck me, just how much I had been dealing with hurt and loss by *doing*. *Doing* was what I was good at. *Doing* that kept my body *and* my mind busy. *Doing* that stopped me being a victim. Doing was who I had become. It had become my identity. And it was starting to really trouble the one who loved me with an unfathomable love. "Let's get still for a while together," He was counselling wisely and longingly, "and let's deal with some of this stuff quietly, together." And honestly, I didn't know if I was capable of that kind of quiet contemplation. I didn't know whether facing full on, what I'd lost, what I'd been through, how I'd felt, the gap I'd been left with; without the aid of a project or an adventure or a distraction.

I suddenly realised that the *you can do this Kid* in me, the problem solver extraordinaire, the Momma who wanted to make her girls proud, had been filling a gap in her heart and indeed her soul, numbing painful thoughts with a nonstop programme of change. And whilst all that change had been positive and productive and involved so much favour and wonderful moments, my Dad was saying, "Baby girl it's time to pause and breathe and reflect and put some of this stuff to bed. I have things prepared for your future, but first let's lay the past to rest properly."

Truthfully, I thought I'd done that, I really did, but in that moment, with all the sickening and unsettling feelings that having to stop and revisit it was dragging to the surface, I knew I needed to allow myself to grieve in a way I hadn't yet. When someone dies, its final. Once the funeral takes place, those impacted begin the process of rebuilding their lives, shaped around their new reality. However, when you lose something from your life that still exists, there isn't that same level of finality; instead of rebuilding the new, you simply plug the old, *just in case*, and I had been plugging my little heart out. And my Dad was affectionately saying to me, 'You've done amazing, but it's time now – it's time to grieve and have a funeral.

The Broom Tree in scripture symbolises two opposing things:

- Despair
- A supernatural encounter with God.

The broom tree grows in dry desolate places. It has exceptionally deep roots which draw water from deep within the ground, allowing it to survive and grow in places where other plants typically can't. It isn't a huge tree, in fact practically, it's more of a bush, but it's branches can provide just enough shade in the desert for people to recover from the blistering heat, until they are strong enough to continue their journey.

The Broom tree is mentioned as a place of sanctuary several times in the bible, in situations where people would have died in the searing heat of the desert, had they not come upon it. In **1 Kings 19,** Elijah found rest whilst trying to escape the threat of death from Jezebel. He was exhausted from battle. Even though he'd seen God perform mighty things on his behalf, in his weariness, the direct threats on his life had suddenly created fear, causing him to panic and run. But God led him to a Broom Tree, where he gave him rest and food and sleep; before speaking with him in a more tender way than He had previously, knowing that's what Elijah needed in that particular moment. And when he was restored and strong once more, God gave him his next set of instructions.

The Broom Tree is also where God led Hagar; where she placed Ishmael in despair; after Sarah told Abraham to get rid of them both **(Genesis 21)**. Sent out into the desert alone and running out of water, Hagar, fearing for her life and that of her baby boy, cried out to God in desperation and God sent a messenger Angel to reassure her that all would be well.

> God will always take us to a **spiritual broom tree** when we are feeling in despair and almost spent. And there, as he **refreshes** and **restores** us, we will have a supernatural **encounter with Him**.

That her Father would take care of them and ultimately, make Ishmael (her boy) into a great nation. Miraculously as she opened her eyes, a well of water sprung up before her. God created a new spring of water from nothing, to meet Hagar's needs.

God will always take us to a spiritual broom tree when we are feeling in despair and almost spent. And there, as he refreshes and restores us, we will have a supernatural encounter with Him.

Although there are times in history, where God sent plagues, I am quite certain that God did not send the virus that was now taking hold of the entire world. But God, as He's promised all along, has a wonderful way of *bringing all things together, for the good of those who love Him.*

In the most unprecedented year, filled with untold heartache, loss, disruption, restriction, readjustment, loneliness, separation, and exhaustion, impacting virtually the entire population of planet earth, God led me and my precious family to a broom tree, where, in the searing heat and barrenness of a merciless pandemic, we encountered His supernatural goodness, grace, protection, favour and commissioning.

This would be a season of shaking and sifting. Of birthing and movement. It would also sadly be a season of death. Many of us sensed that something significant was shifting in the heavenlies, that God *was doing a new thing,* which offered a *once in a generation* opportunity to bring about eternal value, from what was intended to merely kill, steal and destroy. This would be a year that history would never ever (and should never) forget.

> This would be a season of **shaking** and **sifting**. Of **birthing** and **movement**. It would also sadly be a season of death!

For the sake of my seed, this is my own personal account.

The **Novel Coronavirus (Covid-19)** Pandemic was declared on March 11th, 2020

By March 23rd, 2020, the UK had been placed into an initial three-month lockdown.

This is what that lockdown looked like:

- Self-distancing introduced – No person allowed to stand within two meters of another
- Physical touch with someone who does not live in your house - banned
- Away from the home, in any indoor place, masks must be worn by all those aged twelve+
- Everywhere outside, people wear masks and gloves
- All socialising with anyone not in your own household - banned
- Every person to stay at home, other than four reasons - shopping for basic necessities, one form of exercise per day, medical need or to look after a vulnerable person
- People instructed to work from home
- The use of cash - discouraged
- All non-essential travel - banned
- Fuel prices nose-dive as cars disappear from our roads
- Flights and Holidays - cancelled. No air traffic in sky
- School is cancelled – children stay home as parents homeschool
- All high school exams - cancelled
- All sixth form exams - cancelled
- University students - sent home
- Zoom becomes primary channel for business, learning and social interactions
- Non-essential shops and businesses – closed
- Inside remaining shops, tape placed on the floors to socially distance shoppers
- Number of people allowed in shops at any one time - limited
- Long line-ups outside shop doors, manned by security guards

- Online shopping skyrockets. Amazon become biggest winner Long-established high street brands go bust
- Panic buying sets in, with significant shortages of toilet paper, disinfecting supplies and hand sanitiser
- Bread, pasta, flour, beans and chopped tomatoes sell out everywhere
- Supermarket shelves are bare
- Pubs, theatres, restaurants - closed
- Entire sports seasons - cancelled
- Concerts, tours, festivals, entertainment events - cancelled
- Weddings, family celebrations, holiday gatherings - cancelled
- Places of worship - closed
- Graveyards - closed
- Children's outdoor play parks – closed
- Gyms – closed
- Shortage of masks, gowns, gloves for front-line workers
- Shortage of ventilators for the critically ill
- Manufacturing businesses and distilleries switch their product lines to help make visors, masks, hand sanitiser and PPE Closed arenas open up for the overflow of Covid-19 patients
- Temporary hospitals are built
- Family visits to say goodbye to their dying loved ones in hospital – banned
- The sick are treated in ambulances as hospitals run out of spare beds
- The dead are denied wakes or funerals and barely anyone is allowed at the graveside
- Essential key workers are terrified to go to work
- Medical field workers are afraid to go home to their families

- Pregnant women give birth alone as fathers are prevented from labour wards
- Carehomes closed to visitors, due to high numbers of resident deaths
- Fines are established for breaking the rules. Police patrolling the streets
- Daily press conferences from government provide updates on new cases and deaths.
- Government provide *never before seen* levels of grants and loans to businesses to keep the economy afloat
- Government pay 80% of employees' wages as workers are kept at home
- Scaremongering and theories are rife over the origin of the virus

As I write this, just over a year of lockdown has passed, almost **4.5M** people in the UK have been diagnosed (**129M** worldwide) with Covid-19.

Nearly 130 thousand (**2.9M** worldwide) people have heartbreakingly died. At the peak, the average daily deaths in the UK were **1.2k** (**8.4K** worldwide).

It is truly shocking and it isn't over yet. But finally, things are beginning to ease and in the shaking and shattering legions of *new things* have been purposefully and faithfully planted and cultivated.

> *I assure you and most solemnly say to you, unless a grain of wheat falls into the earth and dies, it remains alone [just one grain, never more]. But if it dies, it produces much grain and yields a harvest.*

John 12:24 AMP

It is a fact that a grain of wheat must fall

to the ground and die before it can grow

and produce much more wheat. If it never dies,

it will never be more than a single seed.

John 12:24 ERV

Quietly, behind closed doors, in the omnipresent secret place; all around the world, individual callings, purposes, voices, giftings, missions, ministries; were being awakened, fine-tuned and mobilised.

> Quietly, behind closed doors, in the omnipresent **secret place**; all around the world, individual callings, purposes, voices, giftings, missions, ministries; were being *awakened, fine-tuned* and **mobilised**.

Before all of this, we (the collective *we*) seemed to be dancing to the beat of our own drums. Over-busyness, separately striving, a dependence on 'stuff'. Abusing our bodies with convenient concoctions disguised as food. Focused on our own priorities, lost in our own issues and problems, judging 'different'; the bigger questions – put aside for another day.

Churches, often focused on the size of the physical building or the platform, or who had the most *bums on seats*. Superstar status given to a handful of great orators, rather than on the ONE on whose behalf they spoke. Exhausted people serving from a doctrine of responsibility, all the while,

> But here is the real **miracle** of the season. In the darkness of isolation, separated in body, yet suddenly united in spirit, 'we', humankind, suddenly began to cleave together: United in our battle. **United in our grief. United in our hope.**

their unique treasure, hidden away; unseen, overlooked, uninvited.

Somehow in our human wisdom, we made things hard and exhausting and complicated and divided. The complete opposite of His vision of us all; pouring ourselves out into one another. Equal in His sight.

Bringing what we have. Being who we are. Giving what we can. Loving Him, loving each other, wherever we happen to find ourselves. Interdependent and connected living.

But here is the real miracle of the season. In the darkness of isolation, separated in body, yet suddenly united in spirit, 'we', humankind, suddenly began to cleave together: United in our battle. United in our grief. United in our hope.

And when we looked closely, amazing things were happening everywhere.

- Air pollution drops by 20% as transport on the roads and in the skies dramatically reduces
- Traditional quality *family time* returns
- Simple pleasures, such as long family walks, baking and board games, are rediscovered
- People begin to do more outside exercise, as they look for creative ways to keep fit
- Opportunities to learn new skills are embraced
- Creativity returns, as music and books are written and ideas are birthed
- Neighbours get to know each other, as new relationships & friendships are formed
- Helping others and pulling together becomes everyone's focus
- Weekly doorstep clapping is introduced, to recognise and support the NHS and carers
- Mass movement of people (house moves/job moves) begins as people reassess their lives
- Debts are repaid, from the significant savings made from removal of fuel and commute costs
- Babies thrive, as breastfeeding increases and Mommas no longer interrupted by visitors

- Churches come together to record songs
- Government recognises the Church's outstanding support for communities in need
- Online church becomes widespread, reaching more people than ever before
- Bibles begin to fly off shelves, as people search for hope
- Google searches for 'Prayer' and 'Hope' peak
- Pictures of rainbows (a sign of Gods covenant with His people) are placed in every window
- Aiming to raise £1000 for NHS by walking round his garden, 99-year-old Captain Tom Moore passes £30M, becoming a national hero and a *Sir*
- Scientists worldwide come together in an unprecedented way, to find and test a vaccine

And even more miraculously, for some, this dark place would become fertile and holy ground, in which their outer shells that had been nurturing and holding treasure, kept for this exact moment, would finally burst open, releasing new shoots that would push their way upwards, towards the light. Single grains, that would eventually multiply and yield a harvest.

> For some, this dark place would become fertile and **holy ground**, in which their outer shells that had been nurturing and holding treasure, kept for this exact moment, would finally burst open, releasing new shoots that would push their way upwards, towards the light. Single grains, that would eventually multiply and **yield a harvest**.

Moment of Impact

On April 1st, 2020, (Not An April Fool's) an envelope dropped through my letterbox. Inside was a letter from 10 Downing Street, signed by Boris Johnson, our Prime Minister, advising me that because I had no spleen, I fell into a small group of people who were considered 'clinically vulnerable' to the impacts of Covid-19 and as such, must not leave my home, for any circumstances at all for the next three months.

Unlike most people, I could not do any food shopping, or undertake the permitted *once-a-day* daily exercise. It took a little while to sink in. I lived alone and this meant I was to have no human contact, in any form, for at least three months. I was even advised not to go into my own back garden. On top of that, my Mum who was now eighty-four, was also to be isolated because of her age and that brought a completely different set of challenges. It had all begun to feel like something out of a sci fi movie. Many were likening it to End Times, though for lots of different reasons, I did not go there.

Love Separated

But the *real* gut-wrenching thing, the thing that was breaking my heart into a million different pieces, was the event taking place inside my big girl. In one-month's time, she would become a Momma herself. And that Momma-to-be, needed her own Momma's reassuring hugs and support, now more than ever, as she prepared for this significant moment. Not only that, but there was also talk of her boy not being able to be with her in the hospital. I could not bear the thought of her going through that alone.

As I tried to be strong for her, reassuring her that everything would work out fine, we cried and prayed and cried and consoled each other, realizing that I would also not get to see or hold my baby's baby; my very first grandchild; until he or she was at least two months old. She would not be able to share her joy and her greatest blessing with the one who considered her, 'half of hers.' As a family, we had come through an extended season of unbearable pain and destruction and we had rose victoriously, but this felt like another thing that was being stolen from us.

We had to remind ourselves that even though we weren't 'of' the world, we were 'in' the world and the whole world was going through this alongside us. The pain we felt came only from a deep love and we decided in the end that that this kind of love was a pretty good pain to carry. And so, instead of looking at it as love lost, we called it 'love separated' and that's how we walked through the next three months; like nothing was lost or stolen, just simply, that we were *separated in love.*

And after that, an extraordinary thing began to happen in my heart. Right in this season, before Covid 19 was even a thing, I had determined that despite all the different demands on my time, I would bring my book out of retirement and do my best to finally get it written. As someone who continually, not only gets pulled in multiple directions, but also, due to a highly curious and firecracker brain, can at times be prone to a wee bit of procrastination; the book project's beginning and end were inevitably always going to remain fluid.

But here I stood, with a letter in my hand, telling me that, because of an incident thirty years earlier - an incident that, though considered extremely serious, hadn't really ever impacted my life - until now. And now, because of the absence of that spleen, I wasn't just in lockdown; I was in solitary confinement. For the next three months, I was unable to meet another single human being, unable to exercise outside, unable to food shop. I was, let's say, completely withdrawn from circulation.

> Piece by piece he was *divinely fashioning* and **orchestrating** His strategies and plans, commanding all things that satan had intended for evil to bow to **His eternal purpose**.

A perfect environment to write I'd say.

As I pictured the days ahead, instead of feeling a sense of despair, I couldn't get away from a sense of wonder. I had this absolute certainty and excitement, that my Dad was concealing me. He was protecting me in His secret place, bringing together several sets of unfortunate circumstances, for my good and for His glory. Piece by piece he was divinely fashioning and orchestrating His strategies and plans, commanding all things that satan had intended for evil to bow to His eternal purpose.

THE SECRET PLACE

†

Thirty years earlier

Their beautiful voices filled the room. How He loved to hear them - He was so glad they had come too. This had to be done well, so having the room consumed by Heaven's peaceful sounds was critical. There would be no margin for mistakes.

He guided each tiny movement of the surgeon's hands. It was an emergency, with little time for slow decision making; she had lost far too much blood already and her breathing was deteriorating rapidly from the contamination in her lungs. And there was the clot to deal with too.

He hovered lower, breathing each holy instruction in to his mind; the young wide-eyed students all around, impressed by the skill and wisdom of the tall dark-haired consultant, who was clearly keeping this young woman and her baby alive. They wondered if they would ever be this good?

One or two offered up a small prayer for them both and for their mentor. Unaware of the true-identity of the Great Physician who was *really* working on her.

That will do nicely, He thought (He whispered), relieved; turning and exhaling to the masked and gowned female doctor by his side; 'you can stitch her back up now. The drain will need to stay in there for a few more days. I'll go and give her husband the good news. Mother and Baby both doing well.'

The Great Physician smiled, satisfied; His eyes lifting towards the now hushed incandescent hosts; as if to let them know He was pleased with them. '*There is a time for everything and everything in its time,*' He reminded them. They nodded in agreement.

This is going to work perfectly.

356

†

COMAND HQ

Outside the hospital building, standing in the dark, the penetrating shrill of displeasure did not go unnoticed by those inside, who merely raised their eyes indifferently.

Satan paced up and down aggrieved, he hated to be outsmarted. He would have her one way or another, he concluded. He had plenty more tricks up his sleeve.

He'd choose his moment and next time he would be a little less obvious. Yes, he snarled, he would take a much more subtle approach next time round.

Strangely, I was embracing my concealment. I pressed in and as I wrote I discovered a new sound flowing from my tongue, a sound that was shaping and crafting the words He'd called me to write into something different. A sound that was subtly separating the end from the beginning, the new from the old. A sound that flooded the dry wastelands that were behind me with rivers of living water, changing the landscape as far back as I could see. With all that I had come to see, even the harsh challenging terrain that I'd navigated, seemed suddenly quite beautiful. Nothing had changed, what had gone could not be undone, but in the freshness of the season and with new understanding, wisdom and perspective, I could not escape the preciousness of every step that had carried me here. Here, upon the ancient path – upon The Good Way **(Jeremiah 6:16).**

For I am about to do something new.

See, I have already begun. Do you not see it?

I will make a pathway through the wilderness.

I will create rivers in the dry wasteland.

Isaiah 43:19

And in the midst of it all, this...

Moment of Impact

Into Gods quiver, a freshly formed polished arrow was placed, and on the side in bold letters was etched **VICTORIOUS**

Journal

Thursday 29th April 2020

You called me today· You said you didn't want to get excited as you're not even at your due date yet, but you'd been having some funny little cramping sensations in your abdomen· You've been having Braxton hicks for nearly two weeks, so you sound like you're brushing these off too, but I think we might be starting precious girl· I can feel the tears welling up just thinking about it· Tears of joy, tears of excitement, tears of anticipation· We've both cried together early on about how this virus is keeping us all apart and how hard it will be when the baby comes, not being able to introduce he or she to anyone· The thought of not being able to snuggle or smell my first grandchild or help you in the early days is heartbreaking; but we've chatted it through haven't we· We called it Love Separated, not lost and we will have years to make up for that time of separation·

I am so proud of how you have handled this pregnancy; all the calm and reading you've done on the subject· I hardly recognize my big girl, who once declared she 'didn't read books.' It's been so beautiful to watch the awe with which you've treasured all the changes to your body, the way your bubba is growing and wriggling inside; to see how carefully you've nurtured it with good food, exercise and playing it messages and soothing music through your belly buds· Even now, you're grabbing the last rays of sunshine, your face bronzed and so beautiful from the last few weeks of unusually warm April weather· "It would be great if I had the baby this week Mum", you said last night, "the forecast says rain all this week"· He He, the apple never falls too far from the tree· How we love the sunshine·

I want to be with you, I want to hold your hand and mop your brow and tell you everything is going to be fine; that the pain will be gone soon· I want to see your baby, grown from a seed that was once inside my body; how miraculous is that· I want to see that precious life burst into this world· Of course, I can't, that is the privilege of your boy; *his* right and I'm so incredibly thankful that he is getting to be with you after everything that is going on and all the uncertainty· But you will know when you hold your baby for the first time, the fierceness of my love for you, for your bubba; the inherent need to be there for you, to protect you, to champion you, to encourage you – it's an actual ache sometimes· A glorious ache, one you too will learn to carry·

Calmly, you tell me the twinges are only about 30 minutes apart – no need to do anything yet· "I'm writing it all down in my notebook, Mum, keeping an eye on it, don't stress, I've got this" you say·

Of course, you've got this·

Your little sis is struggling to contain herself· It's a good job we're not allowed to come to the hospital, we'd be way to excitable and giddy·

It's so unlike 'us' isn't it, not being able to just share our hearts with each other at such special moments and there's so much I want to say, but it will get said, it *is* getting said, right here, right now, as my heart bleeds onto the pages of this journal· In this indescribable moment I am capturing this separated love, for you and for your victorious baby, so that it can never be stolen or lost· ♥

Momma (Nannie eeek) x

BTJ burst into the world the very next morning and he was the most delicious bundle of sapphire-eyed, wavy blond scrumptiousness I'd ever seen. In the end and by His grace, the birth had ended up being the most beautiful experience for all three of them and my big girl had been a superstar. We all navigated the ecstasy and the agony of what the season had dealt us the best we could - mostly, courtesy of Facetime, Kleenex and prayer - and as one month became two, God once again graciously showered me with special favour.

The living alone in isolation, that satan would frequently taunt me with, became the one thing that found me and my big girl stood in my hallway, arms locked around one another, BTJ pressed between us as three months of *love separated*, the arrival of the precious boy nestled between our adjoined hearts and the and the unveiling of a girl who went into a cocoon three months earlier and had emerged transformed into the most majestic of Mommas, simply melted away into a waterfall of blended *joy-filled* tears.

Love United.

It was an unexpected gift that I knew many were not experiencing, but a gift I was not about to turn down. In the middle of this pandemic war, when the first wave of isolation was being eased, but in which households were still forbidden to mix, the government created *bubbles*. A solution which allowed anyone living alone to *bubble-up* with another household, as if it were one. A solution that allowed me to hold my grandson for the very first time, whilst I told my big girl how much I loved her and how proud I was of her. It would be many many minutes before we loosened our grip of each other. And as I stepped back a little, creating just enough space between us to lower my head towards the exquisite boy staring up at me from his Momma's arms, I finally got to nuzzle my nose into BTJ's neck and breathe in all of heaven - *then*, look back up into my beautiful girl's eyes and say "How are you doing Sweetie?"

Covid 19 and lockdown ebbed and flowed throughout the year and we all adjusted to this new normal. And in late summer, during a short-lived period where a small group of family members could temporarily meet indoors, TFBB brought us the best kind of news – she was having a baby too. BTJ was going to have a little cousin. In jubilation, her big sis jumped up onto the kitchen worktop and did a celebratory jig, whilst I simply pulled her close, reaching out to take hold of her boy's hand, squeezing it tight. She had been born to be a Momma. As a little girl she'd rocked dolls and pushed around prams continually, chattering away to imaginary babies as she tucked old cast-off blankets around them, simultaneously placing a perished dodie by their head, whilst imitating soothing drifting-off-to-sleep motions, accompanied by the sounds of 'shhhhh shhhhhh.' In her teenage years, she'd spend summer after summer in the States, rocking and feeding real babies and it was only a matter of time before she held her own. She would be a natural.

Despite what was going on outside our family, right here, things seemed just about perfect.

But that was not to last very long.

At ten weeks, in the midst of moving house and temporarily living with me, something didn't seem quite right. Reassuring her that everything would be fine, we made an appointment to go to the hospital for a scan, for peace of mind. Her big sis had gone through something similar and we trusted God that this would be the same.

Only it wasn't.

I could barely hear what she was saying over the phone as she battled to get the words out. "Sorry Sweetie, I can't hear you, say that to me again." I couldn't make out anything she was saying, but everything in me knew from her tone that it wasn't good.

"The baby isn't breathing Mum. They want me to take something to make it... I can't Mum, I can't. What if......, maybe they just missed the heartbeat? I can't. I told them I won't make that decision now."

These are *Mum moments* that bring to bear the full weight of bottomless love. The moments where you want to step in and take their place. But I couldn't. Instead, as this fierce holy anger began to burn inside of me, I did what was instinctive. Once I'd held her and comforted her later, I knelt on the floor in front of her, her boy sat close, holding her hand tightly between both of his, each face stained from the pain their hearts were experiencing; 'Is it OK if I do this?' I asked, looking into her eyes, a sense of knowing this was right, brutally wrestling with a need to protect them both from a second wave of disappointment.

At this stage I wasn't certain of God's plan for this baby, but I knew I had the power to speak life into the tiny seed inside of her, *if* it be His will. She nodded her head slowly, the same conflict etched across her face. I reached up, tenderly placing one hand on either side of her rounded tummy and went into battle the only way I knew how, on my knees, with the power of the Holy Spirit uttering declarations from heaven to heaven, on my behalf, on their behalf and on behalf of the precious treasure within my baby girl.

When I'd finished, I rounded up my army. One was sitting injured in my living room, the other was a phone call away. In two-weeks' time, if the baby had not miscarried, they would check for a heartbeat again. And for the next two weeks, my big girl and I battled in the heavenlies for dry bones to come alive, for the sound of rattling to begin, for the breath of heaven to come down – we were unshakeable and unstoppable.

A new awakening was happening in my big girl, something I hadn't seen before. It was as if a fresh anointing was taking place right before my eyes - an almost *synergy* in battle with me, it was hard to explain, but I wasn't surprised by it, it was something I'd always known was there and now it was being called out. Even BTJ would join us in prayer. Of course, his tiny six-month-old mind didn't understand what was going on, but we needed his victorious spirit in our battalion. Never once, during those two weeks, did we accept that this was God's plan - that would have weakened our efforts - and so, when the second scan came around, we were quite certain the news would be glorious. We were quite certain that as they placed the transducer onto the jelly on her tummy, the sonographer would be astounded to discover their mistake, to discover that wriggling around inside my baby girl was a healthy and happy twelve-week-old bubba...

THE SECRET PLACE

†

Five weeks earlier

Hey, pssss. we don't have long. Dad said it's nearly time for me to go home. How cool is that. Dad said our Momma is going to be really sad when she finds out. And Daddy too. I wish they didn't have to be sad. They seem nice, you're gonna be so lucky to have them. Not as lucky as me though, He He. Kinda confused about why I got picked, but not gonna lie, I'm soooo excited.

He said it's beautiful there. He said it's beautiful here too, but I think *there,* it's like, on a whole other level.

It's been snuggly and fun here, you'll know what I mean when you get to this stage. And it's been so awesome hasn't it, hanging out here together for a while.

I can already feel how much she loves us, by the way she talks to me; all the time, telling me how special I am. It's funny isn't it, she doesn't know you're tucked away back there, waiting to be woven into shape very soon (giggles). Then you'll feel the same wonderful vibrations that I do now, whenever the shadow of her hand passes backwards and forwards on the outside. I'll miss that. It's as if she's saying 'I love you' without making any sound. I'll take that with me and when I finally get to snuggle with her, whenever her time comes, I'll tell her how wonderful that made me feel. Dad said He wasn't able to say when that would be, but He said it will feel like no time

363

at all, because time there isn't like time here and anyway, I'll be so busy doing lovely things, that I won't even notice.

One funny thing I can tell you – our Momma is kinda noisy; well truthfully, they both are (comical eyes) – they sound like fun tho. I hear them laughing a lot. I will miss that (reflective smile), I will miss seeing them, but I will giggle along in heaven, because it sounds like a happy place and I bet I can still hear them laughing from there. I'll watch you all messing around together and smile, cause you were all chosen to be mine. Or I was chosen to be yours. Same thing.

Anyway, Dad said it's not as far away as people think – He winked at me when He said that, so I think I'm going to be much closer than they'll imagine? I hope they feel how close I am. I hope they just know.

Not going to lie, I will miss getting to be your big sis, but He says I'll always be your big sister, it's just we have to wait a little bit to play together properly. We'll do it though, wont we, eventually and I will have had chance to explore properly.

Dad said that I had this kinda secret thing to bring, that people might not see, but that it would cause some important stuff to happen, that's all part of something else. All sounds a bit complicated if you ask me and I don't really understand that stuff, but He said I did good, and that He was super proud of me.

So now, I get to go play forever...

And it sounds *amaaaaazing*.

"Ready Baby Girl?" He smiled excitedly, holding out His hand in a way that she could not resist. She smiled, first at Him, then, briefly backwards; her carefree spirit rising from the unused matter she would never need. A glow; so bright that it lit up the entire sac and flooded the oviducts and small oval shaped chambers either side where the others waited; signalled the *Divine Exchange*.

364

"See you soon then." She breathed, her joy and peace so evident.

"See you soon then." They whispered back.

In another place, not far away at all, a glorious welcome parade was already underway, for one who had successfully run the race set before her.

†

"They said it died at seven weeks Mum." She was worn out, they both were. But somehow, this time she knew it to be true. What a few weeks ago had seemed like an impossibility, like a lie, was now their reality. *Their Bubba* was already with Jesus and had been for a while. And now I was sure too, sure that His hand had been on this all along. My big girl and I, together, with a small number of other faithful and discrete warriors had fought a battle so fierce, that no forces of hell could have prevailed.

Brian and **Candice Simmons** write in **Throne Room Prayers** - *Prayer Warriors are the most powerful world-changing beings on earth. They know who they are. They're the children of God and they act like it. Praying Warriors will storm the citadel of heaven as violent ones who won't take no for an answer.*

And boy did we storm the citadel of heaven; but there are times when our wisdom and discernment must make space for the unseen things of eternity.

So, we let go. And we began with the practicalities.

> There are times when our wisdom and discernment must make space for the **unseen things of eternity**.

Then, we closed in and grieved together, giving thanks for the treasure that had always been **heaven-bound**. Our precious bubba, who had fulfilled its purpose; who's days were written, numbered and perfected. Privately and prayerfully, we would quietly trust what we could not fully understand, hoping and believing *in faith* that healing and new life would come *right on time*.

November 2020

Sweet girl, there is so much I want to say to you, but it isn't the right time. You are dealing with such heartache, that I sense I simply need to let you work through it alone, together, with God. You'll come to me when you feel ready. I know how disappointed you are and being disappointed is OK. You want answers and that desire will push you so deep into God that when its time, there will be a spiritual unleashing within you that you never imagined.

I don't know why this happened, but I do know He is a Good Father and there is always purpose in what He does or doesn't allow. Sometimes, I'm enraged with holy anger over things that I have lost, that we have all lost. It's like I have this fierce, heavenly get off it inside of me. It's not an earthly anger, it's a plundered heaven anger. For some that would turn them from God, but I know it will only draw you closer to Him and make you hungrier, as it has with me. And how blessed is it to know that Heaven holds a perfect, unblemished, piece of you.

We foolishly think we know it all and truly, we know so little. I guess it's a little bit like learning to play the piano, the first little tune you play makes you feel like a brilliant pianist, when really, all you're doing is tinkering. Eventually, after years of practice you sit down and play a concerto, eyes closed. Well, I think we're just tinkering with the power that God had given us and with each authentic attempt to understand His ways and to live the way He wants us to, trusting, accepting, believing with grace and hope, He's growing and shaping and refining us to be the best we can, straining towards our full potential.

You won't ever forget this, but one day you'll hold your baby in your arms and all the sadness will be cradled within

the most beautiful and immeasurable love you could ever have imagined 🖤
Momma x

And right on time, The Lord did what we always knew He would.

As 2021 arrived and I edged ever closer to the completion of my book, I asked God what He was saying about my vision for the coming year. This was His reply:

"Soar on wings like eagles."

I knew this was a well-known passage.

> *but those who hope in the Lord will renew their strength.*
>
> *They will soar on wings like eagles; they will run*
>
> *and not grow weary; they will walk and not be faint.*

Isaiah 40:31 NIV

Of course, I'd heard many eagle analogies over the years, but I wanted to dig-in a little deeper and this is some of what I found.

- Eagles are fierce and strong hunters
- They fly alone – not because they are proud, but because they're not afraid of soaring high above the clouds.
- Their broad wings allow them to lift their prey hight into the air where they are subdued
- Fearlessly, they fly into fierce winds, using the storm current to rise higher, quickly
- The pressure of the storm is used to help them glide, without using up their energy
- Their wing's unique design, allows them to lock into a fixed position amid violent storm winds

We had all privately locked into a fixed position over the past few months (indeed, for the entire past season), but now the storm appeared to be clearing. The clouds were parting, and the sun was teasingly shooting flashes of light out from behind them. The country was finally being given a clear route out of this awful lockdown, and I; well, I dared believe after a year of writing that I might actually make it to the final chapter of my book.

And in the secret place, a brand-new purpose had been defined within eternity's vast roadmap. Formed perfectly and woven skilfully into the precious womb of its Momma, the divine hands of its Creator ensuring that this time, its tiny heart would beat fiercely as it made its nine-month journey to its Momma's waiting arms. He had anticipated everything; even the anguish that would almost certainly try to oppose the joy in my baby girl's heart. The doubt that would grapple with her faith. The fear that would contend with her hope.

If I have done my job well, every single part of my story will ultimately bring your eyes and heart to Jesus. To our indescribable Father, our Dad, our Creator, our Comforter, our Champion. There should be no self-indulgent, inconsequential narrative on my part, only that, which in coming to its full revelation, blows your mind and creates such awe and curiosity (even debate) in you, that in turn, draws you closer to Him. For I believe He is our answer to it all. He is the only answer. Every part of my story, merely the evidence of that. And I conclude - as TFBB's fragile but overjoyed heart dared to hope that this time things would be different, God sent her a dream. She knew immediately; the way I had, the very first time; that this was no ordinary dream. That this was Him, speaking to her, in a very specific way – It's hard to explain to someone who has not yet experienced it, but there can be no doubt when it happens.

"Mum, you're an expert on seahorses, aren't you?" she said as I picked up the phone. "I've had a dream that I need to talk to you about, but first there's something else I need to tell you."

Unbeknown to me, she had woken up a few nights earlier to the sight of something that had taken her straight back to last time. Scared that history might be repeating itself, she'd called the hospital and arranged for a scan. She had just arrived home from the scan when she called me.

"I didn't want to worry you, so I didn't say anything. Then last night, I had a dream. In the dream I got up to use the bathroom and the baby came out. I was holding it in the palm of my hand, looking down at its little head and face and body. It was tiny, but everything was normal, except its skin, which was completely transparent. And through it I could see its spine and everything was perfectly formed. Its little heart was beating away. Then I noticed its bottom half was shaped like a seahorse, which confused me, so I've been crazily trying to google seahorses all morning until I remembered your dream, Mum, and that you'd done lots of research on seahorses.

Sorry, I almost forgot, I had the scan this morning too and the baby is really healthy, and its heart was beating strong. They said it's actually eight weeks, not five, so already past... you know. After the dream last night, I had so much peace going to the hospital, I just knew it was going to be fine this time."

I wanted to cry. I was blown away; the incredibly personal way He'd spoken to her just left me speechless, there was no way to adequately express all that I was feeling towards Him. I had never heard of anyone dreaming about seahorses until me. Yet here He was, speaking to my girl, in a way that I could instantly tell her what He was saying.

That...

> *It is He* who creates

> *It is He* who nurtures and grows and prepares and keeps from harm's way

> *It is He* who births

> *It is He* who releases – determining the precise day, hour and manner....

He was telling her

We've got this Kid

This bubba, that I've placed inside of you, is **KNOWN, CALLED**, has a **PURPOSE** and a **DESTINY**; is **FEARFULLY** and **WONDERFULLY MADE** and is **SET APART** for the Kingdom.

And I will remain right here - nurturing it, protecting it, preparing it – until the time comes, when I will gently bring it out into your waiting arms; breathing my own powerful breath into its lungs, establishing its unique voice; concealed, until its season.

What a glorious father He is to us.

And *this* was my season. The most extraordinary year in which He'd finally called forth *my* unique voice. I hoped I had used it wisely and honourably. I hoped I had listened well. I hoped I had only written truth, the kind that brings life. And I hoped that this truth, His truth, would travel to a million hurting hearts, so that each and every one would get to hear those precious reassuring words, 'We've got this Kid. You and me together, we're going to walk this back to beautiful. Walk this back to you. Walk this back to the *Good Way*.'

I had to admit, my concealment had been a comfortable place - Him leading, me tapping away at my computer. But now, as the time neared to bring my voice out into the open, I was feeling considerably less comfortable. Uncovered, exposed, dissected, rebuked; just some of the words that had begun to cajole an altogether different outcome. 'What if I just keep this book for us, for me and my girls, a legacy handed down the generations? After all, it's primarily my/their story, isn't it? And besides, there are multitudes of other amazing and far better written books out there than mine.' Yes, right on cue, satan rounded up every minion that he could muster, pulling out his best ammo, to remind me of the risk I was taking in telling my story. Doing his worst, to convince me that no one would be interested in what I had to say or in any of the wisdom I had gleaned and felt called to share. Making sure I realised that people were going to mock my views and ridicule my take on events.

He was really going for it, doing all he could to silence the words - to silence my voice.

Until the one who knew me best, who'd called me to it and walked me through it, drew close and reminded me, with the words He knew my heart and my spirit would ever respond to.

We've got this Kid.

Not just that. He reminded me that this is in fact *His* story and that only *by grace*, did it become my story too. My chapter in His story only came into being because, *by grace*, he saw a need (maybe many needs), and *by grace*, He created and delivered a tailored solution to that need (me), into which He placed an indwelling of heritage, identity, purpose, potential and calling. By grace, to further help, He provided a comprehensive instruction manual to cover every eventuality (His Word). And finally, *by grace*, He provided two options for how my chapter could be written - Freehand or Hand-in-Hand.

We get to choose how we write our chapter, but always the story is His.

I believe the '*We*' is collective – ME, YOU & HIM. I believe, every part of Him, the ONE who I've tried my very best to share on these pages; every tender conversation, every loving hug, every wise word, every dream and vision, every mind-blowing gift; is the same ONE who's already there in the midst of your chapter – The chapter with your name on the top. Breathe Him in, sit with Him, talk to Him and write your masterpiece together; *Hand-in-Hand.*

I wholeheartedly believe in this season, in the secret place, our Dad has been stirring up millions of small voices like mine and yours. Turning them in to something He can use 'for good.' Something He always intended to use at this exact-point in time. Individually we are just one small voice, but collectively, we are a *ROAR*. A million different sounds and tones and languages and interpretations and volumes and unique expressions of love and hope and experiential wisdom and knowledge. With one common destiny (Heaven) and one overriding mandate (that none would be left behind).

As we each take our place in *His-story*, grasping finally that our messy life; the hurts, the failures, the victories, the mistakes, the blessings and everything in between, are all divine brush-strokes on the crazy wonderful canvas that He is desperate to unveil; how amazing and transformational would it be, not just for ourselves, but also for those He places in our lives; if we begin to nurture and value our own look, our own style, our own sound, our own beauty? Knowing, that as we courageously release it, we are releasing treasure, that someone else's chapter depends on.

Rasha'

What do you see Y'shua, when you look upon her, as you do so very often? She's a little tatty around the edges don't you think?

A little weary and worn.

A little second hand...

A little past her sell-by date. (laughs arrogantly)

Y'shua

I'll tell you what I see, Rasha',

I see victory.

I see a story unfolding perfectly.

I see a masterpiece, a thing of exquisite beauty.

I see purpose.

I see untapped potential.

I see my precious creation in all its glory.

I see 1000s of batons being exchanged.

And I see you, Rasha', losing your grip *and* your hiding place.

Then the LORD reached out, touched my lips,
and said to me,
"Listen, I am giving you the words you must speak.
Today I give you authority over nations and kingdoms
to uproot and to pull down, to destroy
and to overthrow, to build and to plant."

Jeremiah 1:9-10 GNT

17

Crown Jewels

> You don't know this new me.
> The pieces have been put back together differently.

UNKNOWN

Before we reach the end of this journey, I wanted to briefly press pause and rewind if I could, back to that girl you met at the start - that *'me'* girl - who passionately and enthusiastically seeks out all and any interesting information that might deepen her understanding or corroborate some assumption or other. Google is her best friend, for within Google lies the potential to prove or disprove some exciting fact she just uncovered. A fact, that deep within her heart, she believes lies the power to transform (for the better), well, just about anything.

The 'me' girl, who quite frequently, (most often *truth be told*) becomes so excited by the gift of discovery, that she rushes with immediacy to bless others with *the said* newfound knowledge. Such is her gut-need to share, she barely allows any time or space to absorb the gift herself. Rather like an assembly line that gathers, packages and distributes, but never pauses to inspect the products or for maintenance.

Just recently, the reality of this hit me hard and as I chatted about it with my big wise girl, she spontaneously blew me away with her response. "Mum, that's like binge eating and then vomiting it up without allowing your body to receive any of the nutrients."

Wow... just wow.

Because that is exactly what I've been doing for as long as I can remember.

Gathering, packaging, distributing – binging on awe and wonder, then paying it forward - forgetting that nestled amongst the words and headlines is the nutritionally rich soul-food, prepared especially for me by my Father to *FEAST* on. Wisdom. Knowledge. Truth. Revelation. Instruction. Validation. Love. Life-giving nutrients that require a conscious decision to sit, feast, digest and absorb.

So, in this chapter, I wanted to sit and **FEAST**, taking a little time to soak up every morsel of revelatory nourishment available, before striding forward into the concluding part of my story.

Stewarding Treasure

- **Find:** We owe it to ourselves and to our Creator to fervently search for and show up as the highly prized treasure He knows us and has called us to be.

  ▸ Firstly: In Spirit – We are both spirit and human. The precious gift of Salvation invites us to live a life that is fully alive, free from shame and fear, unshackled from sin, drenched in blessing and favour, marked by grace and shaped by love. A supernatural, promise filled, purpose driven, eternally focused, life.

  ▸ Secondly: In Unity - This is about relationship. It's the organic whole. The Church, the Body of Christ into which we bring our gifts and offerings and love to serve each other, build each other up and serve the world. This is Family and family just isn't the same when someone is missing. Its who we are in Christ and it is our foundational purpose.

  ▸ Thirdly: Individually – This is specific, it's timely, its anointed, it is the reason He placed our feet on this earth. There are pre-prepared and unique things for us to be and do. If not us, *then who*?

- **Embrace:** Once He begins to reveal this to us, we must *throw off all that hinders us* **(Hebrews 12:1)** to passionately and unapologetically accept His truth and calling, stepping into who we already are, but perhaps do not yet realise? Our life should honour Him and bring Him glory and when we embrace that wholeheartedly, we will discover a life overflowing with joy, fulfilment and blessing.

- **Activate:** Over time, we must nurture and invest in who we now know we are (learning to chill over who <u>we are not</u>.) Placing ourselves in situations and among people who can help us grow more fully into our authentic self. Sharpening and refining us and encouraging us to venture into places and situations where, through us, He can show up and show off - where our own special gifts and talents can be used in the amazing ways that He intended and prepared ahead of time.

- **Slay:** Critically, we must quickly learn to recognise and overcome the schemes and strategies of the one who is set on looting and destroying all that is divinely ours.

  > We must learn what is truth. Reveal what is truth. Speak what is **truth**. Live what is truth. And fiercely protect what is truth from the one who would slyly swap it out for a big fat lie and counterfeit treasure.

- **Truth: We must** learn what is truth. Reveal what is truth. Speak what is truth. Live what is truth. And fiercely protect what is truth from the one who would slyly swap it out for a big fat lie and counterfeit treasure.

As you edge ever closer to the final chapter of this book and into the next exciting chapter of your own story, I hope a sense of peace and enlightenment, of restoration and expectancy, of freedom and divine purpose travels onwards with you. I hope the lies and shackles of defeat, deception, rejection, hopelessness and distorted identity that have been falsely laid upon each and every one of us by the enemy of our life and our destiny are *bust asunder*. **(Nahum 1:13)**

And I hope you feel ready and able to rip off the fancy dress you no longer need, as you embark on a fantastical and sacred voyage of discovery, through prayerful and practical application, that will ultimately bring into the light the masterpiece that is *truly* and *uniquely* and *wonderfully you*.

This brief interruption to my story is intended to not only act as a reminder of the beautiful, empowering and life-giving lessons received from our precious and faithful Father, as He tenderly led me from the darkest of valleys to the top of His magnificent holy mountain, but it's also a whistle-stop look at some of the practical steps I took personally and the subsequent outcomes, during my own parallel journey of divine unveiling.

I truly hope it will in some small (or big) way, help and encourage you to begin yours.

Formation of Treasure

So, what exactly is the treasure within us and why is it so important to God *and* to satan in equal measure?

We arrive on earth with a mission - to represent the Kingdom of Heaven. To walk in the likeness and character of our Father; our *Dad*. And the uniqueness in which we are all individually created, means no one else can, has ever, or will ever, represent Him quite like you. I can't remember where I heard this, but I jotted it down because I loved the way it was put:

When you die the part of God expressed in you will never be expressed on this earth again - That's how unique every human being and human spirit is to God. Unique. One if a kind.

We need to 100% grasp that we are divinely shaped and God's word on who we are is truth. Yet, we also have to wake up to the fact that we have an evil enemy, who exists to question truth and distort God's perfect design. He does this so subtlety that we hardly notice, and the second we allow satan even the smallest

The second we allow **satan** even the smallest **foothold** in our mind; to question who we really are and who's we are; is the moment we too begin to **question truth**.

foothold in our mind; to question who we really are and whose we are; is the moment we too begin to question truth.

And this is what satan is after.

YOUR IDENTITY - Who a person is. Self-identity is a person's own perspective on who they are, but true identity is a state or fact which remains unchanged, regardless of varying aspects or conditions.

> *You made all the delicate, inner parts of my body and*
> *knit me together*
> *in my mother's womb. Thank you for making me so*
> *wonderfully complex.*
> *Your workmanship is marvelous—how well I know it.*

Psalm 139:13-14 NLT

YOUR CALLING – Who you are called to be. A strong impulse or inclination. A divine call into God's service. Not a job or a hobby, but a function or station in life to which one is called by God. It's often revealed as our passions, burdens and talents collide with each other.

> *Each of you should continue to live in whatever situation*
> *the Lord has placed you,*
> *and remain as you were when God first called you.*

1 Corinthians 7:17 NLT

He makes the whole body fit together perfectly. As each

part does its own special work, it helps the other parts

grow, so that the whole body is healthy and growing and

full of love.

Ephesians 4:16 NLT

YOUR PURPOSE – The reason a person exists. The function/task/ value offering of the intentional design; the thing God has prepared for you to do; the end goal. It gives meaning.

For we are God's masterpiece.

He has created us anew in Christ Jesus,

so we can do the good things he planned for us long ago.

Ephesians 2:10 NLT

YOUR VISION – The song in your heart. The thing that motivates and releases imagination. The power of anticipating what may come. A sensing that prompts action towards a desired future or outcome.

Each one, as a good manager of God's different gifts,

must use for the good of others

the special gift he has received from God.

1 Peter 4:10 GNT

YOUR DESTINY – Where a person is <u>heading</u>. A divine call into God's service. A predetermined, pre-planned course of events. The root is the Latin word Destinare, meaning 'that which has been firmly established.'

You saw me before I was born. Every day of my life was

recorded in your book.

Every moment was laid out before

a single day had passed.

Psalm 139:16 NLT

YOUR POTENTIAL – The ability to get there. Untapped power. Dormant ability, hidden away; a treasure yet to be discovered. An undeveloped possibility, an unrealised or suppressed future. Potential is who we are, but probably don't know yet. It's what God is continually drawing us towards. Potential is never about what we've already done. Once we've done it, it's done. Potential is about what we are capable of doing or becoming, which, in partnership with God, is limitless. The root is the Latin word potent/posse, meaning to have power, to be mighty.

But forget all that— it is nothing

compared to what I am going to do.

For I am about to do something new.

See, I have already begun. Do you not see it?

Isaiah 43:18-19 NLT

YOUR MISSION – The Behaviours and Values <u>by which</u> a person will get there. What a person does and the way they do it. An important task. The nature of a person's business or duty.

God leads us from place to place in one perpetual victory

parade. Through us,

he brings knowledge of Christ. Everywhere we go,

people breathe in the

exquisite fragrance. Because of Christ,

381

we give off a sweet scent rising to God,

which is recognised by those on the way of salvation —

an aroma redolent with life...

We stand in Christ's presence when we speak;

God looks us in the face.

We get what we say straight from God and say it as

honestly as we can.

2 Corinthians 2:14-17 Message

Oh yes, satan wants your birth right, so we must steward and guard our precious treasure with diligence, alertness, with great wisdom and with respect.

Appraisal of Treasure

God is a gentleman. He doesn't force anything onto us. He lets us choose how we want to do life. We get to make big and small decisions, based on our changeable human emotions and what we believe will make our lives better. However, if there's one thing my journey over the past few years has taught me, it's that it is almost impossible to be truly happy and fulfilled living out a life that I design for myself, independently of God and independently of the purpose and vision He's planted deep within me? A life where I miss out on the immeasurable potential that burns away inside of me. Adventures, experiences, relationships, and unique missions that are specifically mine for the taking – all forfeited for an OK version of life – it seems like such a waste.

What's become increasingly clear to me is that, despite being born with our tailor-made future firmly sealed inside of us, and with all the things we need to fulfil our purpose and reach our perfect and intended destination; that
That mischievous **free will** card is just so darn tempting.

mischievous *free will* card is just so darn tempting. It lures us time after time, into making impulsive choices. Choices which end up becoming the **MOMENTS OF IMPACT** that sadly place us on paths full of hazard warning lights and dead ends. Paths we were never meant to tread, where we drag around on our backs the weight and heartache of our own poor decision, or even worse, of someone else's.

And as the weight gets heavier and heavier to lug around, it becomes impossible to see beyond the pain and the loss of our hoped-for future. Hard to see a way back.

But when we let God into that pain, He begins to put us back together in a way that is beyond our wildest dreams. The cracks and the broken places end up becoming the place where the light enters in, a holy place, where, in the darkness, resurrected hope, understanding and purpose begin to push through. These cracks and scars that we once believed would forever hold us captive and define us, now become the deeper story – the story under the story - the truth underneath the surface of the story we've been telling ourself; the story (and lie) satan has been impressing on our minds for far too long. *That* story is NOT the real story. The real story is way more merciful and powerful and stunning and full of love and promise.

Opportunity lies in failure and mistakes and pain. The struggle is often necessary to birth what is coming and the story of your struggle may just be somebody else's lifeline. We all know that diamonds are formed in the dark, deep within the earth's crust, under conditions of intense heat and pressure; yet they are considered to be one of planet earth's most precious commodities. Bringing the extraordinary presence of God into your situation will ignite a flame within your life that causes you to

Bringing the **extraordinary presence of God** into your situation will ignite a flame within your life that causes you to burn with such brilliance, others will instinctively know there's something different. Something so valuable and attractive, they'll want to reach out and take hold of it.
Then you'll get to tell them what that difference is...
His name is Jesus.

383

burn with such brilliance, others will instinctively know there's something different. Something so valuable and attractive, they'll want to reach out and take hold of it.

Then you'll get to tell them what that difference is...

His name is **JESUS**.

Perspective, perspective perspective. I can't stress enough the important of perspective. How we see something is all about our viewpoint, the angle of our lens, our mindset, our attitude, our objectivity. Let's go back to that sparkly diamond. It starts off in life as a bit of dirty carbon. But add *time, heat, pressure* and *one almighty volcanic eruption* to bring it to the surface and ta da, we call it a diamond. So, what is it really? And why does what it's gone through change everything? When Joseph met his brothers, years after they had thrown him in the pit and sold him into slavery, he said 'You *sold* me', however, by that time he had realised the truth; that God had in fact *sent* him. (**Genesis 45:5**) In what had appeared to be a cruel act of rejection by his brothers twenty years earlier, Joseph had ultimately come to see what had really been going on – that God had actually been orchestrating a divine strategy, which in time would elevate Joseph (whose name means 'increase') and place him in a significant position of authority at the exact time his family needed to be rescued from starvation. Joseph had been on a twenty-year rescue mission.

And then there is the lovely Naomi...

During a brief season of famine, rather than sitting things out, Naomi, whose name means pleasant and lovely, along with her two sons and husband, chose to leave their hometown of Bethlehem, a place that worshiped God, who's name meant Bread/Land of Plenty; a place where their family was considered nobility and honoured; to move to Moab (meaning land of waste) **Ruth 1**. Moab was a land of foreigners who worshiped many gods and over ten years Moab became a place of death and misfortune for Naomi, as one by one, her husband, followed by both her sons died, leaving her with nothing.

Feeling desolate and full of grief, and seeing that the harvest had returned to Bethlehem, she concluded that God had surely deserted her and that the only way to win back God's favour was to retrieve the past. She decided that, once she had released her now widowed Moabite daughters-in-law from their responsibilities to her, she would travel back to her kinsmen in Bethlehem. However, Ruth, one of her daughters-in-law refused to leave her side and committed to go with her wherever she went, so together they journeyed to Bethlehem.

They were surprised by the great celebration that greeted them, as people remembered Naomi and **who she was**, praising the *agreeable* and *pleasant* women, genuinely excited about her return. BUT, Naomi, had so wrongly begun to identify herself with sadness and the misfortune that had befallen her in foreign lands, that she couldn't bear to hear them call by her true nature, instead crying out to them to call her 'Mara', meaning *bitter*. In her deep suffering, Naomi had become bitter (**Ruth 1:20**). And such was her pain and bitterness, that she began to place her identity in it, believing God had brought affliction upon her because of her disobedience.

Nothing could have been further from the truth.

What Naomi could not have known, or ever imagined in her sadness, was the *MAHUSIVE* kingdom strategy wrapped around her *liddle* trip to Moab, because in Moab, Naomi was collecting Ruth, and Ruth was destined to be part of the genealogy of Jesus. Ruth in her own bereavement and her great loyalty to Naomi was about to marry into Naomi's family and would become the Great Grandmother of King David.

Her life had significant *purpose*, she was *called* on Kingdom business, her **mission**, to find the one who would bear a son, who would bear a son, who would bear a king. And her **destiny** was to be used by God for all eternity, to impart the nature and ways of our Father.

And the pleasant and lovely Naomi would nurse and nurture David's grandfather. Naomi's sweet nature would be called upon to rock and sooth and pray over and bless the Grandaddy of King David, through whose bloodline the Saviour of the world would come. I'm getting goosebumps as I type this.

I wonder who we are rocking when we cuddle and pray over our own children and grandchildren. We just never know what God has planned do we?

It turns out that God wasn't mad at Naomi. In fact, God himself had *sent* her. Sent her, refined her in some difficult circumstances, severed and pruned a few branches and then called her back home to fulfil her amazing purpose in His-story. Her life had significant purpose, she was *called* on Kingdom business, her mission, to find the one who would bear a son, who would bear a son, who would bear a king. And her destiny was to be used by God for all eternity, to impart upon us the nature and ways of our Father.

But right in the middle of it all, her vision and her identity got skewed. Her head and her emotions told her heart a big fat lie. *And let's take a guess at who was feeding that lie?* Smack bang in the middle of God's perfectly orchestrated divine plan, she forgot who she was – she forgot *whose* she was, and with the absence of truth in her heart, her sorrow saw nothing but mistakes, loss, failure, guilt, fear, confusion, sadness and bitterness.

In the middle of it all, her vision and her **identity** got skewed. Her head and her emotions told her heart a big fat lie. Smack bang in the middle of God's perfectly orchestrated divine plan, she forgot who she was - she forgot *whose* she was, and with the absence of truth in her heart, her sorrow saw nothing but mistakes, loss, failure, guilt, fear, confusion, sadness and bitterness.

God's perspective is crucial. His ways are so radically different than our ways...

For my thoughts about mercy are not like your thoughts,
and my ways are different from yours.
As high as the heavens are above the earth, so my ways
and my thoughts are higher than yours.
As the snow and rain that fall from heaven do not return
until they have accomplished their purpose, soaking the
earth and causing it to sprout with new life, providing
seed to sow and bread to eat.
So also will be the word that I speak; it does not return
to me unfulfilled.
My word performs my purpose and fulfills the mission I
sent it out to accomplish.

Isaiah 55:8-11 TPT

And there are certain things that can only be learned and prepared for on the front line (or in the darkness of the precious valley floor). All through the ages God had worked His purposes out through ordinary people, often living in complicated circumstances, giving it their best shot; sometimes getting it right and sometimes getting it horribly wrong. He uses our lives to demonstrate *His* nature and *His* power for the glory of *His* name, whether through blessing or through difficulties. Either way, there is a watching world who need to know that our Dad never ever forsakes us and always brings things together for His glory and for our good.

I can't help but wonder; thinking back 30 years to the drama that resulted in my near-death moment and the removal of my spleen; as He'd guided the surgeon's hands to masterfully remove the now squished jelly-like organ, whose first role in life had been to act as a washing machine for my blood; had He already known then, that the space left inside of me would, in time, provide a different kind of space? One in which; *me in Him and He in me;* would sit together, in separation from the world and write a predetermined *good work*? It's a mind-blowing thought. Seeing the reality and truth of this play out right under my nose this past year has helped me see that nothing is ever wasted. Watching bad stuff get flipped on its head to springboard heaven's plans has really helped me to make sense of my life in a way that I hadn't previously been able to. And as I've dug in, unpacking all of the things He's been revealing to me about who He had in mind when He designed me, I'm finally starting to see what He's been trying to show me all along – A Masterpiece: *A beautiful portrait of Cath* – I've always made sense to Him, but now I'm finally beginning to make total sense to me too.

I've been blessed with a secret and the truth is so much simpler than the illusion. Laying ourselves bare, remaining uncovered and visible in the presence of ourselves, of others and of our Creator is so much more liberating and joyful and potent than covering up.

Ask Eve.

Excavation of Treasure

John Calvin wrote: It is certain that man never achieves a clear knowledge of himself/herself, unless he has first looked upon God's face, **and then descends from contemplating Him, to scrutinize himself.**

We are divinely shaped. Of course, we must remember its more about who He is than who we are, but if we don't know who we are. How can we be helpful to Him?

Your *unique* is your winning formula – but we have to first go to God to discover what that winning formula consists of. We can do that through prayer or by delving into scripture - many times the Holy Spirit has confirmed things to me through _repetitive words_/ statements/events etc. when I've been reading my bible. Suddenly

I'll notice common threads or words that just keep coming up over and over again. Let's go back to Naomi. In **Ruth 1:6-15** the words *'go back', 'go home', 'return'* appear eight separate times. His direction is consistent and persistent, we just need to look in the right places and join the dots.

Other times it's been through *dreams*, or in a *Word of knowledge*, or indeed through *other people*.

Check out your *name* too – perhaps it's no mistake you ended up with it?

Something that has been massively helpful for me is to take some quiet time to sit and *write all the things I see in myself*; my core temperament, characteristics, skills, expertise, preferences, dislikes, spiritual gifts etc. I include words that really move my spirit. Words that bring me alive and energise me.

Also, learn from your past. Listen to your life so far; the ways God has shaped you, showed up in your life, the relationships that have moulded you, your accomplishments where you flourished and the experiences that empowered and invigorated you. Let the Holy Spirit remind you where *He* was at work (or not.)

Then, ask groups of friends, family, colleagues, church family to provide *three key words* or statements that they feel describes you best. Where do they see your value, what's your *personal brand* in their eyes? Clearly, you'll have different types of relationships with each group, so the range of words are going to have different inclinations, but quickly, you'll see clear themes developing. It's not unusual to discover a few surprises; what we see and value in ourselves may not always reflect what others see and value in us, and sometimes there's a beautiful nugget of gold or multi-faceted gem just waiting to be brought into the light. Remember God created you on purpose, for purpose and that purpose always involves people, so the observations from the people in your circles of influence are critical in this process. They are going to tell you the value you bring into their life and that's a pretty good indicator of the foundational *you*.

An exercise I did which turned out to be super enlightening, was to take a bunch of my key words and compare dictionary meanings and even biblical meanings where relevant – the extra narrative brought a much more intense colour, richness and clarity to the whole process.

Doing the work is going to require commitment, time and effort and honesty. Get real with yourself and with God. Fully embrace the journey and keep an open heart and mind. And remember, its dynamic – God never stops talking to us and shaping us and surprising and pushing us, so it's never a *once and done* thing. However, as you diligently and prayerfully brings all the insight and pieces of the puzzle together, get ready to be blown away by the results. When it's right, you'll 100% know - it will be soaked in peace, power, liberation and familiarity. Familiarity was the one thing that really floored me. I recognised me. I was able to look at the visual I'd created below and go, yes, that really is me.

> Until we grasp the truth of who we are, we live life exhausted trying to be something we're not, which then bring a counterfeit and messy version of us into our relationships and projects.

Until we grasp the truth of who we are, we live life exhausted trying to be something we're not, which then brings a counterfeit and messy version of us into our relationships and projects. Embracing the work that will lead you back to the whole you, is the wisest and bravest move of all.

Of course, this is going to be a very personal and private journey between you and God. But, in keeping with laying ourselves bare and sharing to encourage and grow each other, I'm choosing to humbly and gingerly share the fruits of my labour below. Much of the content and statements in my cube are the words of others, which resonated strongly, but it has been a team project between me, my tribe and God.

I do sincerely and passionately hope that this portrait of the crazy wonderful me, helps and motivates you to go in search of the Crazy Wonderful *YOU.*

MY VISION

To be a 'city without walls', doing the impossible with Jesus.

To pass through this life freely and spiritedly, splashing 'Him' on people.

No big titles (apart from Momma & Nannie), no big earthly reputation or huge stash of cash (other than what this traveller needs to do life); just that I leave a little of me and a lot of Him behind... and a big love story would be wonderful.

I hope my story tells of the truth, faithfulness, power, and total mind-blowing awesomeness of Jesus and leaves behind a trail of clues along the path to Divine Purpose for future generations.

My real legacy will I pray be a deep, well-watered family root that produces seed after seed, fruit after fruit, generation after generation, for God's Glory and Kingdom Purpose.

MY MISSION

To do the impossible with Jesus and leave a JC trail wherever I go

To be attractive to people because of *His* light in me

To encourage passion and 'wow' in others through my testimony

To impart people's hearts with the truth of the Gospel, sparking a flame that brings new hope

To operate in my spiritual gifts & be powerful in battle

To bring God's revelations to the world

To bless radically and randomly

To encourage others to grow into themselves and into their rightful purpose and destiny

To love fiercely and unconditionally and to forgive easily

To always care more about the wounding than the mess seeping out of the wound

To always find new ways to nurture, encourage and bless my precious family

To live a life full of adventure, fun and childlike naughtiness

To always remain curious

To transform ugly to lovely, ashes to beauty-in a way that causes an emotional response

To always be a fixer of stuff

To keep my hands clean and my heart pure

To live in a freedom that allows me to respond spontaneously

To just be ME; my own kind of crazy-wonderful

I should make it clear, whilst this is the cry of my heart, I most definitely don't always live this out.

PORTRAIT CUBE

A CITY WITHOUT WALLS

COMMON THEMES OF SCRIPTURE/ VISIONS/DREAMS	SPIRITUAL GIFTING/FRUITS	KEY WORDS OVER ME (OTHERS)	TEMPERAMENT ATTRIBUTES
GO "I know who I am"	LIGHT BEARER	SPONTANIOUS	FREE SPIRIT
	WATCHMAN	NOMAD	ADVENTUROUS
	DISCERNMENT	ITINERANT	BOLD
	KNOWLEDGE	FEARLESS	COMFY IN OWN SKIN
	REVELATION	COURAGEOUS/BRAVE	ENERGY/ ENTHUSIASM
	FAITH	ADAPTABLE	NOT DEFINED BY MY SURROUNDINGS
		DECISIVE	ALL IN/ALL OUT
PRAY "never without love and grace"	GRACE/LOVE	FIXER	BARRIER BASHER
	MERCY	PURE HEART	GENEROUS/GIVER
	INCERCESSION	STEADFAST	EXPECT THE IMPOSSIBLE
	FAITH	GIVING OF SELF/RESOURCES	CONVICTION FROM HEART (PURE)
	WARFARE	HOPE BRINGER	WARM/CARING
	DISCERNMENT	INSIGHTFUL	LOVE PEOPLE HARD
	REVELATION	DEEP	PONDERER/CURIOUS
BUILD/REBUILD/ RESTORE "gentle resolve"	MIRACLES	SEE POSSIBILITY	LIMITLESS
	PROPHECY	GENTLE RESOLVE	PROBLEM SOLVER
	SEER – VISIONS/ DREAMS	TRANSFORM	MAKE THINGS BEAUTIFUL
	DISCERNMENT	FRUITFUL	DO-ER
	WISDOM	INDUSTRIOUS	RESOURCEFUL
	KNOWLEDGE	DETERMINED	RESOLUTE
	LEADERSHIP	BATON CARRIER	PEACEMAKER/FORGIVER
RECORD/DOCUMENT/TELL "concerned with it all" "you speak my language"	WATCHMAN	STORY TELLER	
	REVELATION (PROPHET)	HOPE CARRIER	
	SEER – VISIONS/ DREAMS	EMPOWERING	
	LIGHT BEARER	WITNESS BEARER	
	DISCERNMENT	AUTHENTIC	
	WISDOM	CHEER LEADER	
	GRACE/LOVE/ FAITH	TRUTH BRINGER	
	EXHORT	VISIONARY	

393

Earlier, I mentioned using the dictionary (or Google) to dig deeper into some of your personal *buzz words*. Here's a few of mine. Have a read and see how words can really start to come alive as we explore them.

Adventure – To dare; To take a chance; An exciting or bold undertaking with uncertain outcome

Courage – Quality of mind and spirit that enables a person to face pain, danger, difficulty without fear; The heart as the source of emotion; Endurance; Fortitude; Audacity; Fearlessness

Create – To cause something to come into being that wouldn't naturally evolve; To evolve from one's own thoughts; To bring about/make happen

Dew – Purity; Delicacy; Refreshing in quality

Discernment – Acuteness of judgement and understanding

Encourage – To inspire with courage; To stimulate by approval; Assistance

Expressive – Full of meaning; Energetic; Dramatic; Colourful; Passionate; Vivid; Alive; Revelatory

Fruitful – Producing abundant growth; Abounding in fruit

Heart – Spirit; Courage; Enthusiastic

Independent – Not influenced or controlled by others thoughts; not dependent on something else for existence; Free spirit; Unconstrained; Expressive in spirit

Inspire – Exalting influence; To communicate or suggest by divine influence; To arouse a feeling in others; To bring about

Itinerant – To journey; Someone characterised by alternating periods of working and wandering

Light – That which makes things visible; To radiate illuminous energy; A device for the ignition of a spark; An illuminating agent; A sensation produced by stimulating the organs of sight

Nomad – Wanderer; Itinerate; to move from place to place seasonally; Pastoral/outlander; To feed flocks; To graze

Nurture – To feed; To train; To educate; To protect

Open – Available; Generous; Bounteous; Without covering; Without restriction or concealment;

Problem Solve – Remove obstacles; Find Solutions

Pure – Being *that* and nothing else; Untainted by evil; Innocent

Resolve – To separate and make visible the separate parts; To distinguish between; To determine; Firmness; Boldness; Steadfastness; Resolute; Purposefulness

Resourceful – Ability to face and resolve difficulties; Able to deal skilfully and promptly with situations; A resource; Source; Supply; Aid that can be drawn upon when needed; To rise up

Story – A narrative; An account; An Allegation; A Chronicle

Thought-full – To call things to a conscious mind; To remember experiences; To reason; Astute; Attentive; Prudent; To conceive; To make choices; To analyse; Theorist

Transform – To bring about change; To change in condition, nature or character; Recreate; Re-establish

Unguarded - Candid; Pure in heart; Honest; Impulsive; Accessible; Spontaneous; Straightforward

Visionary – A power of sensing with the yes; Anticipating with the mind that which will or may come to be credible, but is not actually present

As you can imagine, I've spent a great deal of time on this so don't panic and take as much time as you need. It's not a race. You're going on a **treasure hunt** - It's a journey and a process and it should be fun. In time, I believe it will bring you wonder, awe, peace and understanding around who you are and why you're here.

> If we don't grasp the truth, that there is a price on our head and a very real **battle for our treasure**, and we don't learn to recognise the difference between the voice of our Dad and the voice of our adversary; then life is going to stay messy and exhausting and lacking in purpose.

As a good girl and someone who likes to please, I can fall into the trap of saying yes to too many people and things, which ultimately breeds frustration and burn-out. Having some kind of visual to refer to really helps me figure out if an open door or a request for help is a God thing or a *suck the life out of me / steel my joy and energy thing* – God things almost always play to our gifts, motivations and passions and if it they don't, we're probably not the best person for the job.

Battle for Treasure

I wanted to wrap up this chapter with a final reminder of something I shared right at the very beginning of the book – Satanic Monitoring. It's definitely a creepy statement. Yet, if we don't grasp the truth, that there is a price on our head and a very real battle for our treasure, and we don't learn to recognise the difference between the voice of our Dad and the voice of our adversary; then life is going to stay messy and exhausting and lacking in purpose.

Sometimes we have to pause and ask ourselves *is* that something the one who loves me most, the one who created me, the one who has my back and wants the very best for me, would say? Would that person honestly put me in *that* relationship, *that* situation, tempt me with *that* thing? Does this feel right?

Practice (and prayer) makes perfect.

Satan does not want us to press into all that God has waiting for us. He wants to tie us to our past, to remind us of it, to define us by it. He is a master at using our emotions and when we let our emotions linger, they steal our courage and our truth.

> Satan is a master at using our **emotions** and when we let our emotions linger, they steal our courage and our truth.

So, we have to know what is true, believe what is true, declare what is true, pray into what is true and overcome every attack of the enemy *in truth.* We need to do this before the battles, during the battle and afterwards, in an act of thanksgiving.

> **Truth combats lies** and the easiest way to speak out truth is to speak out God's word straight from Scripture as if God Himself is speaking it out.

Truth combats lies and the easiest way to speak out truth is to speak out God's word straight from Scripture as if God Himself is speaking it out.

Ephesians 6:11 tells us that God has provided us with His armour to wear daily. It might seem a bit odd at first, but visualise yourself daily putting this on – remember, we are not fighting flesh and blood, it is an invisible and spiritual battle, so we need to fight it with spiritual amour.

- † **Sword of spirit** – The living word of God

- † **Helmet of Salvation** – To protect our mind and thoughts from being taken hostage

- † **Sandals of Peace** – To stay standing on the firm foundations of the Gospel

- † **Breastplate of Righteousness** – Our right standing before God

- † **Shield of Faith** – Protects out heart and vital organs from the fiery darts of the enemy

- † **Belt of Truth** – Keeps our mind ordered and not in chaos, knowing we overcome in truth

Releasing Treasure

And finally, there is a scripture that comes to mind as I think about each of us, right now, excitedly preparing to take our place in His-story, by releasing our own precious treasure to the far reaches of the earth.

> *He gives me words that pierce and penetrate.*
>
> *He hid me and protected me in the shadow of his hand.*
>
> *He prepared me like a polished arrow*
>
> *and concealed me in his quiver.*

Isaiah 49:2 TPT

I can see it now, out of His concealed **quiver,** *you,* **His polished arrows are preparing to come forth,** radiating His light and His glory, ready to release words and actions that will bring devastation to the kingdom of darkness and beauty to the world.

God's choice of words are never an accident.

To physically be made into an arrow, a branch much go through a number of stages:

Changed: A branch must first be cut away from the tree it's attached to; forgetting it's a branch, to become something altogether different.

Pruned: All the obvious imperfections, leaves, twigs must then be removed.

Sanded: Then the more subtle imperfections that may appear small, but would cause the arrow to miss its mark, must be sanded away.

Seasoned: The arrow is then placed inside a dark instrument, where it's flooded with water, before the heat is turned up. This is a critical stage, as too much heat, or not enough heat will result in an arrow that won't perform effectively.

Penetrating Power: A metal arrowhead is added so it can penetrate its target.

The Fletching: The correct placing of feathers provides direction and balance.

The Cresting: Markings are placed on the side to identify to whom the arrow belongs.

In this chapter of your story, you are being set apart, pruned, refined in the fire, seasoned by Heaven and anointed with divine power. He is ready to bring back balance in your life and set your feet upon the firm rock and path to purpose. His mark is ready to be placed upon you and I believe you are about to fly.

Golgotha 33AD, Friday, the 6ᵗʰ hour

Y'shua

(darkness falls) Abba (one in spirit) They have surrounded me and pierced my body. They stare and gloat over me, whilst dividing my garments among them, casting lots for my clothing. But you, my Father, are not far off. O my Strength, come quickly to help me.

Forgive them Abba, for they know not what they do.

[Just before the 9th hour]

Y'shua

(loud cry of dereliction) Eloi, Eloi, lama sabachthani?

Rasha'

He saved others, but he can't save himself. (mocking and inciting the crowds and pharisees) He's the king of Israel. Let him come down now from the cross, and we will believe in him (laughing loudly). He trusts in God. Let God rescue him now if he wants him, for he said *I am the Son of God.*

Abba

Oh, my Son, my precious Son (turns head away in unbearable agony), NEVER will I forsake you. The sin that weighs upon you is their sin. Your sacrifice is more than I can bare; yet, the laying down of your life for them all, is the most beautiful exchange. You are defeating death and darkness, once and FOR ALL. I will raise you up in Glory, above all others. Not long now my Son...

Y'shua (looks below)

I thirst...

[The 9th hour]

Y'shua

Tetelestai (as the lamb sacrifice and prayers are being offered up in the temple). Into your hands I commit my spirit. (takes His last breath)

Rasha'

Checkmate! (cheers victoriously; until sudden fracture within Zion's temple floods him with terror)

Abba

Not so quick Rasha, I have one last move. Posterity will serve him; future generations will be told about Him. They will proclaim his righteousness to a people yet unborn—for he has done it.

And they will forever be free from your curs'ed grip.

I declare from the beginning how it will end and foretell

from the start what has not yet happened.

I decree that my purpose will stand, and I will fulfill my

every plan.

Isaiah 46:10 TPT

18

One More Move

It was a charming puzzlement - finishing, it turned out, was not the end after all.

Au contraire; finishing, had become her beginning.

C.S.

There is a little-known story about two men who are wandering through an art gallery together, admiring a famous painting by Friedrich Moritz August Retzsch called, *Checkmate*. The painting depicts a man playing a game of chess with satan. Typically, satan is grinning ear-to-ear because he has the man cornered. The painting is entitled., *Checkmate*, to indicate that the game is all over, that satan has won. His opponent has no more moves.

As the first man looking at the painting is ready to move on to other paintings in the gallery, the second, an international chess champion, decides he wants to study the painting a little longer, so waves on his friend, saying that he'll catch him up shortly. He continues to stare intently at the old masterpiece in front of him, with a particular interest in the chessboard itself.

Suddenly, he steps back, flabbergasted.

"It's wrong!" he calls out to his friend. "There's one more move."

His friend dashes back and together they scrutinise the painting.

"We have to contact the painter," the chess champion declares, "it's not checkmate...

the King has one more move."

When the concept for this book first drew breath, I publicly committed the last chapter to my heavenly Father. Everything in me was convinced, that by the time I reached the point of writing this final chapter, He would have provided me with an amazing, *wow-worthy Ta Da...* For a while I held a clear sense of what that *Ta Da* would be, but over time, as things (and me) evolved and shifted, I began to allow for God's creativity to show up, embracing a healthy curiosity about the glorious thing He might do in my life; always certain that ultimately, it would happen and I would get to theatrically declare, *Just look what He did.*

So, I got busy doing and writing and waiting in faith for that life changing knock at the door, that surprise email or phone call, that serendipitous encounter; which in my mind, was the destination, the glorious pinnacle, the mountain-top moment; that the entirety of my book-writing journey (from beginning to end) had always been pointing towards.

Whilst *He*, with some amusement and delight I'm quite sure, got busy, quietly restoring His masterpiece.

THE SECRET PLACE

†

He'd designed, constructed and shipped the most impeccable and unmatched solution on that allotted day, with world-class features that carried infinite potential. Little Cath was packed with incalculable ideas and concepts, with an intuitive problem-solving capability, a backlight that ran 24/7 and an internal drive that meant her zest for life and energy pack rarely ran low. Little Cath was also designed in such a way, that she was able to function effectively, wherever in the world she was sent, making her highly flexible and adaptable. Her circuit board, which acted as her main interface, was deliberately embedded in the 'heart' of her architecture, so that her primary power source, her unique features and attributes, plus all of the numerous information channels flowing in and out of it, were optimized. This would also guarantee outstanding results from future second and third generation networking ~ the options would be limitless. And in time, planned upgrades would deliver a dynamic security feature that would trigger alerts whenever potential risks and threats were identified. As with all of the others, He designed little Cath with such meticulous and thoughtful detail, that He knew, only she, in her purest form, could satisfy the exacting needs of the people, places, situations and tasks that He had prepared already, for her time in circulation.

Of course, He had allowed some margin for any blips or stoppage time. Periodic servicing and retuning were always something He factored in.

Layer after layer, he peeled back all that had been covering and disguising and misrepresenting her precious and perfect childlike character; the one that she'd instinctively understood and embraced at the beginning, the one that made Him weep with joy and delight, the one He still desperately needed.

It had all been visible. Until it wasn't. Until her talk got all grown up. Until she lost her wonder and awe. Until she started blending in and fitting in. Until she tried so hard to be good, that being good, became her identity. Until she listened to who *they* said she was. Until the lies and the tricks and all the other worldly things, caused her to forget. Until she labelled her dreams '*childlike*' and '*foolish*'; instead of '*divinely planted*'. Until she began to talk about little Cath as if *she* were actually the problem, rather that *the solution*.

How He had delighted in reminding her. How He had relished feeding her insatiable curiosity and unquenchable thirst to know more. How free she became as she realised the truth. And doing it together had been the best part of all.

He stood gazing on her. His blinding light pulsating in its brilliancy. She was His pride and joy. She always had been, but now, there was a new radiance.

The light, His light, the one He'd always known people would be drawn to, now shone brighter than ever before. It was as if it held the resplendence of seven full days in one.

It was the same with all of them. Once they remembered who they were and more importantly, *whose* they were. Only He, could reveal it to them. It was a radiance that could not be gained in any other way.

†

And true to my word, this chapter is His.

But the *Ta Da? W*ell, as it turns out, that's another story altogether.

Because, as I dreamed up fanciful pictures in my head of the things His divine brush-stroke might bequeath to these crowning pages, He blindsided me with an element *of holy* surprise.

You see, He tells me that *I'm His Ta Da...*

Yup, that's right, the 'Ta Da' *c'est moi.*

Now, our famous Good Girl, would be shrinking away at this point, mumbling with words of false humility and awkwardness. However, it is impossible to have made the journey that I have and not be changed by it. I had a vision about a month ago, where I was in heaven, in the throne room, standing discretely right at the back of the millions of angels who were worshiping and praising Jesus. He was standing facing them, smiling and thoroughly enjoying their praises, when He suddenly spotted me. Beckoning me to come forward, He called out 'Don't stand at the back.' All at once, the angels parted, creating a walkway for me to pass through. As I approached Him, He placed His right hand around my shoulder and together we stood there, father and daughter, side by side, enjoying the beautiful angelic chorus.

So, deep breath...

Ta Daaaaaa!

And here's the thing – whilst I was fully expecting the miracle to come through someone or something; for the meaning and purpose of the rest of my life to be defined or satisfied by an 'add-on' solution; for the value of my book, my testimony, to rest upon the person or thing that rocked up just before I wrote the final chapter - Layer by layer, revelation after revelation, conversation after conversation, prune after prune, blessing after blessing - He was revealing truth - that *I* was the His final word, I was His answer, *I* was the miracle, *I* was the purpose, *I* was the solution.

He was revealing that **I was His final word**, *I* was His answer, *I* was the miracle, *I* was the purpose, *I* was the solution,

I was the *Ta Da*.

I was the *Ta Da*.

For five years (and all those that went before), I have been on the most extraordinary journey, one that a thousand different words could never fittingly capture. A journey; though terribly painful at times; I wouldn't side-step for anything. I thought that the end of my book would herald the end of my story. That the big *Ta Da* would be my signal to show the world how glorious our God is, then step back, job done, live out the rest of my life the way most people do. Only I'm not *most people* and *the end,* is actually only *the beginning.*

What's the famous saying: *Tell Jesus your plans and watch Him laugh.*

I don't think He's laughing, He's much too gracious and loving (and too much of a proud Dad) for that, but here in the final chapter, the one that has always belonged to Him, He's preparing to go *Ta Da* to me *and* to you. He's unlocking the vaults of Heavens and putting on display the Crown Jewells. And though it may not always be easy to see, that priceless treasure is you and me.

I am the Ta Da that my crazy stupid faith was believing for, all along. The signs have been there. He'd been leaving me little post-it notes everywhere; some of which I'd needed to ponder and debate, privately and prayerfully, before I was able to fully reconcile. Sometimes, He tells us things that we're just not

> Hollywood and the world have trained us to fixate on dramatic endings, but *He* is in the business of **spectacular beginning**.

ready to hear. But His patience holds space for us graciously, as we digest His good food, at a pace our bodies and hearts can manage. Hollywood and the world have trained us to fixate on dramatic endings, but *He* is in the business of spectacular beginning. And now, looking back, I see it all so clearly and so beautifully.

As my Dad and I wandered through these pages together, our spirits journeying as one,

Jesus walked me back to myself and helped me remember.

- ✓ He gave me back *my* truth and *His* truth
- ✓ He pruned what was bad and He pruned what was good
- ✓ He bandaged what was hurting
- ✓ And captured every tear
- ✓ He watered and fed what needed to grow
- ✓ Sharpening my sword for battle
- ✓ And fine-tuning my satan-antenna for protection
- ✓ He restored, redeemed, elevated and validated me
- ✓ Identifying and anointing my divine design and call

- ✓ He set me up for greatness
- ✓ And positioned me for purpose

He gave me permission to stay a little bit crazy, to be my own kind of wonderful, to cherish my perfect imperfections, to hold tight to crazy-bonkers faith, to wander wherever my nomadic spirit calls me, to love hard and to use the words and the voice He placed within me 'for good'.

And most of all, He gave me permission to shine; so very brightly, that in the afterglow, others will see Him.

This story may be mine, but I believe He's inviting you to make it yours too. I'm not a trained writer, I'm just a girl who's always loved telling stories, not realising that one day, she would become the story. Though my style of writing may not be your style, it's the only way I know to tell my honest truth; so, I hope my words have done enough. In living it and recording it, I hope I've been able to inspire you to believe again, to dream again, to look inside to the one who waits there, beckoning you to come forward and not to stand at the back, to be moved enough, to risk taking your own personal walk with Him - back to the future, back to you. Not the *you* as the world has labelled you, not even the you as *you've* labelled you - but the YOU that you truly are. The original, the blueprint, the prototype. Remembering and claiming back all the divine dreams that the uncontained, spontaneous, intuitive and fearless child within, misplaced somewhere along the way.

You have an identity that can only be found in Him. That identity is very real and very specific. It's not just a buzz word.

If you never pick up the baton that has your name etched into the side of it, what then?

I pray you *throw off everything that hinders you, so that you run your very own, unique, adventurous and limitless race* (**Hebrews 12:1**), doing it boldly and differently and intentionally and joyously, *with perseverance* and freedom; the way your Dad designed and created you to do. I pray you are brave enough to lay down and *let go of all that is behind you* and give God a clean slate to work with. Oh, how I struggled at first with abandonment, because abandonment is an exchange transaction, but what we get is so much better than what we trade.

We, my friends, are the miracle in the middle of our own stories. *We*, are the *Ta Da* to the world. *We*, are Heaven's solution. Our perfect imperfections were designed on purpose, for a purpose. No mistakes, no misfits, no spares, no copies. Every single one of us, a *one-off*. And once we truly grasp that; surely then, we owe it to this wonderfully messy, painfully broken, stunningly beautiful, desperately in-need, hopefully expectant world; *and* to our own irreplaceable and promised-filled story and the stories of those whose paths are predestined to cross ours; to make sure that we show up as '*us*'?

> We are the *Ta Da* to the world. We are **Heaven's solution**. Our perfect imperfections were designed on purpose, for a purpose. No mistakes, no misfits, no spares, no copies. Every single one of us, a *one-off*.

Let's do it together.

Then maybe one day I will get to read your story, told in a way that only you can.

There is a quote that I love which says *Mix our pages, bleed our ink; write your story into mine, so there are no beginnings and no endings; just pages of us.* (**Atticus**) – Isn't that just a fabulous picture. Let's mix our pages and bleed our ink, let's desire; that as we all find our way home to our childlike self again, revealing the ONE, that THE ONE imagined, designed, built and sent; on purpose, in purpose; let's desire that our paths cross serendipitously (a pre-destined happy collision), in a way that makes our Dad smile with pride and delight, declaring, 'Now that's what I'm talkin about.'

Be bold, be different, be the change, be the ONE - You'll never influence the world or change it, by being just like it, like everyone else. YOU, my amazing friend, are designed and created to be different, unique, to stand out, to stand up, with all of your own kind of crazy wonderfulness and light.

Abandonment is an exchange transaction.

And when you realise all of this,
dat light is gonna shine

SEVEN TIMES BRIGHTER

Moonlight will shine as bright as sunlight, and

the sun's glare will become seven times brighter,

like the light of seven days rolled into one, when The Lord

binds up the wounds of His peple.

Isaiah 30:26 TPT

So that, through you, others will one day, see Him.

One final word, for those days when showing up as the crazy wonderful you that you are, feels just too hard and too confusing and too lonely and too messed up – When the constant marketing hacks and lies and labels from the great deceiver makes you want to yank those familiar disguises back up and hide away (or even worse, give up altogether) - Never, ever forget that this chapter, as hard as it's been (*maybe even still is*), is simply that; one difficult, but perhaps, necessary, chapter within your amazing and divine story. It may be a chapter you choose to forget? Or it may be a chapter you revisit many times? It may even be a chapter you find yourself reading aloud to others down the line, because that's how we grow and that's how we harvest.

But one thing you can be sure of, it's most definitely not the end of your story.

What if you played around with *today's* wrap-around narrative? What if you set your *curious* loose and tried to look at things with slightly different eyes?

What if you discovered, like Naomi, that there's a lot more to the plot of this chapter than you ever dreamed possible?

Look closer, study it, then study it some more until you see it. Dare to align your creativity (even your faith if you can) with His. Allow your heart to gaze beyond what your eyes think they see, into the secret place where your Father works day and night. And let the remnants of your *all but invisible* flame be supernaturally fanned, *whoosh*, back into life - small at first, dancing unseen in the dark, of course - yes; but then in no time at all, a little taller, a little stronger, a little more mischievous, a little more hope-filled; until your beautiful *ORA* sends shards of light and radiance across the pages of the next chapter.

Remember that old three-wheeler bike in my dad's garage – well your next big reveal is on its way too. Hidden away in His workshop, *your* Dad has been discretely and skilfully arranging the unique fragments of your heartbreak, that awful rejection, the huge disappointment, that sense of failure, your deferred hope, your shattered dreams – all of the unplanned and undesired parts of your last chapter - into the most beautiful story you every read. The story of you.

With His usual gentleness and precision, He has been lovingly and skilfully transforming your broken pieces into an even more beautiful version of you – 'a gift, as if seen for the very first time,' perfect for this very moment. Below your layers of scuffed and chipped paint the original 'fearfully and wonderfully made' structure is still fundamentally the same – YOU are still YOU - but your heart, your soul, your spirit, your wisdom, your testimony tell a much greater story.

And in this next chapter all will be revealed, because...

The King (your Dad)

always has One More Move!

EPILOGUE

A last-minute message had unexpectedly popped up on her phone, just as she was about to leave. *They would be there.* She caught her breath briefly, imagining how it might play out. But, by then it seemed too late to change her plans, and for some strange reason, she hadn't wanted to?

Only a few months earlier, this would have shaken her to the core, perhaps even caused her to stay home, but somehow it felt like it was time. She had noticed a shift in the atmosphere these past few weeks. Deep down she knew something was happening. Getting ready. In preparation for what, she wasn't sure, but she found her spirit suddenly dancing to the beat of expectancy and promise. Maybe this was all part of it? Closure. Healing. Finality?

In reality, nothing significant had changed, and yet, it seemed like everything had changed.

There wasn't a specific moment that she could pinpoint, she was simply aware that things no longer felt lost or stolen, the way they once had. The way they had for too long. The giant suddenly looked small and far away.

And so, she'd come. Here. Not hidden, not fearful, not rejected, but brave and bold and strong and beautiful and excited. It felt like a passing-out celebration. A victory parade in her honour. She chuckled at that thought – it was crazy, yet in the dimmed, holy space she felt celebrated, upheld, exalted. There really was only one explanation – Him.

Sitting in the beautiful presence of her Father, the most unusual comfort bubbled up inside. How could that be? Her past, a mere thirty meters away? If she turned her head, she would be able to see them, but somehow it didn't seem to matter anymore. So much of what had been a part of her, part of all three of them; part of everything she'd loved dearly – here, in her Father's house, the gap between them had become an ocean. The familiarity, strangely evaporated. The anger and pain, the bitterness and remorse; those things belonged to another time, another place, another part of her life. And somehow, without her noticing, it had stopped hurting.

Her face glowed with such reverence for the one who had brought her here. Her hands high in the air, declaring the glorious majesty of the way-maker; the miracle worker.

A joy that could never be naturally explained, poured out into every word she sang. The unborn baby girl, waiting patiently for her own new beginning in just a few more weeks, leapt inside the belly of its Momma, *her* own baby girl; who worshiped alongside her. It had been one heck of a journey.

Things hadn't turned out the way she'd expected, the way she'd so passionately prayed for, but it seemed to her in that moment, that they had worked out just the way they were meant to.

She was quite sure it wasn't normal to feel as giddy as she did in such complicated circumstances, but then, there had never been anything *normal* about her... and there certainly had never been anything normal about her Father.

CITATIONS

Cheque Book of the Bank of Faith – Daily readings by CH Surgeon

(2014, Preface)

CH (Charles Haddon) Spurgeon

Christian Focus Publications – Scotland UK) - ISBN: 9781845500702

Discernment – The Essential Guide to Hearing the Voice of Gpd

Jane A Hamon

(2019, p, 95-96)

Chosen Books (Baker Publishing Group): Minnesota – ISBN: 9780800799557

Throne Room Prayers – Praying with Jesus on The Sea of Glass

(2018, p.80, 89)

Brian and Candice Simmons

BroadStreet Publishing Minnesota – ISBN:9781424557820

Institution of Christian Religion - John Calvin's Institutes

John Calvin

(Chapter 1, para 2 : THE KNOWLEDGE OF GOD AND OF OURSELVES MUTUALLY CONNECTED. —NATURE OF THE CONNECTION.)

Originally written in Latin by M. John Calvin in 1500s, and translated into English according to the Authors last edition, Original Translation into English Thomas Norton in the mid/late sixteenth century. 4th Translation into English printed by Arnold Hatfield London, for Bonham Norton. 1599. *These were Her Majesty's printers for the Hebrew, Greek, and Latin tongues, the other her Highness' printer of the books of Common Prayer.* There have been many published and reproduction version since. Full copies can be found online.

Cath Sheridan is a ridiculously proud Momma, a Business Strategist, a Storyteller, a Nomad, a Ponderer and a relentless and passionate Pursuer of Purpose! Her goal in life is to make sense of the fabulous, the not so fabulous, the unconventional and the downright peculiar, that is 'US' (you & me). Then fearlessly embrace 'Life on Purpose' (in purpose), as 'Cath' - the Crazy Wonderful, Perfectly Imperfect Cath, who He skilfully designed, packaged, ordained and sent - encouraging others to do the same. Cath is a longstanding member of Crossgate Community Church in Preston - Lancashire, UK, where she leads the Intercessor ministry. She's also part of the wider Speaking team and has run classes on Discovering Purpose, led various small groups and continues to be heavily involved in the building design and creative team. In addition, for the last 25 years she's also had significant involvement with Adullam International Ministries (AIM), based in the USA, Moldova and Kenya. Everything else there is to know about her (EVER!) is in the book!